MW00572564

Published by Straight Talk Books
P.O. Box 301, Milwaukee, WI 53201
800.661.3311 · timeofgrace.org

Cover image: Shutterstock/Mikhail Klyoshev

Printed in the United States of America
ISBN: 978-1-949488-49-4

life
TO
THE
full

**DEVOTIONS TO HELP YOU
SEEK GOD EVERY DAY**

January

Do nothing out of selfish ambition or vain conceit.
Rather, in humility value others above yourselves,
not looking to your own interests but each of you
to the interests of the others.

Philippians 2:3,4

Resolve
Christine Wentzel

The ticktock countdown finally reached the midnight hour. While the echo of "Auld Lang Syne" burned off in the rising sun of the dawn, the world sighed, "Happy New Year."

Living in the midst of humanity's hopelessness are people who see their need for renewal, acknowledge their sinful lives, and are transformed by the forgiveness found only in Christ Jesus. Grateful for the transformation, they follow in his footsteps to carry the message of true hope found in Jesus' resurrection from the dead.

"If then you have been raised with Christ, seek the things that are above, where Christ is, seated at the right hand of God. Set your minds on things that are above, not on things that are on earth" (Colossians 3:1,2 ESV).

Forget the New Year's traditions that hang on luck and whose resolutions highlight more self-improvement than selfless improvement. Instead, resolve to deepen your restored relationship with God our Lord and Father, God our Redeemer and Friend, and God our Comforter and Guide! Resolve to feed your faith daily with his Holy Word. Resolve to gain understanding from his learned teachers who open the treasures of heaven found in its pages. Resolve to gather in the communities of his faithful family. Resolve to show the proof of his activity in your changed life.

The lost will seek Christ's mercy and grace in us. Resolve to be readily available—we meet them every day. Time is running out.

Talk to yourself (about God!)
Pastor Mike Novotny

Do you ever talk to yourself? You should, especially if you're a person with a big heart.

I've met some bighearted, compassionate, empathetic, sensitive, Christ-like brothers and sisters in the faith. While I tend to be more intellectual, they lean toward being emotional and relational, which is a true gift to the Christian church. I think of my mother who would gladly sacrifice sleep to alter a bridesmaid's dress or sew up a ripped seam. Seeing her compassion is a small glimpse of the bighearted love of our Father.

The challenge, however, is not letting those emotions take control of what's true. Have you ever been there?

The prophet Jeremiah was an emotional man too. How did he combat those deceptive feelings that robbed him of his joy? He explains, **"I say to myself, 'The Lord is my portion'"** (Lamentations 3:24). Notice the start of that sentence—"I say to myself." Jeremiah talked to himself! About what? About God!

We're wise to do the same. When you're scared, uncertain, or anxious about your day, tell yourself about God. Remind your shivering heart what God is like and how his character affects your situation. Through faith in Jesus, you'll go through today with a God who can, who cares, who controls, who knows, who's near, who's enough, and who endures. Slow down—right now—and read through that list again, spending 30 seconds on each truth about your God's character.

If you talk to yourself about what kind of God you have, you'll be more than okay.

What to do when life is a mess
Pastor Mike Novotny

Have you ever found yourself in a total mess? When your past choices have left you with present consequences that probably won't change for the foreseeable future?

Maybe your body is broken down because, in part, you messed up. All those morning workouts skipped and desserts ordered caught up to you, leaving you with a sluggish heart that can't be quickly fixed. Or maybe your connection to your parents, your siblings, or a coworker is strained, stripped down to the bare minimum of communication. You were so focused on your goals and your life that you forgot that real relationships require time and sacrifice. There's no text you can send to instantly create closeness.

So what do you do when your sin has made a mess of things? You imitate Jeremiah. He wrote, **"Yet this I call to mind and therefore I have hope: Because of the Lord's great love we are not consumed, for his compassions never fail. They are new every morning; great is your faithfulness"** (Lamentations 3:21-23).

Instead of fixating on his failures, Jeremiah forced his mind to think about God, his great love, his unfailing compassion, his great faithfulness. That's what restored his hope.

Could you do the same thing today? Call to mind everything you know about God. His grace. His mercy. His patience. Meditate deeply on our Father's heart, his Son's sacrifice, and his Spirit's presence. Your day can wait. Because that's how you deal with the mess. That's how you live with hope.

Focusing on Jesus, not self
Andrea Delwiche

"I will bless the Lᴏʀᴅ at all times; his praise shall continually be in my mouth. My soul makes its boast in the Lᴏʀᴅ; let the humble hear and be glad. Oh, magnify the Lᴏʀᴅ with me, and let us exalt his name together!" (Psalm 34:1-3 ESV).

Let's try this: Set everything aside and focus on Jesus. Let's bless him and praise him for his goodness.

Consider the stories of the gospels—feeding the five thousand, stilling the storm, and defending the woman brought to Jesus by those who hated him. Consider his teaching about loving one another above ourselves. How about his gentle instruction to pay attention to God's beautiful world so we can be reassured about God's love for us? Consider additional signs of his power: raising people from the dead, offering his own body for us, coming back to life on the third day.

Which story resonates with you today? What would it have been like to follow Jesus in that particular moment? How would he have acted? What did he say? Bless Jesus for his goodness and the wonderful ways he works.

Consider whatever good and lovely thing you've treasured in these few minutes. How can you let it be the lens through which you view the rest of your day? With the psalmist, you can say, **"I sought the Lᴏʀᴅ, and he answered me and delivered me from all my fears. Those who look to him are radiant, and their faces shall never be ashamed"** (Psalm 34:4,5 ESV).

God and your great-great-great-great grandpa

Pastor Mike Novotny

As you look around, how many things do you see that were around when your great-great-great-great grandpa was walking the earth? My great-great-great-great grandpa would have been born 150-200 years ago, give or take a few trips around the sun. Was my laptop around in the early 1800s? Nope. My desk? This book? The church where I'm writing these words? Nope, nope, and more nope. The city where I live (Appleton, WI) was founded in 1857, so that might not even make the cut!

But I do see something out my window that my ancient ancestors saw—the sun. Like few other things in my life, the sun and the moon and the stars seem to endure forever.

I think that's why the author of Psalm 136 wrote, **"To him who alone does great wonders, His love endures forever. Who by his understanding made the heavens, His love endures forever. Who spread out the earth upon the waters, His love endures forever. Who made the great lights—His love endures forever. The sun to govern the day, His love endures forever. The moon and stars to govern the night; His love endures forever"** (verses 4-9).

The author points to nature as the closest example of any created thing to the love of our Creator. Just like the sun keeps showing up on good and bad and hopeful and hopeless days, God's love shows up too. That fact made some of our great-great-great-great grandparents worship. Think about it a bit, and it will make you worship too.

January 6

Learn to R-E-A-D your Bible
Pastor Daron Lindemann

Can I share a spiritual habit that has helped enrich my Bible reading?

R-E-A-D your Bible. This acronym helps me daily to meditate more deeply on God. Before you even open your Bible to read, try this:

Remember God. I use a simple breathing technique so that my devotional time with God is less about me and more about him. **"I remembered you, God"** (Psalm 77:3). I exhale in confession, exhale what I'm trying to control, exhale my fears and disappointments. In turn each time, I inhale while remembering all that is true about God. Who he is. I say, "God, you are _____."

Enjoy God. The one **"who meditates"** on God is **"like a tree planted by streams of water"** (Psalm 1:2,3). That's one happy tree—always nourished and fresh, content and confident as God's breeze tickles its leaves.

Appreciate God. I give thanks for five recent blessings. They're different each day. It puts the focus on God's work and God's glory and helps keep me from complaining. **"Give thanks to the Lord, for he is good; his love endures forever"** (Psalm 118:1).

Direct your attention (1 Samuel 3:10). Shut off your devices. Find a quiet place. In your schedule and heart, set apart free time for this moment so that you don't worry about the next thing. Ask, "God, what do you want to tell me today?"

Don't just read the Bible like you read your mail. R-E-A-D the Bible.

The gift of a good group
Pastor Mike Novotny

When I was growing up in the church, I had no idea that I needed a group. Thanks to my mother, I would show up at church every Sunday to hear about Jesus, a habit that led me to open my Bible at home and read more about Jesus. But did I connect with other Christians to pray for each other, confess our sins to each other, and forgive each other in Jesus' name? I didn't even think about that.

But the Scriptures mention it all the time. Listen to how one believer gushed about such groups: **"How good and pleasant it is when God's people live together in unity!"** (Psalm 133:1). It is both morally "good" and emotionally "pleasant" when Christians can do life together without cliques, divisions, or unaddressed hurts but rather with mutual commitment, honest concern, and genuine love.

Make no mistake—a group like that is hard to create and maintain. Satan knows its power, so he fights and lies to prevent it, convincing too many of us that we are fine with a "personal relationship with Jesus." But God knows its power too, so he gives us this clear reminder and promise to be with us as we take the next step to living in true Christian unity.

So what could you do today to be a living example of this passage? What step could you take to connect with another Christian and do life together? I'm not sure what that step is, but I do know it's good to get one step closer to living together as the people of God.

God cares (even now)
Pastor Mike Novotny

In a book by Tim Keller, I read the tale of a witch who turned unsuspecting travelers into stone. She had a cottage with a comfortable bed that she offered to anyone who needed a place to stay for the night. But the bed was enchanted, and anyone who was asleep in it when the sun came up would become a statue in the witch's collection. In that same house was a servant girl who had pity on the unsuspecting travelers. So when a young man stopped at the cottage for the night, the servant girl threw sharp sticks and stones into the bed before he settled down for the night. When he tried to sleep, the stones and sticks stabbed him, keeping him awake. He cursed the girl who had prepared the bed. Little did he know how much she actually cared.

Sounds like God. While we don't understand the sticks and stones of life, he does. He knows, he allows, and he even plans our pain because he cares. We assume we'd be fine with more blessing. But God knows. Sometimes God doesn't do what he can simply because he cares.

"Humble yourselves, therefore, under God's mighty hand, that he may lift you up in due time. Cast all your anxiety on him because he cares for you" (1 Peter 5:6,7). Be humble enough to believe that God allows things to happen, not because he can't control them but because he cares for you.

Hope
Sarah Habben

I hope this horrible situation ends soon.

I hope she'll keep her word.

I hope my new job works out.

In a perfect world, we wouldn't need to hope. But in this broken world, we hope all the time. We hope things will get better, work out, go our way. Our hopes are pinned to imperfect people and circumstances, so they often shrivel like an old balloon. We learn to hedge our bets.

Does that kind of "iffy" hope creep into our faith lives? "I sure *hope* God will provide my daily bread . . . forgive my sins . . . see me through this challenge." Iffy wishing is not what Paul was describing when he wrote, **"And we boast in the *hope* of the glory of God. And *hope* does not put us to shame"** (Romans 5:2,5).

That kind of hope isn't centered in things or people. It's a hope that boasts in God. We can replace the word *hope* with the words *certain confidence*. We have *certain confidence* in God's glory, and that confidence won't disappoint. Not because our confidence is unshakeable but because our God is.

If you're still hedging your hopes, go back to the cross. Christ hung there in our place, to win our peace with God. His gift of peace gives us hope—*certain confidence*—that God's unshakeable, glorious grace will provide for us on earth and deliver us safely to heaven.

If your hope fails you, it's because it's the wrong hope. Hope in the Savior; God will never disappoint.

"If I were king . . ."
Pastor David Scharf

"If I were king . . ." Perhaps that line reminds you of the cowardly lion from the *Wizard of Oz* singing proudly, "If I were king of the forrrrest, not queen, not prince, not duke . . ." The song is about what a frightened lion would do if he weren't so frightened. Everyone would bow to him!

What would you do if you were king? You could enjoy the pleasures of living in the lap of luxury. You would have the best foods, accommodations, and entertainment, not to mention the prestige and respect. And you know what? That would be your right! After all, you would be the king!

Revelation describes the King of kings, Jesus: **"To him who loves us and has freed us from our sins by his blood, and has made us to be a kingdom and priests"** (1:5,6). Christ rules in our hearts through faith, rules the church by his grace, and rules the whole world by his power. Yet the most incredible thing about our King is in how he showed his power. He laid it aside on the cross so that we might be kings and priests. You have no cowardly lion for a king. Instead, you have the Lion of the tribe of Judah as your King—the One who never backs down in his protection of his children, in the preservation of their faith, and in the pursuit of their salvation!

There's no reason to be cowardly with a King like Christ!

Arguing with God
Pastor Mike Novotny

Do you ever argue with God about how big and complicated his calling is and how small and unprepared you are? Maybe you've read those simple words in your Bible—"Give to the poor. Seek justice. Forgive those who sin against you. Respect your husband. Love your wife. Honor your father and mother"—but immediately objected, "How God? How could I ever do that?"

If you ever argue with God, you're going to love Moses. Most people picture Moses as the Ten Commandment-carrying, confident, called, bold, bearded, "Let my people go!" guy. But he wasn't. In fact, he was the opposite of most of the descriptions you just read. Moses was reluctant and afraid. His big toes were red and raw from dragging his sandaled feet when God called him to confront the pharaoh.

So how did Moses end up doing it? Here's how: **"But Moses said to God, 'Who am I that I should go to Pharaoh and bring the Israelites out of Egypt?' And God said, 'I will be with you'"** (Exodus 3:11,12). That was God's answer to Moses' argument. "No, Moses, you are not all that special or strong or gifted, but that's okay. Because I'm going with you."

God still says that, you know. When forgiving her or loving him or helping them feels impossible, our Father responds, "You're right. It would be impossible for you. Thankfully, you won't be alone. I will be with you." That's how God ends the argument. He promises to be present.

How would things change if you remember that today?

Dealing with death
Pastor Jon Enter

At most Christian funerals, the peace-filled words of Psalm 23 are spoken: **"The Lord is my shepherd; I shall not want"** (verse 1 ESV). Jesus loves you, provides for you, and is there for you. Such comfort! Such peace!

Then verse 4 hits: **"Even though I walk through the valley of the shadow of death"** (ESV). If you've been to a funeral, you've likely felt these words thud in your heart. One cold, harsh word jumps out. *Death.* How could it not?

But death wasn't the focus for God or King David as these words were written. We make it the focus with our sadness, but it's not. God calls death a "shadow." That's all it is! A shadow can't hurt you. It has no substance. A shadow can only scare you if you let it, but it can't hurt you!

That's why God proclaims in 1 Corinthians 15:55, **"Where, O death, is your victory? Where, O death, is your sting?"** Death is a shadow for a believer. It can't hurt you eternally in Jesus.

The pain you're feeling from the loss of a loved one is real. And it's difficult. And it hurts. But there's an end; there's peace in Jesus as you walk with him through that valley of sadness knowing *and remembering* our loved ones who die in faith *live!* They live! They live forever already with the Lord.

May that truth give you peace as you walk with your Good Shepherd, Jesus!

Your name in the book of life
Pastor Mike Novotny

I have a vivid memory from the late 80s of two people sitting at our kitchen table—my mom and Bob. I can hear those two voices, first my mom's and then Bob's, as I eavesdrop from my spot on the living room couch. My mom was teaching Bob how to read. Bob was a quiet, kind, and compassionate man from our community who had never learned to read, so my mom volunteered to teach him. For years, Bob humbly showed up to learn, and my mom humbly gave her time to teach.

That memory reminds me of Jesus. Jesus gave us his time, not just an hour each week but his entire life. He humbled himself both in life and death, volunteering to help us with our biggest problem—the book of life. Without his sacrifice, no sinner would find their name on heaven's reservation list. But through Jesus, a miracle is true.

Some of the Bible's final words, a glorious description of eternity with God, describe this miracle: **"Nothing impure will ever enter it, nor will anyone who does what is shameful or deceitful, but only those whose names are written in the Lamb's book of life"** (Revelation 21:27).

One day, every Christian will see their name written in that book. With inexpressible joy, we will sound out the syllables of our names. With gratitude, we will worship the Lamb who gave up everything so that we could be saved.

Rejoice with me today at the thought of our names in Jesus' book!

Sir, we would like to see Jesus
Pastor David Scharf

Jesus was in Jerusalem. His name was being talked about all over Israel. It was the week he was going to die, and he knew it. To say the least, he had a lot going on. Some Greeks who had heard of Jesus' message and the wonders he performed came to Philip with a very simple request: **"'Sir,' they said, 'we would like to see Jesus'"** (John 12:21). Greeks were non-Jews, so it was rather unheard of for them to ask to speak with a Jewish teacher. And with that, Philip was given an incredible opportunity to show Jesus to someone. What did Jesus tell them? He told them about what his impending death would mean for them. It was an eternity-changing encounter.

This is now your purpose in life. We as royal priests exist for this purpose. Our task is very simple: to bring people to see Jesus. Do you have a neighbor whose car stays in the garage on Sunday mornings? Is there a parent who needs you to encourage them in their faith walk? Do you have a friend or coworker who's shown a curiosity about religion? Show them Jesus. How? **"Philip went to tell Andrew; Andrew and Philip in turn told Jesus"** (John 12:22). Notice that Philip didn't need to flex his theological prowess. He simply brought them to see Jesus.

Show Jesus with your life. Speak freely about what Jesus means to you. Then invite someone to church. And don't just invite but bring someone with you so that they too can see Jesus!

Cell phone vs. God's Word
Pastor Clark Schultz

Do you know how many times a day the average person picks up his or her cell phone to check messages, scores, or other addicting games with the word *candy* in them? 110 times. Compare that to the number of times a person picks up his or her Bible daily. (Insert good old-fashioned Christian guilt here.) I'm just as guilty as you are, but let's work through this thought process together. Cell phone—outdated the moment you purchase it. God's Word—timeless. Cell phone—causes anxious thoughts. (Why hasn't that person texted back yet?) God's Word—gives us answers per his timing and wisdom. Cell phone—battery runs low unless charged. God's Word—doesn't drain us but charges us up.

Still not convinced? As a fellow smartphone addict, I've found that my stress level increases the more I use it. On the flip side, a psalm or passage from Romans calms my anxious heart. If I lay my phone down, it becomes an overpriced decoration. In the Word, I'm told I'm forgiven and a precious child of God. I'm more than a decoration. Cell phone—costs $$. The Word—tells of the cost of God's Son to make me priceless in his eyes. Last but not least, some phones have the feature to know where you are at all times, comforting or frightening? God's eyes watching and knowing you since conception, comforting or frightening? **"The Lord will guide you always"** (Isaiah 58:11).

Just because
Jan Gompper

One thing that brings me great joy is my dog. No matter how long I'm gone, when I return, Lacie runs to greet me with tail wagging, body wriggling, and voice squealing. No matter what, she can't wait to shower me with dog-love . . . just because.

Don't you wish people loved this way? Can you imagine if your spouse or kids squealed with excitement every time you came into their presence? Okay, maybe that sounds weird, but knowing we're loved makes us feel good. And knowing we're loved unconditionally makes us feel amazing.

That's exactly how God loves us. We've done nothing to earn his love. In fact, we've all done things that should cause him to bare his teeth or run in the opposite direction. Even when we've ignored, disappointed, or hurt him, God still loves us. How do we know? **"God showed his great love for us by sending Christ to die for us *while we were still sinners*"** (Romans 5:8 NLT). No strings attached . . . just because.

No matter how long we may have been away from him (two months, two years, a lifetime), whenever we approach him, he wriggles with joy and reaches out with open arms. **"This is real** [unconditional] **love—not that we loved God, but that he loved us and sent his Son as a sacrifice to take away our sins"** (1 John 4:10 NLT).

I can't help but think that God created dogs to remind us of his unconditional love. After all, D-O-G is G-O-D spelled backward. ☺

Ordinary Christianity
Pastor Mike Novotny

I wonder if the devil loves extraordinary Christianity. By "extraordinary," I mean those stories you read in Christian books about people who prayed for three hours a day and shared the gospel with thousands and impacted the lives of millions. I wonder if the enemy loves the extraordinary because most of us are ordinary. (No offense.) We wake up with bedhead, try to keep up with email, and attempt to work out more than we eat dessert. Ordinary. The problem with extraordinary Christianity is spectator spirituality. Ordinary people like me and you sit in the stands and watch the "real" heroes do great things for God.

But—listen—that misses a massive teaching in the Bible—God uses the ordinary to do the extraordinary. People like me. People like you. Two ordinary midwives saved the life of Moses (Exodus 1:17). A bunch of ordinary fishermen were Jesus' first draft picks (Matthew 4:21). Or, my favorite, this truth from Paul: **"Brothers and sisters, think of what you were when you were called. Not many of you were wise by human standards; not many were influential; not many were of noble birth. But God chose the foolish things of the world to shame the wise; God chose the weak things of the world to shame the strong"** (1 Corinthians 1:26,27).

So don't worry if you're not the smartest, the skinniest, the strongest, or the latest social media influencer. God isn't looking for that. He's looking for you, ordinary you, to do his extraordinary work of loving people in Jesus' name.

You are gifted
Pastor Mike Novotny

Do you know the gift(s) you've received from God? In four key chapters of the Bible (1 Corinthians 12, Romans 12, Ephesians 4, and 1 Peter 4), God speaks to us of the "spiritual gifts" that he has given to each of his people. They are called gifts because we don't deserve them, and they are called spiritual because the Holy Spirit brings those gifts when he enters into a Christian's heart.

If you're unsure of your gifts, listen to Peter's words: **"Each of you should use whatever gift you have received. . . . If anyone speaks, they should do so as one who speaks the very words of God. If anyone serves, they should do so with the strength God provides"** (1 Peter 4:10,11).

Peter gives you a clue to figuring out your gifts when he talks about speaking versus serving. Some of us do the most good when we use words. We preach sermons, teach classes, counsel a strained marriage, write sympathy letters, text a struggling friend, welcome a church guest, and share wisdom with a grandchild. Does that sound like you? Others of us do the most good through work that involves few words. We clean the church, design the space, fix the widow's car, build quality homes, make the meal that brings people together, and show up during their grief. Does that seem to fit?

Figuring out your God-given gifts is the first step in serving others to the glory of God. So, what are your gifts?

Don't skip God
Pastor Mike Novotny

The other day I pulled out my absurdly thick, 4-inch graduate school binder that contains my theology notes from my second-year doctrine class. About halfway through the semester, we tackled the person and work of Jesus—how he is our truth-telling Prophet, our self-sacrificing Priest, and our death-conquering King. Eternal, life-saving stuff!

But as I paged through those notes, I noticed that I had missed something—God. The very first items on the class outline were about God—his essence, his attributes, and his qualities. Much like the Apostles' Creed, that ancient statement of the Christian faith, my professors wanted me to begin by thinking about the glory and majesty of God. After all, the whole point of Jesus' life, death, and resurrection was to give sinners like us a chance to be with God forever!

I love how the prophet Jeremiah focused on the importance of being with a God that glorious: **"I say to myself, 'The Lord is my portion'"** (Lamentations 3:24). What gets us through the painful, lamentable seasons of our lives is knowing that the Lord is our portion, that right now (*is*, not *will be*) God is what we get, and that God is enough. Through faith in Jesus, God has come to be with us and dwell in us in this very moment!

Please don't miss what I missed! Because of Jesus, God is here. The Lord is your portion! Imagine it! Picture him! You won't regret it!

In Christ Jesus our Lord
Pastor Daron Lindemann

In Christ Jesus our Lord, death is dead. It cannot kill.

In Christ Jesus our Lord, life is bigger than your surrounding circumstances. You are not defined by what happens to you.

In Christ Jesus our Lord, angels clash with demons in spiritual warfare to protect you. And angels always win!

In Christ Jesus our Lord, today is a gift. That's why we call it the present.

In Christ Jesus our Lord, the future isn't something to worry about. Nothing that happens to you tomorrow or next year beats him to the scene.

In Christ Jesus our Lord, powers of this world are pawns for his kingdom. And you belong to his kingdom. You're on the winning team.

In Christ Jesus our Lord, your whispered prayers reach higher than high stress, high taxes, high blood pressure, high demands, high risk, and high hopes.

In Christ Jesus our Lord, your faith digs deeper into his life-giving water than any depths of despair.

In Christ Jesus our Lord, there is nothing that you do, nothing that happens to you, nothing you forget to do, and nothing you neglect that will make him love you any less.

"For I am convinced that neither death nor life, neither angels nor demons, neither the present nor the future, nor any powers, neither height nor depth, nor anything else in all creation, will be able to separate us from the love of God that is in Christ Jesus our Lord" (Romans 8:38,39).

Replaying the past
Pastor Jon Enter

My daughter just learned (hopefully) a life lesson. While visiting friends on vacation, she yelled out in front our hosts, "I refuse to sleep on that air mattress!" She got to sleep on the floor. For over 20 minutes, she sulked. "WHY DID I SAY THAT?" But she did. It couldn't be undone.

None of us can change the past. When we try, we spiral into a vortex of negativity. "What if I had only—ONLY—done something differently?" But what-if questions don't change anything; they steal happiness and contentment.

If the apostle Paul focused on his past, he never would've served Jesus. Focusing on our past's brokenness never brings happiness or contentment. Paul didn't live in the what-if world; he knew God was bigger and more grace filled than his past. So he confidently wrote, **"Forgetting what is behind and straining toward what is ahead, I press on toward the goal to win the prize for which God has called me heavenward in Christ Jesus"** (Philippians 3:13,14).

Forget your past; you don't live there anymore! The what-if questions don't work. So change the question from what if? to what now? what next? Control the controllables. What does God ask me to do now? What does God ask me to do next?

The answer is in God's Holy Word. Simply do a Google search—"Bible passages about . . ."—to find God's guidance, grace, and help in your life. What now? What next? Jesus will not fail you.

The only thing I need to know for sure
Pastor David Scharf

What do you need to know for sure? That you turned the coffee maker off this morning? That you closed the garage door when you left for work? No. It's not the end of the world if you come home to the coffee crusted to the bottom of the pot or even that a bicycle is missing from your open garage. So much of what we think about doesn't matter. There's only one thing I need to know for sure: that I am forgiven.

In A.D. 430 when the church father Augustine was near death and his strength was ebbing away, he begged one of his friends to paint on the wall opposite his bed the words of Psalm 32: **"Blessed is the one whose transgressions are forgiven, whose sins are covered. Blessed is the one whose sin the LORD does not count against them"** (verses 1,2).

The dying Augustine laid there gazing at those words as the darkness closed in. There will be nothing else worth clinging to in the end than those words. Look at Jesus' cross and know that as Jesus hung there dying and the darkness was closing in, he was thinking of you. He was saying already then, "Your wrongdoings are forgiven by my cross. Your sins are covered by my blood. I don't hold anything against you." Look at the cross and know you are forgiven. It's the only thing you need to know for sure!

Approachable
Pastor Daron Lindemann

"Thank you for seeing me, sir."

"Hello, it's a pleasure to meet you, sir."

As she waited for the job interview, Jeanie just couldn't decide what she'd say. Maybe a simple, "Hi," would be best. Or would that be too casual?

"Mr. Millard will see you now," the pleasant receptionist informed Jeanie with a smile, gesturing toward the VP's door. As Jeanie stepped closer, the door opened. A smiling, relaxed man extended his hand and said warmly, "Welcome, Jeanie. Have a seat and tell me more about . . ." She spoke her first sentence naturally and comfortably.

What have you said to God lately? Maybe you don't know what to say. Then remember that God makes what you say to him easy and enjoyable. How? He's broken the ice by speaking to you first and warmly engaging you in dialogue. **"We cry, '*Abba*, Father.' . . . We are God's children"** (Romans 8:15,16).

God has made himself easily approachable. He has welcomed you by opening the door through Jesus Christ. To sinners seeking his love, he speaks with terms of endearment, gently inviting with words like *child* and *lamb*.

And God even offers to translate your mumbling, bumbling prayers into heavenly language and direction: **"The Spirit intercedes for God's people in accordance with the will of God"** (Romans 8:27).

God is eager to listen to your voice. He enjoys your words. Praise him. Pray to him. Give thanks to him. It starts with letting God have the first word as he opens the door.

Hidden treasure
Sarah Habben

"The kingdom of heaven is like a treasure hidden in a field. When a man found it, he hid it again, and then in his joy went and sold all he had and bought that field" (Matthew 13:44).

Most of us understand Jesus' parable like this: The man in the parable represents believers. The point is that God wants believers to give up everything joyfully to follow Jesus, our greatest treasure.

That's a good, biblical interpretation. But it's worth noting that the parables surrounding this one in Matthew 13 focus on *God's* activity and attitude, not that of believers.

What if we look at the parable in that light—as *God's* activity and not our own?

Now the man in the parable is Jesus.

And the treasure . . . could it be? . . . is *you!*

When I read the parable the first way, I feel like a dud. I just can't compare to that man. Oh, I give up my Sunday pillow time to attend church. I give my time and talents. But give up *everything* for Jesus? *Joyfully?* Nope. The parable shows me just how far I fall.

But now let's picture the man in the parable as Jesus, who gave up everything *joyfully*. Not just his pillow but his throne, the angels' accolades, and his life—all to buy back the crown of his creation.

The One who bought us at such great cost will never be careless with our needs, fears, or prayers. We are Jesus' priceless treasure.

And he is ours.

Submission mode
Jason Nelson

"Submit to one another out of reverence for Christ" (Ephesians 5:21).

Ladies and gentlemen, boys and girls, I have an announcement to make. We're all in submission mode. Because I'm in submission mode, it's not my place to tell you how you should do your submitting. I'm still trying to figure out my own. I don't have time to look over your shoulder and tell you how to put yourself one down. But if you want some hints from God about submitting, keep reading in Ephesians. Wives are to submit to their husbands. Husbands are to sacrifice themselves for their wives. Children are to obey their parents. Jesus gave himself up for all of us. This is a profound mystery, and we're all in this together. We're all in submission mode. Any attempts to isolate one Christian's way of submitting from another's are failures to submit.

What does a mutual submission society look like? No one pulls rank because there isn't any. There is orderliness because we agree upon it and submit to it. It can get a little awkward at the entrances and exits to our endeavors. Courtesy can jam things up. "Let me get the door for you." "No, let me get the door for you." "You go first." "No, you go first." "Who's in charge here?" "I don't get the question." "Well, then, who takes the credit?" "I still don't get the question."

The amazing Merlin
Pastor Mike Novotny

Recently, I met an amazing man named Merlin. Merlin is an 81-year-old woodworker who can outhustle a team of 20-something construction workers. During our church's recent building project, I watched Merlin donating his God-given gift for our new worship space. The all-wooden stage? Merlin's work. The 24 beautiful cafe tables for the lobby? Merlin's work. The 12-foot conference room table that takes your breath away? Merlin's work.

In the middle of the project, I asked our general contractor how much money Merlin was single-handedly saving our church by donating his time and talent. "50 thousand dollars," the contractor replied. Stunned, I went to find Merlin to thank him for his generous heart. Eventually I found him, sitting on the floor in his sawdust-covered jeans, quietly eating a sandwich out of his old-school lunch box. He smiled at me, nodded a "You're welcome," and went back to work.

Merlin makes me think of Peter's words about the goal of our God-given gifts: **"Each of you should use whatever gift you have received to serve others . . . so that in all things God may be praised through Jesus Christ. To him be the glory and the power for ever and ever. Amen"** (1 Peter 4:10,11).

In the years to come, many people will share a coffee in the lobby, share ideas in the conference room, and preach/sing the gospel from our church's gorgeous stage. They might forget Merlin's name, but I pray that we all remember the glorious name of Jesus. And I pray that your gift does the same.

Heads up!
Pastor Clark Schultz

If a fly ball is hit into the air, you might hear the words, "Heads up!" to warn you. If a friend or coworker wants to inform you of something so you don't make a fool of yourself, he or she says, "Hey, just a heads-up." In Psalm 24:7, the psalmist David gives us both a heads-up of information and of warning: **"Lift up your heads, you gates."**

The context of this psalm is the celebration of the ark of the covenant (a symbol of God's presence with his Old Testament people) and its display and then resting place in the pre-temple (tabernacle). David's point from verse 1 of the psalm is to say, "Heads up! Don't get caught up in all the pomp and circumstance and forget where and who we should be looking to."

Fast-forward to an application for our lives. We have our to-do lists . . . some legitimate and some may even be for religious purposes, but do we have a heads-up to why we're doing them? Or do we get caught up in the pomp of what we're doing? David directs his readers to have a heads-up to the coming King. He isn't referring to himself but to the King of kings, Jesus.

As you go about your weeks, months, and years, keep the words of David on your mind: "Heads up!" Look to the Word and to the skies for your King to return.

I just don't understand!
Pastor David Scharf

If you're looking for an entertaining mind boggle, ask someone to try to explain the Trinity. You might hear comparisons like, "God's like an egg—shell, yoke, and white—three parts but just one thing." "No, he's like water—it can take the form of liquid, ice, or vapor." Nice try, but not quite.

There's no dividing God. The Father is all God, the Son is all God, and the Holy Spirit is all God. 1+1+1=1 is terrible math but great theology! We have one indivisible God who is revealed in three distinct persons, each one fully God. If at this point your mind is saying, "I don't get it" . . . now you're getting it. Our finite minds just can't wrap themselves around God. That's a good thing. We need God to be infinitely greater than us!

However, we do understand what we need to understand about the Trinity: the indivisible triune God loves us. How? The day the Father forsook his Son on the cross was the first and only time that eternally indivisible circle was broken . . . to let you in. This fact is perhaps the only truth of Scripture harder to grasp than the Trinity. God loved *us* enough to do this. He let us in when we were baptized into **"the name of the Father and of the Son and of the Holy Spirit"** (Matthew 28:19). We'll never get every detail of God, but these truths of what his heart led him to do for us, that we can understand . . . and that's all that matters!

How God made you
Pastor Mike Novotny

It took me over 30 years to figure out how God made me. You would think that my strengths and weaknesses would be obvious after a few decades of spending every second with myself, but they weren't. Only after some serious exploration did I discover how my Creator wired me in unique ways.

I've learned that I am gifted at learning. Reading a book a week, podcasting hours of sermons a day, and pursuing advanced degrees is easy/fun/invigorating for me. But solving complex counseling problems and being a shoulder to cry on feels like I'm pitching with the wrong hand. Year by year, I'm learning to look for ways to use my gift while I humbly learn to delegate the tasks that are not my gift.

How about you? You, if the Holy Spirit lives in your heart, are gifted too. Peter writes, **"Each of you should use whatever gift you have received to serve others"** (1 Peter 4:10). Each of you. Not some of you or certain folks among you. Each of you. That means you too.

So how did God make you? Think about what comes easily to you, what you tend to do first on your long list of to-dos, what makes people gasp, "I could never do that!" Pray for open eyes to see your gifts. Ask trusted friends where you are gifted (and where you aren't!).

Then, to thank Jesus for the gifts of grace, mercy, and salvation, use your gifts to serve others.

Take their jewels
Jason Nelson

I'm grateful to a couple professors I had in college who taught me how to "plunder the Egyptians." They had keen intellects and broad knowledge of Christian thought. They were confident in the power of the gospel. They weren't afraid to discuss ideas from outside of their theological framework. They weren't looking to make mischief, but they preferred educating students over indoctrinating them. They were secure enough in their beliefs to pilfer gems from other Christians.

God gave the Israelites the economic capital to get established in the Promised Land because **"they plundered the Egyptians"** (Exodus 12:36). After ten convincing plagues, the circumstances were right for a give-and-take to occur between Egyptian masters and Jewish slaves. Their conversations may have gone something like this:

"Boss, that's a nice-looking ring you have there. I've been admiring it for some time now." "Here. Go ahead and take it. It's yours. Take the necklace too. Just get out of here."

So the Jews left Egypt much richer than when they arrived.

The treasury of spiritual capital holds deposits from all neighborhoods in the church. It would be the height of arrogance for any of us to think that out of two billion Christians in the world, we are the only ones getting it right. We can learn something from one another. Jewels are jewels. If you're not a slave, you'll know what you can take from someone when you see it.

You should love this Bible nerd
Pastor Mike Novotny

The other day I sent my wife a text with some in-depth, granular, Hebrew-based research I had done in the Bible. She replied (as only my beautiful bride can) with a picture that said, "Neeeeeeeeerd!"

Okay, she might have had a point. I was calculating the ratios of specific Hebrew words used throughout the various books of the Old Testament, which is a bit nerdy. But check out what I discovered:

The book of Psalms only contains 7% of the total words of the Old Testament, yet it has 59% of the uses of *praise/give thanks*. So why the disproportionate amount? Because two other words constantly show up in the psalms: 52% of the total Old Testament appearances of the word *love/mercy* and 44% of the *forever*s are in the psalms. Apparently, when God inspired these ancient songwriters to talk about his forever-enduring love, their pens instinctively scribbled, **"Give thanks to the God of heaven. His love endures forever"** (Psalm 136:26).

Doesn't that truth do the same to you? Your eyesight, hearing, heart, joints, and memory won't endure. But God's love does. When you buy your first bifocals or schedule your first bypass, God's love endures forever. When your mom needs a new knee or your father's mind is fading, God's love endures forever. No matter what you lose, you won't lose his love. Because it endures forever!

I can't think of news much better than that. Do you agree? (I thought you would. I'll let my wife know you're on my side. ☺)

February

All your words are true;
all your righteous laws are eternal.

Psalm 119:160

Today, not someday
Pastor Clark Schultz

I grew up in a small town in Wisconsin called Johnson Creek. My nearest friend was miles away in another "metropolis," Helenville. The busy road I lived on didn't allow the option of biking because my mother was concerned for my safety. With older siblings either out of the house or too cool to build forts and play Star Trek (yup, I'm a Trekkie), I was alone. I remember saying, "Man, if I just had someone to hang out with, I wouldn't feel alone."

Sadly, this feeling doesn't always go away when we grow up. You can be in a crowded school and have this feeling. You can roll over and place your hand in the empty spot on your bed where your spouse now dearly departed or fighting overseas used to sleep.

I bet the thief on the cross next to Jesus felt that loneliness. He chose his life of sin, and he was going to die with no assurance of what comes next. We can easily feel like we're living on our own lonely, sin-drenched island. But Jesus' words to this thief give us great comfort: **"Truly I tell you, today you will be with me in paradise"** (Luke 23:43). TODAY, not someday. Today Jesus is with you, dear reader. "Will be" isn't a maybe; it's a done deal. He is with us now, every day of our lives, always by our side, and will be with us when we reach paradise. Why? Because Jesus experienced the ultimate loneliness for us so we can be with God forever.

Jesus breaks chains
Pastor Mike Novotny

Have you ever felt chained to something? Like you just had to _____. There wasn't any choice but to _____. Have you ever heard something in church or read something from Jesus and thought, "I could never _____"?

For example, do you feel the pressure of being successful? When it comes to your grades, your salary, your resume, or your latest post, you just can't be ordinary or average or unnoticed. Or do you feel the pressure of making everyone in your life happy, feeling guilty that you couldn't do that and that and that for him and her and them and be here and there and everywhere at the same time? Or have you ever believed that you have to be a good person, a better person, to go to a better place and be with God?

Where did all these "chains" come from? Perhaps from the half-truths that they contain. We should strive to do our best and serve other people and do good for God. But that's not the whole truth. And a half-truth is a chain, a chain that can enslave you to guilt, exhaustion, and despair.

This is why I love how Jesus breaks chains. From every lord and master that would scar us, from every half-truth that would chain us, from any idea that would mess with our eternal future, Jesus went to war to win you back. **"So if the Son sets you free, you will be free indeed"** (John 8:36).

Don't let the father of lies chain you today. You are loved. Through Jesus, you are saved. Through the Spirit, you can do all things. That's the truth that sets you free.

Toxic friendships
Pastor Jon Enter

I attended a leadership conference as a senior in high school. The speaker focused greatly on the importance of friendships. He kept repeating, "Show me your friends, and I'll show you your future."

It's true. You undoubtedly know people who joined the wrong crowd, wrecking their future. "Show me your friends, and I'll show you your future" isn't just a catchy quote. It's biblical. It's practical. Proverbs 13:20 declares, **"Walk with the wise and become wise, for a companion of fools suffers harm."**

When you have a bad day, show me the friends you talk to about that bad day, and I'll show you your future emotion. Do you surround yourself with negativity? Is your trusted circle quick to judge, get mad, get even, get drunk, get destructive spiritually? "Walk with the wise and become wise, for a companion of fools suffers harm."

Show me your friends, and I'll show you your future. And if the friend you show me is Jesus, I know your future. It's an eternal future changed because of Jesus' love, forgiveness, and guidance. A true friend comes in when the world goes out. That's Jesus! Jesus came into this world for you! Jesus went to the cross for you! Jesus entered into your heart to save you!

Look at your chosen sphere of influence. Do they pour positivity in forgiveness or negativity by enabling bad choices? What friends uplift you, pointing you to Jesus?

Show me your friends, and I'll show you your future.

Gifted for God's glory
Pastor Mike Novotny

You are gifted for glory. The word *glory* means that someone or something makes you gasp, "Wow!" A sunrise, a newborn baby, or the love of Jesus might spark an instinctive "Wow!" within you. That's glory.

According to the apostle Peter, you are gifted for glory. The goal of your skills and talents is to make other people think of God and say, "Wow!" **"Each of you should use whatever gift you have received to serve others . . . so that in all things God may be praised through Jesus Christ"** (1 Peter 4:10,11). Notice the phrase, "in all things." Whatever your gift/"thing," the purpose is the praise of our Lord.

Because when you use your gift, people get a glimpse of God. When your smile, energy, and warm welcome make a guest in your church feel at home, you are a glimpse of the kindness of God. When your words encourage, teach, and keep your kids on the right track, you are a glimpse of God's fatherly wisdom. When you work hard, finish the project, and refuse to give up despite the obstacles, you are a glimpse of the Savior who fixed his eyes on the cross and didn't quit until he cried, "It is finished!"

Ponder how your gifts might give others a little glimpse of the wow-ness of our God. While you're meditating, think about the people in your life who are using their gifts to help you remember how glorious our Savior actually is.

Because God's glory is the goal of every gift.

A walk in my shoes
Jan Gompper

When I was little, I loved putting on my mom's high-heeled shoes and imagining I was a grown-up. I remember looking out the car window when passing the "projects" area of Chicago, wondering what it would be like to wear the shoes of a kid who grew up there.

As an actor, I've had to step vicariously into the shoes of characters I've played. Many times, I've had to dig deep to try to understand what made the person I was portraying think, believe, and act.

We can only imagine what it's like to walk in the shoes of another. But Jesus actually did it. The apostle Paul writes, **"He gave up everything, even his place with God. He accepted the role of a servant, appearing in human form. During his life as a man, he humbled himself by being fully obedient to God, even when that caused his death—death on a cross"** (Philippians 2:7,8 ERV).

Jesus became one of us so we could *know with certainty* that he fully understands how difficult our earthly walk can be. He did it so we could *trust with certainty* that he not only sees our pain but has also felt it. He did it so we would *believe with certainty* how much he loves us.

We will never be able to understand completely what it's like to walk in someone else's shoes. But might not the racially and politically divided world in which we currently live greatly benefit if all of us did our utmost to at least try to slip them on?

Your version of God
Pastor Daron Lindemann

We create our own versions of God and then point fingers of blame at these versions of God.

"God let my sister die. He doesn't care."

"God allowed a pandemic. He's cruel."

"God needs to be number one all the time?! He's such a narcissist."

These inaccurate versions of God aren't real, however. God is not busy or senile or narcissistic. God is perfect. We are flawed. Our versions of God are the problem.

So now what?

Grace. It's the chief characteristic of God. The big promise. The number-one truth he reveals about his will, his plans, his desire to connect.

Sure, we're flawed and he's not. As long as we recognize that, he doesn't point a finger of accusation at us but opens a hand of invitation.

"Come to me" (Matthew 11:28). Like Jesus invited people. Sinners. Prostitutes. Criminals. Tax collectors. Beggars. Ceremonially unclean lepers.

Just as you are. You don't have to clean up first. You don't have to listen to Christian radio first or send your kids to a Christian school or hire a Christian plumber.

Come as you are. Grace can handle it. Grace that is beyond your understanding—it exists in God's heart while viruses and storms and violence exist in this world. You'll understand why these happen only when you first let go of creating your own version of God.

And let him be himself with you.

Not the end
Sarah Habben

Our hearts tell us that death is loss. A body buried can no longer taste a ripe tomato, smell the rain, entwine someone's dear fingers in their own. The dead are deprived of speech and motion, of future hopes. Those measuring their last breaths and those standing at a grave both know: Death is loss.

And yet the Bible contradicts our hearts! In prison the apostle Paul wrote, **"For to me, to live is Christ and to die is gain"** (Philippians 1:21). He'd done some suffering. He'd thought about life and death. And he concluded they are both blessings.

To live is Christ. Christ is to a believer what oxygen is to lungs. Empty of air, lungs are useless. They can't do the work for which they were designed. Empty of Christ, we're no good either—we're unforgiven enemies of God, of no benefit to anyone. Our Savior animates us with his love and fills us with his power. He enables us to serve each other with joy. Even when we stumble under sorrow and trip over trials, nothing can separate us from his love.

To die is gain. In this world we're born to trouble. The blessings we enjoy exist side by side with sin, temptation, sorrow, death. And death is hard. But in Christ, it isn't loss. Dying doesn't *end* our hope or our future—it *achieves* them. In crossing death's threshold, we gain a perfect life in heaven—the end of weakness, deliverance from evil, a joyous reunion of saints, and the fulfillment of our chief hope: to be with Christ.

God is always here
Pastor Mike Novotny

A few years ago my wife and I saw *Dear Evan Hansen*, a musical about a teenage boy who's lonely, socially awkward, and depressed. But then Evan tells a lie that changes his life, granting him instant internet fame and even the attention of the girl he likes. But, of course, the lie gets exposed and everything falls apart. Crushed and alone, Evan runs back home, where his mother wraps him up in her loving arms and assures him that she's not going anywhere, that she will always be there for him.

Kim and I loved the musical, but I have a love/hate relationship with its message. On the one hand, I love how Evan's mom forgave her son and loved him even when no one else did. On the other hand, I hate how she made a promise to him that she couldn't keep. Because she couldn't "always" be there for him. In fact, part of Evan's loneliness came from the fact that she was rarely there for him due to her hectic work schedule as a single parent.

Thankfully, we have this: **"God is our refuge and strength, an ever-present help in trouble"** (Psalm 46:1). Our Father is our refuge, the one we run to in times of trouble. And notice that life-saving adjective—*ever-present*. He is present every time, everywhere, every when.

Like Evan, we all need someplace to go when we mess things up. Thankfully, we have a place. Always. That's no exaggeration. Which is why the gospel is such good news.

Be still

Pastor Mike Novotny

One of the more quotable, peace-inducing passages of the Bible comes from Psalm 46:10, which says, **"Be still, and know that I am God."** Have you heard that verse before? It's hanging on hundreds of artsy wooden signs in Christian homes.

The Hebrew verb for "be still" literally means to completely relax your muscles, to let everything go limp, like there are no bones in your body. If you're clenching your fists and fighting or gripping a sword and swinging, to "be still" means to put everything down and just relax. How? By knowing that he is God. The exalted God of the nations. The almighty God who fights and wins our battles. When you know that he is with you, you can relax. You can be still.

So let's practice that. I want you to think about your fears for a second. What might happen with your body, your family, your financial future? What if the economy . . . ? What if the election . . . ? What if you . . . ? As you think about those fears, I want you to tense your body. Clench your fists. Curl your toes. Squeeze your face. And now . . . relax! Breathe out and release every muscle. Be still. As you breathe deeply, remember what your God is like—loving, gracious, forgiving, powerful, in control, wise, patient, holy, just, eternal, present.

You have no reason to freak out today. You can be still if you know that he is God.

That's just who I am
Pastor Daron Lindemann

She overspends the credit card again. When confronted, she excuses her impulsive shopping: "That's just who I am."

People explain away anger, unfaithfulness, porn, and even addiction with the excuse, "That's just who I am." That's an identity crisis. Because no Christian's identity is sin. **"It is no longer I who do it, but it is sin living in me that does it"** (Romans 7:20).

Your identity is healthiest when you believe that what God says about you is absolutely true. Not the version of you that others see. Not even the image of yourself that you see.

"Then the disciple whom Jesus loved said to Peter, 'It is the Lord!'" (John 21:7).

If you were to ask John who he was, his answer would have focused on *whose* he was.

In writing the book of the Bible that bears his name, the disciple John identifies himself as the one whom Jesus loved.

You are loved. No matter how little you believe it, how sinful you are, or how disappointed you are in God—you are loved. You can't change who you are in the eyes of Jesus and the heart of God.

Loved. *Hmm.* Maybe that's my new answer to people who ask, "How are you today?"

"Loved."

It would say a lot to them. And to me. I need that; don't you?

Start with sameness
Jason Nelson

Imagine an alien invasion. I mean the kind with green skin and arriving in spaceships. I would expect earthlings to unite on the basis of our sameness and resist them just like in the movies. Even if the aliens say, "We come in peace," I think we would be suspicious of them because it would be obvious that they are not like us.

Perceptions of differentness are relative and evolve in our consciousness. I was attracted to my wife because of her appealing differentness from me. But now we have so much in common. Our neighbors are different from us until there's a referendum we agree on. Then they're just like us. Less than two centuries ago, black people were auctioned off like livestock because some white people focused on their different skin color and dehumanized them. A couple of centuries ago, Native Americans were treated like other wild things settlers had a right to remove from the landscape. You would think our history would cause us to be more enlightened in our views of each other. But too many earthlings still want to emphasize the differences among people for their own advantage.

What if we celebrate our sameness first and go from there? God said, **"I made the earth and created humans on it"** (Isaiah 45:12 GW). There's only one origin of all species—God. There's no natural selection that makes some humans more valuable to him than others.

Our great heritage!
Pastor David Scharf

Who first told you? Who first told you that Jesus died on a cross to take away all of your mistakes or that God made you his child in Baptism? Who first told you that you're going to heaven or that you can be sure of your salvation because Jesus won it entirely for you?

The writer to the Hebrews said, **"Remember your leaders, who spoke the word of God to you. Consider the outcome of their way of life and imitate their faith"** (13:7).

Who first told you? Maybe it was Mom and Dad, a friend, a pastor, a teacher, or a coworker. Thank God for that person right now. That person has handed down an invaluable heritage. It's a heritage that means hell is not the end. It's a heritage that lasts forever. Thank God for the leaders who spoke God's Word to you. Then do what God asks you to do: imitate their faith.

That's the beautiful part about this heritage. You get to pass it on as many times as you can. Who can you encourage today with the Savior who hears the prayers of his people and answers every time? Who can you comfort with the news of a Savior whose hand is scarred with nail marks of love and is always held open to take our hands? Whether it's for the first or the millionth time, who can you tell?

You give them . . .
Pastor Jon Enter

Recently I read the account of Jesus feeding the five thousand. Something jumped off the pages of Scripture that never did before. Different truths hit your heart because of the different circumstances you're facing in life. God's Word is living and active!

After the crowd of thousands sat all day in the hot, searing sun hearing Jesus teach, they were famished. The disciples approached Jesus to send the crowd away to get food. I love how they blame the crowd for shutting down the all-day church service. "You know, Jesus, this has been great. We would keep going, but the people . . ."

Do you remember Jesus' reply? **"You give them something to eat"** (Matthew 14:16). You. What Jesus said, he meant. You likely know the story. The disciples brought a boy's Happy Meal lunch of five small barley loaves and two small fish to Jesus. Jesus blessed it, broke it, and gave it to his disciples to distribute. Each disciple had only half of a small roll or half a small fish. After giving a tiny nibble to the people, they likely ran out after 17 people. But when they went back to Jesus, there was more and more and more.

"You give them something to eat." They did the work of *bringing*; Jesus did the work of *blessing*. The same is true for you. Do the work God has entrusted to you. Bring your best effort to Jesus to be blessed, trusting the results to his miraculous, loving hands.

A Valentine from Jesus
Christine Wentzel

Valentine's Day . . . bleh! My first experience with love's missed arrow happened in high school. In the cafeteria, a Valentine's booth took floral orders for almost a week before the big event. Valentine's Day revealed the chosen few proudly carrying wilting flowers all day long. Ugh, the shame of empty hands.

For good or bad, this ritual of people's fickle affections is still on the calendar. Take heart—it's only one day. Here is the real deal from your True Love for all eternity: **"I have loved you with an everlasting love; I have drawn you with unfailing kindness"** (Jeremiah 31:3).

God honors us with something greater than wilting flowers. He draws us to himself with the purest form of love. His love rescues us from pain and death. His love restores us to who he wanted us to be when he first knew us before time began.

He nurtures, strengthens, and sets us on our feet readied with the gospel. With arms full of mercy and grace blossoms that are fresh every morning, we daily hand to the brokenhearted a genuine valentine from Jesus.

"This is love: not that we loved God, but that he loved us and sent his Son as an atoning sacrifice for our sins. Dear friends, since God so loved us, we also ought to love one another" (1 John 4:10,11).

Under God's care
Andrea Delwiche

"The LORD makes firm the steps of the one who delights in him; though he may stumble, he will not fall, for the LORD upholds him with his hand. I was young and now I am old, yet I have never seen the righteous forsaken or their children begging bread. They are always generous and lend freely; their children will be a blessing" (Psalm 37:23-26).

We don't always value the wisdom of our elders. But it can be good to hear from someone who has seen *more* than we have seen and not only survived but thrived. King David, the writer of Psalm 37, is such a witness.

What had David learned over a lifetime of following the Lord?

God's provision and love allow his followers to live with a heart free from burden. We don't need to fret or be envious of others. Instead, we can spend that time delighting in God and committing to following him.

God always provides for his children out of his endless supplies, and so we can be generous and show selfless love to others.

When life is difficult and we struggle to see the way forward, it is good to **"be still before the LORD and wait patiently for him"** (verse 7). He will guide us forward.

God's provision is so much bigger than what we can see or understand. We are always under God's care and have both now and eternity to grow and flourish in his grace. This earth is only the beginning of this adventure with our good God.

God's weird (but beautiful) Word
Pastor Mike Novotny

Psalm 133 might be the weirdest/most beautiful analogy in the Bible. It says that living in unity with God's people **"is like precious oil poured on the head, running down on the beard, running down on Aaron's beard, down on the collar of his robe"** (verse 2).

Imagine pouring a bottle of extra virgin olive oil over your buddy's head and watching the thick liquid glisten in his beard and slip under the collar of his shirt. Isn't that a wonderful image?

Maybe I should explain. Back around 1500 B.C., God chose Aaron to be the high priest. Aaron would pray for the people and bring sacrifices for the sins of the people, a little preview of Jesus, who would help us in our relationship with God too. When Aaron started his work, the people would pour a special blend of oil over Aaron's head as a unique way to say, "This is the one whom God called to help us spiritually."

Now that's a beautiful picture, isn't it? When you do life together with other Christians, you don't have to figure out faith alone. Instead, you're surrounded by people who help you, calling you out when you're on the wrong path and bringing you to the cross when you know you've messed up.

If you have relationships like that, praise God today because not everyone does. If not, pray to God to open doors so you can do life together with others who love Jesus.

Ashes, ashes, we all fall down
Pastor David Scharf

"Ring around the rosy, a pocketful of posies. Ashes, ashes, we all fall down!" Few people realize that this nursery rhyme dates all the way back to 1347. The Black Plague in Europe claimed more than 25 million lives. "Ashes, ashes" (or "atischoo, atischoo") is an imitation of the sneezing sounds of the infected person, followed by people "falling down" in death. The season of Lent, perhaps more than any other season of the church year, confronts us with our sin.

As we walk with Jesus in Lent, we will contemplate his suffering in our place. We will put on "sackcloth and ashes," reminded that as sinners before God we are nothing but "dust and ashes" (Genesis 18:27). We will contemplate the inexpressible love of Jesus who died for ashen sinners on Good Friday. However, Lent is not the end. Rather, it prepares us for Easter. Through our risen Savior, we too rise from the ashes. **"[He will] bestow on [us] a crown of beauty instead of ashes, the oil of joy instead of mourning, and a garment of praise instead of a spirit of despair"** (Isaiah 61:3).

Evaluate your life. Repent of all the ways you have missed the mark. Completely despair of saving yourself so that you must look to Jesus, the only One who can save. Then be at peace with God, knowing *all* is forgiven.

February 18

God is love
Sarah Habben

"God is love" (1 John 4:8). What a beautiful truth for sinners who wonder if God can forgive them. What a bonfire of comfort for the Christian walking in death's cold shadow. It's true: God's love is his *essence*.

But what does that love look like when you're giving in to temptation—having sex before marriage or cheating at school or lingering over bad websites or drinking too much? You might find yourself thinking, "So I'm a little messed up, no biggie. God is a God of *love*, not judgment!"

Does God's love look like a benevolent wink? Verse 10 of this same chapter gives us context. It says, **"This is love: not that we loved God, but that he loved us** *and sent his Son as an atoning sacrifice for our sins."*

God's love looked on humanity and *judged* us. We're not a little messed up. We're desperate, lost, hell-bound sinners, each of us chasing after what is best for "me." God's essence is love, yes. But it is also holiness. Holiness and sin cannot coexist peacefully any more than fire and paper. Sin must burn. What does God's love look like in the face of our sin? It's not a chummy wink. It's a public execution. It's God's dear Son being punished in our place.

Lord, when I'm tempted to think of your love as a free pass, draw me back to your cross. Show me there how big my sin is. Show me there how much bigger is your love. Amen.

Light in the darkness
Pastor Clark Schultz

I'm afraid of the dark. Are you? Our home has a night-light in almost every room. I'm proud to say a small plane could land safely with the lighting we have. What is it about darkness that's so frightening? Is it the fear of the unknown or being unable to see?

The fear of being unable to see describes many of the Jews at Jesus' time. They couldn't see that Jesus was the promised Messiah.

This passage from Matthew cites directly from Isaiah to show Jesus was the fulfillment of the Old Testament prophecies: **"The people living in darkness have seen a great light"** (4:16). But the Jews who prided themselves on Moses and the Prophets couldn't see the connection—Jesus is the Light.

Now before I jump all over them, I have to admit I too can't always see the Savior in the Scriptures. I let doubt or my to-do list cloud me from seeing Jesus for who he truly is. My concerns, worries, and sinful habits block my vision of seeing Jesus as the fulfiller of prophecy; the light in my dark world; the Savior of all; the forgiver of my sins; the One who stretched out his arms to die for me, to reach for me, and to tell me all will work out for my good. To Jesus the Light of the world, I say thank you and pray for the strength to shine to others in the dark who need to know who he really is.

Know anyone who could use some light?

Lead your heart
Pastor Daron Lindemann

Disney movies, graduation speeches, motivational blogs, and even some well-meaning mommies preach, "Follow your heart."

Let's appreciate the idea that our head knowledge can't always engineer in our minds what we truly need to understand. After all, love is more than a legal contract. It's truly a matter of the heart.

But that doesn't mean that the human heart should be calling the shots. **"The heart is deceitful above all things"** (Jeremiah 17:9). If you follow your heart, it's going to lead you astray sooner or later. And you may not realize it until it's too late.

Now, don't be heartless. Employ your heart. Involve your heart. Put your heart into the service of God's kingdom work around you and in you. Yes, go at it with **"all your heart"** (Mark 12:30).

In the same way, you love and serve God with all your money, but your money isn't telling you what to do. You love and serve God with your body, your time, and what you eat and drink. But these must not be your masters. No, you manage them. You are the steward of them as gifts from God employed for his glory.

"Above all else, guard your heart, for everything you do flows from it" (Proverbs 4:23). You lead. Your heart follows. From the outside of your heart, you take a position of guarding and protecting it so that it can serve you.

Don't follow your heart. Lead your heart.

God works for our good
Sarah Habben

"We know that in all things God works for the good of those who love him, who have been called according to his purpose" (Romans 8:28).

We often want this verse to mean, *God allows hardship so he can give me something better.* For example, a flooded basement means God has a better house in mind for me. A failed relationship or job means God's got something happier planned. God's "good" is something tangible, material, immediate . . . right?

Sometimes. Sometimes not.

When we put verse 28 back in context, we see the little word "for." **"For those God foreknew he also predestined to be conformed to the image of his Son"** (verse 29).

God works in all things—the heartbreaking and joy-making—for our good. But God's promise here is not to mop up our spilled ice cream and hand us a bigger cone. His promise is to make us more like Jesus—loving, faithful Jesus who obeyed his Father all the way to the cross.

- God's primary concern is our *holiness*, not our prosperity.
- God will work things out for our *spiritual* good, not always our material good.
- God's promise is *eternal* life, not an easy life.

Strangely, it's a relief! We don't need to doubt God's love when we see no tangible good wrestled from evil. We don't need to wonder if he's punishing us when things go wrong. We KNOW God is working for our good. How? He's shaping us to be like Jesus. He's preparing us for our heavenly home.

Rest and . . . grow
Andrea Delwiche

We have an opportunity right now to journey into the heart of God's kingdom plan for us. Take a few minutes to quiet your mind with the Spirit's help, and then dwell on these words: **"How precious is your steadfast love, O God! The children of mankind take refuge in the shadow of your wings. They feast on the abundance of your house, and you give them drink from the river of your delights. For with you is the fountain of life; in your light do we see light"** (Psalm 36:7-9 ESV).

Can you picture yourself resting in the shadow of God's loving protection? Can you picture God's house, perhaps set in a green valley with light shining in the windows? Can you see the front door open and God inviting you inside to share a fireside dinner with him? Can you picture him handing you a sturdy-handled cup and encouraging you, "Here, drink from the river of my delights!" Can you visualize the fountain of life, the living water promised by Jesus himself?

What we are offered by the triune God is no less than a reservoir of new life that we can drink from right now and into eternity. Now, through Christ, we are invited to rest our weary selves and grow as new people, Christ's followers in Christ's kingdom.

This is reality: quiet springs of protection, rest, and renewal. In his light, we can see light.

The hurt of forgiveness heals
Pastor Daron Lindemann

Just forgive and forget. Have you heard that advice? It likely developed as encouragement from people who don't know grace.

Joseph knew grace. God's story of Joseph reveals a privileged young man who taunted his older brothers. So they hurt him, bullying him and bartering him off to slave traders.

Through more injustices, Joseph learned more about hurt. It opened the door for God's providing grace. **"The LORD was with Joseph so that he prospered"** (Genesis 39:2).

Like scars, the hurt Joseph experienced did not disappear from his memory or story. But by faith he came to learn that the hurt, the pain, the injustice would not be the author of his story.

Scars help us reframe the hurt by God's healing grace. They tell not just our story but God's story.

When Joseph, who became a ruler in Egypt, saw his brothers later in life, he remembered the hurt. How could he forget? But by God's grace, his hurt had been healed. He forgave his brothers.

"'Don't be afraid. Am I in the place of God? You intended to harm me, but God intended it for good to accomplish what is now being done, the saving of many lives. So then, don't be afraid. I will provide for you and your children.' And he reassured them and spoke kindly to them" (Genesis 50:19-21).

Forgiveness doesn't always forget. It always trusts God's grace.

I love bread!
Pastor David Scharf

I love bread! I love it toasted and slathered with real butter. I love it at those nice restaurants doused in olive oil and vinegar. I love it covered with bacon, lettuce, and tomato (but mostly the bacon!). My apologies to anyone struggling to stay true to the Atkins diet, but are you hungry yet? Come to think of it, I'm not sure it's the bread I love or what I put on the bread.

Jesus said, **"I am the bread of life. I am the living bread that came down from heaven. Whoever eats this bread will live forever. This bread is my flesh, which I will give for the life of the world"** (John 6:48,51). I love Jesus, but I love him more topped with material comfort in life. I love Jesus covered in personal success. I love Jesus slathered in the approval of family, friends, and coworkers. Do you see my point? We need to strip away the toppings and just crave the bread . . . the Bread of Life, that is. This bread is Jesus.

It's easy to get entranced by what the world says we need and fail to appreciate that there is only one thing we need. We need bread . . . spiritual bread. We were starving, so Jesus came down from heaven to satisfy our need. This bread gives us the message of the cross in his Word that feeds us so we can live forever. Are you hungry yet? Me too!

Thought leaders wanted
Jason Nelson

I was watching a slideshow predicting which jobs won't exist in the future and which jobs will be the hot ticket. It doesn't look good for coal miners. It looks promising for climate scientists. I didn't see it on any list, but it seems to me that a good field to go into would be thought leadership. Good ideas are always needed, and good thinkers are in short supply.

Archimedes was an early Greek thought leader who lived a couple hundred years before Jesus. He was a mathematician, engineer, physicist, inventor, and astronomer. He said, "Give me a long enough lever and a place to stand and I could move the earth." Thought leaders know more than a little about a lot of things, and they see what you could accomplish if you put the pieces together. They thoroughly enjoy the moment of discovery. When Archimedes first realized there was this thing called buoyancy, it's said he ran naked from his overflowing bathtub and was heard to say, "Eureka!" ("I found it!").

Thought leaders are products of a well-rounded education. May every classroom be a think tank. Pray God would raise up new generations of thought leaders who can improve our churches, our schools, our government, our medical outcomes, and our download speeds. We know he can do it because his heaven is higher than our earth. His ways are higher than our ways. And his thoughts are higher than our thoughts (Isaiah 55:9).

God's timing
Pastor Mike Novotny

I had zero idea what would happen the Saturday after the Tuesday that I released my book. Back on January 7, 2020, I released 3 *Words That Will Change Your Life*, a book about the power of God's presence, how God is the refuge we can run to no matter how bad life gets. But I had no clue what would happen four days later. On the other side of the planet, on January 11, the first-known coronavirus patient died. And our world, as you now know, fell apart.

God must have known that we would need a safe place to hide when things were turned upside down. **"God is our refuge and strength, an ever-present help in trouble. Therefore we will not fear, though the earth give way and the mountains fall into the heart of the sea, though its waters roar and foam and the mountains quake with their surging"** (Psalm 46:1-3).

I love how graphic those final words are. Even when the earth gives way and the mountains fall apart (or when the economy gives way or your family falls apart), we don't need to be afraid because we have God. Our refuge. Our strength. Our 24/7 help in times of trouble.

Maybe you're reading these words today for a specific reason. Maybe God is preparing you to face the next season of your life, no matter what happens, without fear. Through Jesus, his presence is your refuge. Run to him today, and know that you will never be alone or unloved.

No separation anxiety
Jan Gompper

I was in a department store one day when suddenly I heard a bloodcurdling scream, followed by relentless sobbing. A little boy had gotten separated from his parent.

Separation anxiety is real. Small children, people who've lost a spouse, divorced people, and even dogs experience it.

Those of us who believe in heaven and hell have images in our minds of what those two places will be like. In fact, Scripture gives us pictures of both. These are just some examples of what hell will be like: the rich man whose thirst could not be quenched (Luke 16:19-31), a lake of fire (Revelation 20:10), a fiery furnace (Matthew 13:50), chains of gloomy darkness (2 Peter 2:4), etc.

But that little child's terrified cry made me wonder if those images are not even the worst part of what hell will be like. The worst part will be living in a constant state of panic and anxiety that will never be quelled. We will be separated eternally from the gracious presence of God.

Thankfully, we have the assurance that God will *never* let go of our hands. He has promised, **"Never will I leave you; never will I forsake you"** (Hebrews 13:5). Even when we "wander off" or sometimes try to push him away, Jesus grasps our hands even more tightly, and he will never let go until we are safely back in the arms of our heavenly Father.

Because of faith in Christ, we will never experience eternal separation anxiety.

Remind me, Lord
Andrea Delwiche

In these times, feeling safe and secure can seem like a relic of the past. Perhaps we used to be able to brush off our worries, but no more. Our hearts race with fear. The muscles of our neck tighten as we dwell on our mental list of problems. Troubles are as stark as the newsprint in the morning paper. The diversions that we've used to cover over injustice and hatred, excess and comfortability are being exhausted. Saving ourselves and our families through our own means begins to look as laughable as it truly is.

We don't need to save ourselves. We can't save ourselves. Not day to day. Not eternally. The same Lord Jesus who saved us to spend eternity with him lives inside each of us today and works in, with, and through us to care for us now. He keeps our feet on level ground and guards our hearts, minds, and bodies with his immeasurable love.

"Reassure me; let me hear you say, 'I'll save you'" (Psalm 35:3 MSG).

The psalmist's request of the Lord can be our prayer too. He says, in effect, "Lord, remind me that you alone are my salvation." We need to be reminded of this—maybe even on an hourly basis some days.

In the past week, how has God provided you with reminders of his salvation? Can these gifts spur a prayer and expression of thanksgiving? How about a foundation for deep peace?

May God help you rest and live joyously, wrapped in his love.

March

If we confess our sins, he is faithful
and just and will forgive us our sins and
purify us from all unrighteousness.

1 John 1:9

The finish line of life
Pastor Mike Novotny

When Bill Broadhurst entered the 1981 Pepsi 10K in Omaha, he stood no chance of winning. Ten years earlier he had a brain aneurysm that left him partially paralyzed, which made every step of those 6.2 miles feel like a marathon. But Bill still signed up because his hero was racing that day. Bill Rodgers, the world-class athlete who had just won his third straight Boston Marathon, made the trip over to Omaha, a race he would easily win. But "easily" would be the last word to describe Bill Broadhurst's run. After 2 hours and 29 minutes, a 24-minute mile average, he crawled across the finish line, dragging his exhausted body, finishing dead last.

But guess who appeared? Bill Rodgers strode toward Broadhurst, gold medal around his neck, and smiled. "Here," Rodgers said, taking the medal off and placing it over the heart of the man who had finished last.

Isn't that just like our story? We spiritually stumble through our lives, falling short and falling down. We struggle to do the right thing, to say the right thing, to think the right thing. We sometimes feel dead last in the race for the perfect Christian life. But then Jesus appears, the Jesus who ran the perfect race, the Jesus who endured every step of the way. And he takes his prize—his constant connection to God—and he says, "Here." It's his gift. And it is ours through faith.

"For the wages of sin is death, but the gift of God is eternal life in Christ Jesus our Lord" (Romans 6:23). What a gift! What a Savior!

Forgiving yourself
Pastor Jon Enter

When you've done wrong and it's altered life, wrecked relationships, and can't be undone, guilt comes. It suffocates and steals joy. Guilt presses you down into despair.

What do you need to forgive yourself for? What careless comment did you spew or destructive deed did you do that changed your life?

King David knew his multilayered answer to that question: An affair. A drunken cover-up. A carefully planned and concocted murder. David ran from the responsibility of what he did until confronted by God's prophet: **"Then I acknowledged my sin to you and did not cover up my iniquity. I said, 'I will confess my transgressions to the LORD.' And you forgave the guilt of my sin"** (Psalm 32:5).

David acknowledged his sin without excuse. God forgave him, and here's the key part: God forgave the guilt of his sin.

I'm guessing you've confessed to Jesus that big, ugly sin you committed, likely apologizing many times over. Why are you apologizing again for something God already forgave? It's forgiven and forever removed!

You keep apologizing and don't feel forgiven . . . the guilt remains . . . because you haven't forgiven yourself.

When the devil attacks with memories of what you did—and he will because it works—tell off the devil with these words: "Devil, I'm forgiven. That's not me anymore! I'm forgiven by God, and I forgive myself." Treat yourself with the same grace and goodness that God gives you. For God has forgiven even the guilt of your sin.

The story of Stacey King
Pastor Mike Novotny

Have you ever heard of Stacey King? He was a rookie for the Chicago Bulls in 1990 who almost lost a game against the Cleveland Cavaliers. King missed a few key free throws, finishing the game with only a single point. Thankfully, however, another king was on the court that night—Michael Jordan. MJ had one of the best games of his career, ending that night with a whopping 69 points and leading the Bulls to an overtime victory.

After the game, a reporter asked Stacey King about his night on the court. King replied, "I will always remember this as the night that Michael Jordan and I combined to score 70 points."

Ha! Isn't that great? I love that quote, but I love the truth that it reminds me of even more, namely, that we go through life with the King of kings by our side. Jesus is even better than Jordan, and his presence comes with power. What struggle are you facing that's bigger than Jesus? What situation is stressing you out that's bigger than Jesus? What sin have you committed that's bigger than Jesus?

When Jesus said, **"Surely I am with you always"** (Matthew 28:20), he made a game-changing promise, a promise that would enable the apostles to make disciples of nations, the same promise that enables us to do things that seem impossible without him.

So don't be afraid. Despite your weaknesses, Jesus is with you. This just might be the day that you and Jesus combine to do something extraordinary!

I look good!
Pastor David Scharf

Sometimes my wife grimaces when I exit the bedroom in the morning. "What's the matter? Doesn't this match?" I ask. "Nope! Not even close!" She replies. That's my cue to turn around and try again!

I wonder how often people who know I'm a Christian look at my life and grimace because I don't match. That is to say, what I do and what I believe don't always match. I say I'm a Christian, but sometimes others could rightly say of my life, "Nope! Not even close!"

That's a problem. You and I need the right clothes to get into heaven. It's like a fancy restaurant that requires the gentlemen to wear suit coats to dine there. Without the right clothes, you can't get in! When it comes to heaven, nothing short of the perfection of Jesus will do.

Here's God's solution: **"For all of you who were baptized into Christ have clothed yourselves with Christ"** (Galatians 3:27). Do you see what God's done for you? He's dressed you in an immaculate outfit. He's clothed you with Jesus himself in your baptism! You're right now wearing the most beautiful clothing ever, made from the threads of Jesus' perfect life and woven together on the loom of the cross. Your clothes match the perfection of heaven. Now, when you look in the mirror today, you get to say (and mean it!), "I look good!"

Ordinary is how God ordinarily works
Pastor Mike Novotny

I bet you'd love to make some extraordinary changes in your life. Maybe to unconditionally love the people in your family, even that sibling who never sees eye to eye with you. Or maybe you want to trust God so much that you hold on to your peace no matter what happens. The kind of faith that says to sickness, to cancer, or the latest political mess, "God knows about this. God's got this. I'm good." Or maybe you want to put God first in your budget for the first time. Or forgive the one who abused you so many years ago. Or be courageous enough to share your faith with an old friend. These are all extraordinary acts of faith!

But do you know how God tends to do extraordinary things in our lives? Through ordinary stuff. Like going to church. Like thoughtfully praying the Lord's Prayer. Like reading (and truly thinking about) a daily devotion. Like asking good questions and listening to people's answers. Just like the tallest tree became extraordinary through thousands of ordinary days and hundreds of ordinary rain showers, God loves to use simple, easy-to-miss habits to shape us into Christ-like people.

"[The kingdom of God] is like a mustard seed, which is the smallest of all seeds on earth. Yet when planted, it grows and becomes the largest of all garden plants, with such big branches that the birds can perch in its shade" (Mark 4:31,32).

So don't miss the power of the ordinary. Ordinary is how God ordinarily works.

A little bit racist?
Jan Gompper

A song in the Broadway musical *Avenue Q* kind of shocked me when I first heard its refrain. The lyrics say that everyone is a little racist sometimes and that we've all made judgments based on race.

Racist? Me? Impossible. Or is it?

If we're honest, we *are* all a little bit racist. And even the things we think "don't count," like a little racial joke or a stereotypical comment about a particular race, have helped fuel the division and hurt we see across the country.

Of course, we don't *want* to be prejudicial, but we are because of sin. That's not an excuse; it's a fact. And the sad truth is that we will never live in a world free of racism and prejudice this side of heaven. Owning up to our sin of racism, however, is one step toward breaching the divide.

Until heaven *is* our home, we must never stop chanting our country's mantra of "liberty and justice for all." It's a mantra our heavenly Father penned long before our constitutional forefathers did: **"There is no longer Jew or Gentile, slave or free, male and female. For *you are all one* in Christ Jesus"** (Galatians 3:28 NLT).

I long for when I will finally be able to experience what the apostle John envisioned in Revelation: **"After this I saw a vast crowd, too great to count, from *every* nation and tribe and people and language, standing in front of the throne and before the Lamb"** (7:9 NLT).

One thing is certain—God is not racist—not even a little bit.

Upgraded wardrobe
Pastor Clark Schultz

If you look at a calendar in August or January, you won't see it like you do other major holidays, but the first day of school is dubbed "Wear Your New Clothes" day. Flashback to my eighth-grade year when a friend asked me, "Hey, are those a new pair of corduroy jeans?" My answer, "Why no they're not." His response: "Oh, because I see the sales tag and sizing sticker are still attached to the back of your pant leg." Gulp! Embarrassed or not, there's pride/confidence in showing off the new kicks, flat brim hat, jersey, or jeans.

This same confidence can be said of the new threads you wear spiritually. Jesus gave you an upgrade in your wardrobe. **"I delight greatly in the Lord; my soul rejoices in my God. For he has clothed me with garments of salvation and arrayed me in a robe of his righteousness"** (Isaiah 61:10).

This wasn't always the case. By nature, we're soiled in sin. But God in his mercy clothes us in his Son's robe of righteousness (we're holy and sinless because of Jesus!). It's a robe we didn't earn. One drop of Jesus' blood is the ultimate stain cleanser. Total forgiveness. We're not covered in designer clothes that go out of style or are later sold online. We have divine clothes from the ultimate fashion/creation designer, God himself.

On the first day of school, work, or week, walk with confidence in what you wear!

Risk factor
Christine Wentzel

"I'm not judging you; I'm just sayin' . . ." is a trendy, risk-adverse attempt to vent one's opinion without the added bonus of dealing with a guilty conscience. The devil is eager to help people dodge the consequences of this sin, much to their shame.

No one likes to be corrected. But we need checks and balances grounded in the Scriptures and carried out in a trust-filled community of our peers. Jesus is clear on how to deal with sinful behavior in the church (Matthew 18:15-20). In verse 15, he starts with: **"If your brother or sister sins, go and point out their fault, just between the two of you. If they listen to you, you have won them over."**

It's at this crucial first step where self-righteous temptations can trip us up. For some, "I come in Christian love . . ." can mean the same as, "I'm not judging you; I'm just sayin' . . ." Checking our motives before starting this process will make all the difference in the world to winning repentant hearts or making matters worse. Humbly recognizing our own sinful hearts and remembering Jesus' mercy and forgiveness is crucial before we take the first steps in Christian correction. Give the benefit of the doubt by making space for grace in which the two of you can work it out for the glory of God our Father. Leave the risk factor for how it turns out in his perfect hands.

"For where two or three gather in my name, there am I with them" (verse 20).

A mission that's worth it!
Pastor David Scharf

Jesus said, **"Go and make disciples of all nations . . . and surely I am with you always, to the very end of the age"** (Matthew 28:19,20).

But it's hard to tell people about Jesus, isn't it? I think William Carey would agree. The year was 1793, and William Carey kept asking, "Why is no one sharing the gospel with the millions of people in India?" And his friends said, "That's a great idea, William. Why don't you do it?"

And he did. He left behind a comfortable life in England to go to a land he'd never seen with languages he'd never heard to share the message of Jesus with millions of people who had never heard it. Not only that, if they did listen, it would mean that they would suffer social disgrace and be cut off from their families. He had no place to live and no place to work when he landed in Calcutta. The odds were not in his favor.

But he preached anyway. He preached for six years, and no one came. Finally, after seven years and learning seven languages, God blessed him with one convert— Krishna Pal. Was it worth it? Well, today there are over 28 million Christians in India. God doesn't ask us to be successful. He asks us to share the message, assures us of his presence, and promises to take care of the rest. Who can you tell in your mission field today? It's a mission that's worth it!

The most shocking thing about Jesus
Pastor Mike Novotny

The most shocking thing about Jesus might not be his death. I can't imagine his death on a cross—the crown of thorns, the nails, the pain—but what really shocks me is Jesus' life. Because for his entire life, his love endured forever. He didn't run out of love a single time. He never, ever, ever said, "I'm done." He never rolled his eyes at Mary or talked back to Joseph (not even when they told their 12-year-old to do his chores). Jesus loved and then loved and then loved some more, a walking and talking Psalm 136. He obeyed his Father, then obeyed the next day, and then obeyed his whole life. He remembered our sinful situation, our lives filled with temporary love, so he lived for us. Jesus constantly loves for us. His love endures forever. **"Give thanks to the God of heaven. His love endures forever"** (Psalm 136:26).

That means that through faith in Jesus, you get love that endures forever. No matter what fails or sputters or ends, the best part of your life never will—God. The God who can calm your storms, who cares about your anxiety, who controls the economy, who knows every last hair on your head, who's enough for your heart, who's near in your struggles is the same God whose love endures forever.

There are many reasons to praise Jesus. But Jesus' life of constant love just might be the most shocking thing and most praiseworthy thing about him.

Don't despise ordinary things
Pastor Mike Novotny

I almost got depressed the other day in church. As I was preaching, I said, "After six years as your pastor, I have preached 200-300 sermons in this church. Show of hands—how many of you remember all of them? half of them? 100 of them? 10 of them? any of them?" I wish I could tell you that excited hands filled the air with each question, but the air stayed empty until a smattering of people reacted to my final question.

I was almost depressed. It takes me 10-15 hours to prepare each sermon, so I had spent 2,000-4,500 hours on those messages. And only a few people remembered a few of the things I said. Ugh.

But, thankfully, God reminded me that he loves to work through ordinary things. Defenseless toddlers become strong teenagers through 10,000 meals that they will mostly forget. And children of God become strong in their faith through 300 sermons whose themes they won't be able to name. That's okay. In fact, that keeps us humble and ensures that God gets the glory.

Like me, you will do a lot of good things that people won't remember in a few years . . . or hours. But don't get depressed. The prophet Zechariah once wrote, **"Who dares despise the day of small things?"** (Zechariah 4:10). In the kingdom of God, small things do great things. Don't despise them, even if others forget them.

What small thing might God be using in your life today?

Living forgiveness
Pastor Jon Enter

What is it? What past failure do you still feel awful about? When the memory of that horrible decision hits, it can make you feel worthless, unworthy of God's love.

Don't live in the past! Pastor Paul wrote to the new Christians in Philippi, explaining how to live differently, to live in forgiveness: **"Brothers and sisters, whatever is true, whatever is noble, whatever is right, whatever is pure, whatever is lovely, whatever is admirable—if anything is excellent or praiseworthy—think about such things"** (Philippians 4:8). Why just think about them? Why not command us to do them? Because Paul knew how God built us. Where our focus is, there we follow. If you focus on the negativity of your past, you'll be negative, hurting yourself and others. But if you think about what is true, noble, right . . . that's what the Spirit will lead you to do!

Live unshackled; live freely forgiven both by God and by yourself!

I have a challenge for you. It'll be awkward at first, but soon it will transform you. Each time you're in the bathroom, look at yourself in the mirror. There's no place to hide. Say to yourself, "I'm forgiven by Jesus. I forgive me. I'm worth it." It's personal and powerful.

Your mind knows you're forgiven and changed. Your heart is where the battle rages. Speak to yourself, to your heart, that you are worth it. If you doubt your value, look to the cross, and you'll see just how much you're truly worth!

The joy of forgiveness
Pastor Daron Lindemann

"Let me hear joy and gladness; let the bones you have crushed rejoice. Hide your face from my sins and blot out all my iniquity" (Psalm 51:8,9).

Todd helped me break the first bone I ever broke. I broke my finger. Oh, that hurt! A month later I bumped it and, "Ouch!"

I was so glad when it finally healed. The sign to me that it had finally healed was I didn't notice any pain when I bumped it. The bone that I crushed (with Todd's help) rejoiced!

See the word "bones" in this psalm; it's plural. Many bones. Imagine if every bone in your body (the human body has 206 bones) was broken. Ouch! It would hurt for months, but then there would be healing and rejoicing!

They probably wouldn't heal at the exact same time either, so you'd experience multiple moments of joy.

Look again at this psalm verse. There is one "iniquity." That word means "guiltiness." One, massive, shameful piece of sin is what we were. But in Jesus Christ, God forgave us in one massive work of salvation when Jesus paid the price for our sins. He died and rose.

Now, instead of just saying, "I forgive you" one time and telling you that you better remember it or you'll be sad, God says, "I forgive you" for each one of your sins. And says it often.

Every bone rejoices! Every one of your sins every day is fully forgiven, specifically, individually, again and again! That's joyful forgiveness!

Your (extra)ordinary Savior
Pastor Mike Novotny

Did you know that one of the most common names for Jewish boys in Jesus' time was Jesus? I'm not making that up. Check out this passage: **"Pilate asked them, 'Which one do you want me to release to you: Jesus Barabbas, or Jesus who is called the Messiah?'"** (Matthew 27:17). Or this one: **"Jesus, who is called Justus, also sends greetings"** (Colossians 4:11). No wonder they called our Savior—Jesus of Nazareth. There were a lot of Jesuses running around!

But that man with the ordinary name would do extraordinary things. Jesus of Nazareth lived for us, died for us, bled for us, and substituted himself for us so that anyone who believes in him, any ordinary sinner, could have eternal life—a place in the presence of God, a life where spiritual happiness wouldn't be interrupted by tragedy or loss. Through faith, we spend every moment of our entire lives with the God of all creation at our side! Extraordinary, isn't it?

We are relatively ordinary people. We have names that dozens of others in our towns share. We do work that could be duplicated by millions of other people. We live in homes that, perhaps, others lived in before and still others will live in after we are gone. Yet there is something extraordinary about us. We have God. God with us, for us, and working through us.

All because that guy with the ordinary name offered us extraordinary grace.

Unchain my soul
Jason Nelson

I am yearning to be free. I am yearning for a better society, and I think we could have one if we all wanted it and talked openly about it. I am yearning to be free to discuss how God's grace flows into and out of human potential. I don't want to debate which humans have potential. I don't want to worry about falling into theology traps that restrict Christian commentary to a narrow range of topics that is summarized with a set of low expectations. I am yearning to pursue lofty ideals. I like people and want to appeal to their better angels. I am yearning to urge people to be good and do good because God is good.

When Jesus showed up in a body, he accepted our brotherhood and sisterhood and even promoted it. He redeemed us with his blood and taught us how to live with one another along the way. When did we stop emphasizing, **"Do to others as you would have them do to you"** (Luke 6:31)? Was it just too simple? Was it not obscure enough for religious elites because we wouldn't need anyone to explain it to us? Who had a meeting and decided the Golden Rule was sappy moralizing and not a moral imperative from the very lips of Jesus himself? I am yearning to be free to do for others what I want them to do for me. I am yearning for you to do the same.

Your group and more fruit
Pastor Mike Novotny

There's an obscure but incredible reference in the Bible to the power of doing life together with other Christians. Psalm 133 says that God's people living together in unity **"is as if the dew of Hermon were falling on Mount Zion"** (verse 3).

I told you it was obscure! "Hermon" is a reference to Mt. Hermon, a towering peak north of the Sea of Galilee, which gets about 55 inches of precipitation each year (50% more than the city of Seattle). "Mount Zion" is a nickname for the city of Jerusalem, which soaks in 22 inches of rain annually. Jerusalem is not a year-round desert. During the rainy season, it turns green and produces fruit. But can you imagine how fruitful it would be if the dew of Mt. Hermon moved south and fell on Jerusalem's hills?

What a perfect analogy for us! Like Jerusalem, you can be fruitful (patient, loving, joyful) without a group of Christians. Attending church and reading devotions at home is, without a doubt, a way that the Spirit strengthens your faith. But when you add others, when you share burdens and prayers and reminders of God's love, you burst with life in ways that you didn't before. A friend's faith can increase your joy. A brother's burden can be your chance to show more kindness and love. A sister's confession of Jesus can restore your peace.

Do you have a group yet? If not, ask God to help you get a group and increase the fruit of your faith.

Search me, God
Andrea Delwiche

Someone hurts you, and you're embarrassed, wounded, and betrayed. You tell yourself and others that you've forgiven them, but you nurture your grievance deep in your soul. You have not forgiven. The debris of hatred and anger begins to accumulate. The flow of God's cleansing water is diverted. You may not even realize it.

Psalm 139 goes into great detail about God's ability to know, with his loving Father-heart, where we are: **"You have searched me, Lord, and you know me. You know when I sit and when I rise; you perceive my thoughts from afar. You discern my going out and my lying down; you are familiar with all my ways"** (verses 1–3).

God knows more than our location on Planet Earth. He deeply understands where we are in regard to our relationship with him and others. Scary thought or lifeline?

Lifeline. When we ask him, **"Search me, God, and know my heart; test me and know my anxious thoughts"** (verses 23,24), we are asking him to shine a light into our dark corners and sweep out any accumulated debris. Then God's waters of life flow freely.

What if you sat quietly today with the Lord and invited him to "search you" to see if there is any grudge that you hold against another person? Picture him looking in the corners of your soul. As he reveals sore spots to you, ask him to **"lead [you] in the way everlasting"** (verse 24) and help you sweep away anger and hatred and let his healing love flow.

Why a burning bush?
Pastor Mike Novotny

Sometimes I don't ask the most obvious questions until decades later. Like the burning bush. I've known the story of Moses and the burning bush since I was in Sunday school, but it wasn't until recently that I asked, "Why a burning bush?" God could have spoken to Moses in a tornado or a dream or through a donkey, so why a fiery bush that didn't burn up?

The more I pondered that question and reexamined the old story, the more I saw three truths: First, just like fire, God is dangerous. **"'Do not come any closer,' God said. 'Take off your sandals, for the place where you are standing is holy ground'"** (Exodus 3:5). You can't just run into a fire without serious protection, just like you can't run into God's presence without the protecting blood of Jesus. Second, just like fire, God is life giving. **"I have come down to rescue them from the hand of the Egyptians"** (Exodus 3:8). Just like the fiery sun gives us life, God's rescuing hand gives us eternal life in his presence. Third, just like that bush, the eternal God doesn't burn up. **"God said to Moses, 'I AM WHO I AM'"** (Exodus 3:14). Our God isn't "I Was" or "I Will Be for a Bit" but the always-around "I AM."

When God appeared to Moses that day, he wanted to stress three of the most important things in the universe. And while we haven't seen the same miracle, the same God is here today—holy, life giving, with us always.

Unbreakable
Sarah Habben

In the humid climate of the Caribbean, closed-toe shoes were something I only wore under duress, like when I had to renew my visa and comply with the Immigration Department's dress code. One such day, I was schlepping several blocks between Immigration and Treasury in my "immigration shoes" when the toe of one shoe started flapping. I shuffled back to my car, hoping the sole wouldn't peel off before I could get home and find a different pair.

Glue unsticks. Stitches loosen. Nails rust. Friendships flop. There isn't a bond that can't be broken. Except one: God's love for sinners like you and me. The apostle Paul wrote, **"For I am convinced that neither death nor life, neither angels nor demons, neither the present nor the future, nor any powers, neither height nor depth, nor anything else in all creation, will be able to separate us from the love of God that is in Christ Jesus our Lord"** (Romans 8:38,39).

Note that list of challenges. God's love doesn't guarantee an easy life! Christians die; face temptation and uncertain futures; and live with evil governments, bad bosses, and deep losses. But not one of those hardships means God's love for us has come unglued. The best proof of this is Jesus' outstretched arms on the cross. He embraced the whole world with those loving arms, forgiving us even for the days we scorn his love and put our faith lives on the back burner.

Lord, keep your unbreakable love before our eyes so that we never tire or turn from it. Amen.

Do you believe in arranged marriage?
Pastor Daron Lindemann

Some cultures today practice the custom of arranged marriages. It's much different than our modern American culture.

Either is acceptable to God. But know this: God has arranged a marriage that outshines, outloves, and outlives any other marriage or marital status (single, divorced, widowed, married, or remarried).

God chose all believers to be his own bride. He chose us even though our sins make us unattractive. He knew he was "marrying down" but also knew that this marriage would change us, transform us, and not just make us a bit better but holy!

The Bible refers to believers as the bride and Jesus as the groom. Jesus **"gave himself up for her to make her holy, cleansing her by the washing with water through the word, and to present her to himself as a radiant church, without stain or wrinkle or any other blemish, but holy and blameless"** (Ephesians 5:25-27).

She glows. People stand when she enters the room. She walks elegantly down the aisle, and all eyes are on her stunning beauty.

That's you and all believers. No matter what your marital status on this earth, you have the best marital status as the bride of Christ.

Dear God, yes! I approve your arranged marriage. I love Jesus, the perfect Groom who loves even me. I can glow in holy beauty. I am elegant in his grace. I can face today believing that you already approve of me and Jesus is fully committed to me. Amen.

Are you ready for the minefield?
Pastor David Scharf

When you reached over to turn off the alarm this morning, did you hesitantly place one bare foot on the floor and then the other, wondering what the devil has in his bag of tricks for you today? The evil one has had all night to plant a minefield of temptation. Did you wonder how it would begin today?

If you are like me, the temptation minefield has been filled with unexpected traps this morning. Have you been fighting them? Or have you been inviting them? The reformer Martin Luther once said, "You cannot prevent the birds from flying in the air over your head, but you can certainly prevent them from building a nest in your hair." You can't stop the temptations from coming, but today you can avoid inviting situations that you know will capitalize on your weaknesses.

Jesus said, **"This, then, is how you should pray: 'Our Father in heaven . . . lead us not into temptation, but deliver us from the evil one'"** (Matthew 6:9,13). It is daunting to think that we are doing battle with the devil. But as daunting as that knowledge is, know that you are not alone in the fight. You have a Father in heaven who knows your weaknesses and will always provide a way out.

As he leads you through the devil's minefield today, keep your eyes fixed on the cross of Jesus for the strength to resist the devil and for forgiveness when you succumb to him.

King by force
Pastor Jon Enter

I always wondered why the Bible numbered only men in the feeding of the five thousand. The Jewish culture was a patriarchal society, a man-driven culture, but women and children weren't property. They counted. Jesus loves, forgives, and wants all to be saved, not just men. So why didn't God count the women and children?

The answer might be found at the end of this account. After Jesus miraculously fed the masses, we're told, **"Jesus, knowing that they intended to come and make him king by force, withdrew again to a mountain by himself"** (John 6:15). The force they were going to use wasn't against Jesus; it would've been against the Romans. One of the toughest parts of sustaining a military campaign against an enemy was feeding your army. They didn't have to worry about that anymore. They had Jesus' power!

And they had the numbers to start a revolution. Five thousand men was the size of a Roman legion. By the time they traveled from the Sea of Galilee, those numbers likely would've doubled or quadrupled. Plus, it was almost the Passover, so Jerusalem would've had an additional 80,000+ loyalist Jews there along with those living in the city already.

But Jesus withdrew. He knew that wasn't the plan. He came to save the people spiritually, not politically. And he did! Jesus marched into Jerusalem on a different Passover as the Lamb of God who takes away the sin of the world. Thank you, Jesus, for being the Savior we need!

Cry for a moment
Christine Wentzel

"Jesus wept" (John 11:35).

Oh, the bittersweet joy this sentence gives! We draw comfort knowing Jesus was emotional enough to cry. His pain was enough to make him weep. In two words we know our Savior felt compassion, empathy, and sorrow for all his hurting people. As the Son of Man, he is human, just like us (yet without sin). His body reacted to strong feelings, just like us.

However, there is one undeniable difference between how he handled his emotions and how we handle ours. He remembered the sacred joy in the suffering of his mission. He believed his obedient life was our liberation from sin. He knew he was our only chance to live happily ever after.

On your journey to your forever home in heaven, go ahead and cry. Not only does it release built-up tension, but it shows your ability to feel. It gives your family in Christ a chance to comfort you, which strengthens your relational ties.

But don't get lost in the crying. Just like everything else in life, crying has its seasons. Jesus promises to wipe your cheeks dry. He sets you back on your feet. Your sure trust in God's care now means you do not surrender to hopelessness.

Cry for the moment. It's okay.

Can I have your attention?
Pastor Daron Lindemann

Before smartphones and Facebook, humans could focus on something for at least 15 seconds before our minds began to wander.

Today, researchers say that we have the attention span of a goldfish—8 seconds. Scientists are now experimenting with the fruit fly's brain—very similar to the human brain—and those little buggers have an attention span of 3 seconds.

Hey. You. Stay with me here.

As a society, our attention span is compromised by so many shiny things. So we just see less. We notice less. We pay less attention.

Advertisers know this, so they create YouTube ads that grab our attention before we can hit the "Skip" button.

Jesus knows this too. Attention in our lives is lacking. Jesus gives us his attention. He knows us. He likes and follows us. He friends us. He sees us. He loves us. All the time.

Even though we don't deserve to have Jesus turn toward us in love, he does. Like to one man who questioned him: **"Jesus looked at him and loved him"** (Mark 10:21).

Jesus sees you. He sees your hurt or loneliness. He sees your sin and shame and even rebellion. He doesn't just pretend it didn't happen or hope you'll be okay. He notices. He looks at you and loves you.

The Bible calls that mercy. Put down your phone today—for at least 8 seconds—and take the time to see someone who needs your mercy too.

Pass the salt, please
Pastor Clark Schultz

"You are the salt of the earth" (Matthew 5:13).

Normally when someone looks at you and says, "You're being a little salty," it's not meant as a compliment. Jesus, who liked to be different than the religious leaders of his day, was encouraging his listeners to be just that . . . salty. But he didn't mean it in a negative way.

Salt preserves, salt (when taken in the appropriate dose) is good for you, and salt even adds a little flavor. Earlier in the book of Matthew, Jesus said that the people of this world who reject him are in the dark. So he encouraged his listeners to be a light to this dark world. Like peanut butter is to jelly, with letting our lights shine, Jesus also encouraged us to add a splash of salt to our lives of living for him. We can use the salt of the gospel to show God's preservation for us and for others. We can give a good sprinkle of the law and the gospel over our daily conversations. And when others are being negative, we can spice things up by being a salty Christian. A Christian who's not a perfect know-it-all but one who realizes he or she is a lost and condemned creature, a follower of God who needs a whole lot of flavoring in his or her life, a flavor that only Christ can give.

So grab the shaker of the gospel God has given you and, like dinner, feel free to pass the salt.

A dull ache
Jan Gompper

Loneliness is real. The world is filled with people who live with a dull, nagging ache inside them much of the time.

Many of us get so busy with our own lives and families that we fail to notice the person at church who has nowhere to go for Thanksgiving dinner. We bypass the classmate who's eating lunch alone. Perhaps other people's loneliness makes us feel uncomfortable because we may feel at a loss as to how to help.

Fortunately, Jesus understood loneliness. He understood it because he felt it more than any of us have ever felt it. How lonely he must have felt when he cried out from the cross, **"My God, my God, why have you forsaken me?"** (Matthew 27:46 ESV).

Yet, despite the loneliness he no doubt felt (or, more likely, because of it), Jesus was "tuned in" to the loneliness around him. He not only offered words of comfort; he took the time to be present with the lonely.

Reminding the lonely person that God will never leave them or forsake them (Deuteronomy 31:6) is definitely a wonderful source of comfort. Yet words alone, even God's words, can still feel empty to a lonely person. Instead, for the person whose heart is filled with the dull ache of loneliness, offer a hug, a dinner invitation, an hour spent at a coffee shop. God said, **"Let us not love with words or speech but with actions and in truth"** (1 John 3:18).

Guess who's coming to dinner?

I serve
Pastor David Scharf

If your life had a motto, what would it be? Here's a better question. Would the motto you give your own life match the one your loved ones would put on your life?

Ich dien (German for "I serve") is the proud motto of the Prince of Wales, which can be found on his seal. In our world, that is a shocking sentiment! Every day we see people vying for positions that will enable them to command and compel others to serve them. Service to self is often the only thing I see in the world. Sadly, I see it in my own heart as well.

Jesus says to us today, **"Not so with you. Instead, whoever wants to become great among you must be your servant, just as the Son of Man did not come to be served, but to serve, and to give his life as a ransom for many"** (Matthew 20:26,28). How countercultural! *"I serve"* is to be every Christian's motto. Why will we want to serve?

Ich dien—I serve. This was the motto of Jesus' life for you. He lived perfectly, not for himself but for you. He died to pay for sins, not his own but yours. This serving love is shocking! *Ich dien.* The person whose heart speaks these words as its motto rises to heights of true nobility. Remember the One who served you and *Ich dien* will be your life's motto as well.

Whom can you serve today?

The only enduring thing
Pastor Mike Novotny

I bet what breaks your heart, maybe more than anything, is when something doesn't endure forever. Like when you finally have a little money in the bank, but then—ding!—that little dashboard light lights up because that pricey part of your car didn't endure forever. Or when the guy you were dating—the guy who seemed so perfect, so sweet, so committed—didn't endure forever. Or when you were making progress with your mental health, staying positive and strong, but then things slipped right back to where you were. Mental health, marriage, our own morality—the heartbreaking problem is the same: Nothing seems to endure forever.

But that's why I love the most repetitious chapter in the entire Bible, Psalm 136. It starts, **"Give thanks to the Lord, for he is good. His love endures forever"** (verse 1). Just in case you didn't catch it the first time, the psalm writer goes on to repeat "his love endures forever," not once or twice but 25 more times!

Isn't that the best? When your car battery dies, God's love endures forever. When your family isn't as picture-perfect as you prayed for, God's love endures forever. When anxiety gets the best of your heart, God's love endures forever. I could go on (like the psalmist!) but these devotions are supposed to fit on one page.

Just remember that God is good today. Why? Because his love endures forever.

Jesus sets you free
Pastor Mike Novotny

In 1863 an escaped slave named Gordon appeared in Baton Rouge with the scent of onions on his skin. He had been running from his master, the cruel John Lyons, who owned a plantation 40 miles away and wasn't about to let "his property" escape that easily. Lyons had sent a bloodhound pack to track Gordon, which explained the onions. Gordon rubbed his skin with the fragrant onions, reapplying after crossing every creek or stream, to throw off the dogs, allowing him to reach his refuge among the Union Army. When he arrived, a photographer snapped a picture of Gordon's back, grotesquely scarred from Lyon's whip, a picture that silently preached of the horrors of slavery.

Slavery is one of the pictures that the Bible uses to describe our story. **"Jesus replied, 'Very truly I tell you, everyone who sins is a slave to sin'"** (John 8:34). Whenever something other than God is in control of our lives, we are slaves. That something might be the pursuit of our dream career, the perfect family, or a relaxing retirement. While these seem so unlike John Lyons, they can prevent us from reaching the freedom of heaven.

This is why Jesus went on to say, **"So if the Son sets you free, you will be free indeed"** (John 8:36). Through Jesus' scars, we escape the devil's plantation and reach the promised land of heaven, where God is always present and where we are free indeed.

Take a moment to ponder the life of someone enslaved to sin. Then worship as you remember that Jesus set you free.

Forgiveness doesn't count
Pastor Daron Lindemann

Jesus told a parable that purposely made no economic sense. A lesson about forgiving grace that can't be calculated like a day's wages.

Forgiveness is not something you (or a person who has hurt you) must toil and sweat to earn. Jesus made this point clearly by an employer's response to the complaint of a full-day regular being paid the same as part-timers: **"I am not being unfair to you, friend. Didn't you agree to work for a denarius? Take your pay and go. I want to give the one who was hired last the same as I gave you. Don't I have the right to do what I want with my own money? Or are you envious because I am generous?"** (Matthew 20:13-15).

The gracious employer in Jesus' story handed out the same paychecks to early risers and latecomers alike. Forgiving grace is not about finishing last or being first. It's about not counting. Forgiveness is a gift, which is why it contains the word *give*.

Mercy like God's is not our kind of math. It's not always the best economical decision or the most prudent political path. It's not always ledgered accurately on business plans and spreadsheets. It's not always exerting authority and discipline in doses that make the most difference.

The mercy of God doesn't add up, doesn't count, and is never deserved. That makes each of us forgiven and then able to forgive others.

March 31

Your (extra)ordinary Bible
Pastor Mike Novotny

About 125 years ago, most scholars thought the Bible was filled with extraordinary words. The Greek New Testament has about five thousand different words, and about five hundred of them were believed to be extraordinarily unique. They didn't appear in any other ancient Greek literature besides the Bible. It was almost as if, the scholars suggested, that there was a special language for this special book. But then one day in the late 1800s, two archaeologists were digging in an ancient garbage heap near the Nile River in Egypt. As they sifted through scraps of old papyrus— receipts, shopping lists, personal letters, etc.— they started to recognize a few words, the ones they thought were unique to the New Testament. First one, then two, then dozens, then hundreds! It turns out that the language of the Bible was ordinary language, that God was communicating with the words of the marketplace and the fishing dock. Because ordinary is how God ordinarily works.

That snippet of history reminds me of Jesus' words: **"I praise you, Father, Lord of heaven and earth, because you have hidden these things from the wise and learned, and revealed them to little children"** (Matthew 11:25). Apparently, you don't need a PhD to read your name in the book of life. Just simple trust. Just the faith of a child.

That's the extraordinary grace that you can find in your ordinary Bible.

April

In your hearts revere Christ as Lord.
Always be prepared to give an answer
to everyone who asks you to give the reason
for the hope that you have. But do this
with gentleness and respect.

1 Peter 3:15

I am Barabbas

Ann Jahns

It was the week of Jesus' death. During a sham of a trial, he stood before Pontius Pilate accused of crimes he didn't commit, based on trumped-up charges.

Since Jesus' trial took place during the annual Passover festival, it was the custom that week for the authorities to free one prisoner of the Jews' choosing. Their choices? Jesus, the sinless Son of God, or Barabbas, a murderer. In a frenzy of hatred, the crowd screamed for the release of Barabbas. Even Pilate knew that Jesus was innocent: **"'What crime has he committed?' asked Pilate. But they shouted all the louder, 'Crucify him!'"** (Matthew 27:23).

Can you see yourself in this story? I sure can. I am Barabbas. You are Barabbas. We were prisoners on death row. But Jesus quietly took our place on the cross because he loves us that much.

I'd like to think that Barabbas grabbed his unexpected freedom and undeserved grace with both hands and it changed his life. Did he live out his days testifying to this Jesus who took his place? The Bible doesn't say.

But what we do know is that we have been given a new lease on life. We were dead in our sins, doomed before a perfect God.

But then Jesus traded places with a man named Barabbas, and he also traded places with us. He paid the price for our sins. We now stand with confidence before our holy God, cloaked in the perfection of Jesus. We are free!

What are you going to do with your freedom?

Tetelestai
Pastor Daron Lindemann

Does Jesus need your help?

On the cross he was beaten and bloody. A victim of injustice. Did he need your help on that dark Friday? Did he cry out to his disciples or the angels to lend him a hand or call forth Moses or John the Baptist from the dead?

No. Jesus didn't need your help to pay for sins then. And he doesn't need your help today.

"It is finished" (John 19:30), he cried from the cross. He spoke a word that in Greek is *tetelestai*. It was a word used by painters when they had finally completed a work of art. A word used by merchants when someone paid a debt in full.

Done. Accomplished. Nothing more.

Do you ever feel like Jesus did a lot of good but there's just a little you need to contribute in order to get God's approval? *Tetelestai* says that's a lie. Don't believe it.

Done.

Accomplished.

Nothing more.

God promises that your forgiveness is a free gift. And it was completed at the cross. *Tetelestai*.

Jesus, you need nothing from me, but you want me and want everything in me. You forgive me without needing anything from me. You saved me without my help. You sacrificed yourself for me. Your love for me makes me love you too, Lord. I want to serve you. Amen.

The problem with getting older
Pastor Mike Novotny

Now that I'm 40, the devil loves to use my experiences, hard-won wisdom, and lessons learned to convince me that I don't need to pray.

Here's an example—A couple is on my calendar for marital counseling. But after hundreds of such meetings, I can probably guess the issues that are wrecking their intimacy and, in addition, I already have a few classic Bible passages to turn to. Therefore, I just go about my day, writing sermons and returning emails until the second the couple knocks on the door. I don't need to pray for wisdom or the right words. After thousands of hours of experience, I got this.

See what I mean? Getting older can be spiritually dangerous. After caring for so many patients, teaching so many classes, writing so many emails, attending so many funerals, you got this.

But without God, you and I don't got this. We need his strength and his Spirit every day in order to avoid a disastrous word that we can't take back or a decision that will come with consequences. Perhaps this is why Jesus taught us to remain as helpless and dependent as little children. **"Therefore, whoever takes the lowly position of this child is the greatest in the kingdom of heaven"** (Matthew 18:4).

No matter how long it's been since your baptism, remember how much you need God. And, even better, remember God is always willing to listen and to answer your humble prayers. That's the promise Jesus gave after he made you God's dear child.

A Lenten reflection
Jan Gompper

During high school, I loved the church season of Lent (the time leading up to Easter). As a way to remember Jesus' sacrifice for us, most of my Catholic girlfriends would "give up" eating dessert, which meant I generally got extras. Back then, my hips could handle the added sugar.

Though I enjoyed the extra sweets, I thought my friends' practice of giving something up for Lent was silly. It seemed to stem from believing they had to *do* something to earn God's favor. I knew salvation was a gift of God's grace, and no matter how many desserts they gave up, God would not love them more than he already did.

Reflecting on my friends' Lenten practice, I now sometimes ponder, "What *would* I be willing to give up for God?" Not to earn his favor but because I love him. Giving something up implies making a *sacrifice*, which is defined as "an act of offering something *precious*." Would I be willing to give up something that is truly precious to me for God? I don't know about you, but I can't even consistently give up a few hours of TV watching to spend more time with him.

What a relief God is not like me! He *was* willing to give up something precious. He **"did not spare his own Son, but gave him up for us all"** (Romans 8:32). God sacrificed his holy, precious Son because we are also precious to him.

Do not fear! An angel is here!
Pastor Mike Novotny

I didn't want to be critical, but it seemed like Matthew spent too much time on the Romans. If you read the last pages of Matthew's gospel, you find the Romans at the end of chapter 27, then again at the start of chapter 28, and then again in the middle of chapter 28! Come on, Matthew! The gospel is supposed to be about Jesus!

But then it hit me. For Matthew's earliest readers, Roman guards and crosses represented their greatest fears. Maybe that's why Matthew wanted the early church to read, **"The guards were so afraid of him that they shook and became like dead men"** (Matthew 28:4). The guards—the armed, trained Roman guards—practically wet themselves when they saw "him." Who's the him? Not the resurrected Jesus. Not the entire army of heavenly angels. No, just one angel. One. The superpower of the first century quaked with fear from the sight of a single angel.

Okay, I'll take my critique back. Matthew was trying to teach Christians from every generation that we have nothing to fear. Our God is so strong and mighty that we never need to be afraid.

So what do you fear the most these days? Whatever your answer, remember this: Your fears are nothing next to God. Scratch that. They are nothing next to the angels of God. Scratch that. They are nothing next to *one* of the angels of God!

Do not fear. The God of glorious angels is here.

Do not fear! Jesus isn't there!
Pastor Mike Novotny

If my investigation was accurate, the angel was right. **"The angel said to the women, 'Do not be afraid, for I know that you are looking for Jesus, who was crucified. He is not here; he has risen, just as he said. Come and see the place where he lay'"** (Matthew 28:5,6).

In early 2020, I had a chance to check into the angelic report. Some historians believe Jesus was buried at the Garden Tomb, just north of downtown Jerusalem. Others think the resurrection happened at the Church of the Holy Sepulchre, nestled inside the Old City of Jerusalem. So I decided to check both for the body of Jesus.

Normally, tourists flock to both of these sites, hoping for a glimpse of the place where our salvation was completed. But I was there just as the coronavirus was changing the world. Therefore, tourism had plummeted, giving me way more than a quick glimpse inside the tomb. I was able to linger, to look around as the angel instructed, and to confirm that Jesus was not there.

Obviously, it takes way more proof to prove something as wonderful as a resurrected Savior and, thankfully, we have it. But my day exploring Jerusalem reminded me that the Easter story is more than a story. It's history. It's true.

Which is why you truly do not need to be afraid. Your Savior is risen, just as he said. He is with you today!

Do not fear! Grace is here!
Pastor Mike Novotny

One of my favorite parts of the Easter story is Mary's place in it. Before any of the apostles saw the empty tomb or the risen Savior, Mary Magdalene did. She got to the tomb with the other women. She heard the angel's message. She saw Jesus' face when he appeared to her. **"Mary Magdalene and the other Mary went to look at the tomb. The angel said to the women, 'Do not be afraid, for I know that you are looking for Jesus, who was crucified. He is not here; he has risen, just as he said'"** (Matthew 28:1,5,6).

Why should that make you smile? Because Mary had the messiest story of them all. We sometimes think of proud Peter as the biggest sinner. Or doubting Thomas. Or Matthew, the ex-tax collector. But, according to the Bible, Mary had an even messier past. She was once possessed by seven demons (Luke 8:2)! Demons! Seven of them! Yet the one with the most in her closet was closest to Jesus.

I love that fact. You may have a messy past too. A legal record. A broken home. A dark secret. A wayward child. A hidden struggle. A failed marriage. But don't be afraid. Jesus was crucified and raised, just as he said, so that you could have a place in his story. So that you could see his smiling face. So that you could fall at his holy feet in worship.

If your life is messy, remember Mary. Remember Easter.

Do not fear! Jesus is here (early)!
Pastor Mike Novotny

Jesus is never late. In fact, he sometimes shows up early. Remember what happened on Easter morning? **"So the women hurried away from the tomb, afraid yet filled with joy, and ran to tell his disciples. Suddenly Jesus met them. 'Greetings,' he said. They came to him, clasped his feet and worshiped him"** (Matthew 28:8,9). Just when the women thought they would have to wait until Galilee to see Jesus, he showed up early!

Jesus still does. You might assume that you have to wait until heaven to be with him. Many Christians assume that only once you die do you get to be with God. But that's not true. It all starts now! Eternal life begins when you first believe. Jesus said, **"Very truly I tell you, whoever hears my word and believes him who sent me has eternal life and will not be judged but has crossed over from death to life"** (John 5:24). True, we can't see Jesus' face like Mary did on Easter morning, but faith promises that he's still present with us, right here and right now.

That's why you can worship today. You can shake off your fear of what might happen because Jesus is already here with you. You can walk into the doctor's office for your exam, have that tough conversation about your child's behavior, or read the news without being consumed by worry. After all, the glorious Son of God, the One who left the tomb empty and works out all things for our good, is here.

Thank God for a Savior who shows up early!

Unboxing
Linda Buxa

Did you know unboxing videos are a thing? People love taking videos of themselves opening up gifts in the mail or their box-of-the-month club. They love discovering—and sharing—what's inside.

My favorite unboxing ever happened on Easter, but there was no video. Three days after Jesus was hung on a cross and took the punishment for all the things I've ever done wrong, **"there was a violent earthquake, for an angel of the Lord came down from heaven and, going to the tomb, rolled back the stone** [unboxed it, if you will] **and sat on it"** (Matthew 28:2).

That angel opened up the tomb and told the people who expected to see a dead body that there was nothing inside because **"he is not here; he has risen, just as he said"** (verse 6).

This empty box changed everything for those people, and it changes everything for you.

You are no longer at odds with Jesus but at peace with him. You are no longer an enemy but a child of God. You aren't alone in this world, but the Holy Spirit lives inside of you, filling you with daily gifts of love, joy, peace, forbearance, kindness, goodness, faithfulness, gentleness, and self-control.

Now you get to use these gifts; you get to be a gift to the world. You get to unbox the Scriptures for others, explaining what's inside. You get to tell others that the tomb is empty and that God's good gifts are available to them too.

You can even make videos about it.

Be still
Ann Jahns

When my husband and I were young parents, taking three little boys under the age of four to church was an adventure, and not the fun "let's go backpacking through Europe" type of adventure. Armed with soft books, washable markers, and crushable Cheerios, our goal was to make it through the service—with no need for stitches. And because it's not acceptable to yell in church, especially by parents who know better, we'd find ourselves stage-whispering constantly, "Sit still. Be still!"

God also whispers to us, his children, **"Be still"** (Exodus 14:14). But what does that even mean for us right here, right now? The world we live in is anything but still. It's constantly moving, constantly changing, constantly shifting. The 24-hour news cycle. Endlessly updating social media feeds. Work and activities and kids' sports and obligations and [fill in the blank]. Who has time to be still?

Exodus 14:14 explains why we should be still: **"The Lord will fight for you; you need only to be still!"** The reason that we can be still is because God is God, and we are not. Thank goodness. Those who believe in Jesus, who have tasted the sweetness of the gospel after feeling the sting of the law, can be still. We have a stillness in our souls. The world we live in might be racing out of control, but it's like we're standing still as it swirls around us, confident in the power of our God.

Be still, believer. Take a deep breath. Our God is in control.

Victor not victim
Pastor Daron Lindemann

Easter makes you a victor! Here's how.

Jesus took on death, not just as your enemy but his. He took on sin, not just as your enemy but his. He became their victim and then rose from the dead.

Easter means that Jesus made sin a victim. Jesus made death a victim. And Jesus became the living victor. **"Death has been swallowed up in victory"** (1 Corinthians 15:54)!

Whose victory? Because Jesus is more than inspiration, he gives you his own death, his own resurrection, and his own life. He gives you the mercy of forgiveness and the promise of answered prayer. Jesus gives you the victory.

"But thanks be to God! He gives us the victory through our Lord Jesus Christ" (1 Corinthians 15:57).

Jesus raises your hopes, your strength, and your new life of drive and determination to trust him and follow him every day. More than that, Jesus will raise your dead body to eternal life: **"The dead will be raised imperishable, and we will be changed"** (1 Corinthians 15:52).

Because Jesus rose, death itself is the victim, sin is the victim, and you are not. Because Jesus rose, you are the victor. Now live like it!

And yes, you can even die like it! Christ is risen!

Pelted by pain
Pastor Jon Enter

A young family's picnic was suddenly shut down by rain. After they hurried to the car, Dad pointed out a tender sight. A baby bird too young to fly in the rain was shivering and shaking in fear from the powerful rainstorm as momma bird held her protective wing over her young.

Why did the baby bird still quake in fear? Well, the winds still howled. The water splashed up into its face. Raindrops pelted the slightly uncovered corner of its wings. Only a tiny fraction of the true danger that surrounded was felt, yet the baby bird was terrified.

The spiritual forces of evil surround you! This world is only evil all the time. Worry howls. Disease and death splash into your life. You get pelted by pain and problems. Yet these are only a tiny fraction of what threatens to destroy you! Why? Psalm 91:4 brings truth and daily comfort: **"He will cover you with his feathers, and under his wings you will find refuge."**

How often Christians walk blissfully unaware of danger that surrounds them. We complain against God, "Where were you?! Where was your protection?!" when only a splash of one raindrop's worth of hurt hits us while a monsoon of misery rages around us. You and I are covered and cared for by the Almighty. If you're scared right now, don't focus on the sound of the storm; nestle into the embrace of the One who calms the storm. And peace will follow in your true Refuge.

Never take grace for granted
Jason Nelson

I can't touch your heart unless I open up mine. I'm a baby boomer, middle-class, American, white male. I had nothing to do with any of it. I've benefited from all of it. It's been grace to me. I'm troubled that so many people in the world, who have no more control over their circumstances than I did, experience life so differently. I know God loves them just as much as he loves me. They don't have the shelter from storms that I have. I need to manage a few inconveniences. They need to manage devastation on a regular basis. I can't imagine what that does to a person's soul. So I ask this question about what I haven't gone through: Why me?

I've been involved in church-related work for many years. I can get the answers right on the doctrine test. In one way or another, I've passed those answers on to others. I used to think that was an accomplishment. Not so much anymore. It's a hollow victory to pass the doctrine test but not show up for the reciprocity test. **"From everyone who has been given much, much will be demanded"** (Luke 12:48). My contributions in God's kingdom have been safe and sanitary. If God wanted more from me, it's getting a little late now. There it is, my guilt laid bare. My point is, never take grace for granted.

Anxiety is like a rocking chair
Pastor Daron Lindemann

There's much to be anxious about these days. If you feel pressure, it doesn't make you bad, sinful, or weak. It's no different than your ears popping when your Boeing 737 climbs to a higher altitude.

I'm studying the word *anxiety* in the Bible, oftentimes translated *worry*. But get this. Its base meaning isn't a negative one at all. It has the sense of care or concern.

It's used positively in 1 Corinthians 7:32, where the apostle Paul mentions a man being **"concerned about the Lord's affairs,"** and in 1 Corinthians 12:25, reminding believers with different abilities and interests to have **"equal concern for each other."**

So how does concern turn into anxiety? It's like a rocking chair.

Care or concern rocks gently, content in the moment, not even realizing that it's rocking. Slow. Peaceful. Relaxed. Mindful of the pressure points but not mastered by them. Happy to be rocking.

Worry or anxiety rocks fast and furious, trying to actually get somewhere, do something, make things happen. And the more it tries to control these, the more overwhelming it feels. So it tries even harder and rocks even faster. Lots of activity but getting nowhere.

So how will you handle the pressure today?

There are many things God can do better without your help. Rock gently. Relax in this moment, and see what God can do.

There's power in the blood
Ann Jahns

"Thank you. Your blood donation today will save at least three lives," said the cheerful young woman as I tried to ignore the large needle in my arm at a recent blood drive.

Even better than the little bag of chips and the can of juice that I was rewarded with for my efforts was knowing that my blood was potentially a lifesaver. And what did I really give up for my efforts? About a pint of blood and about an hour of my time. Not too much.

But what about the blood of Jesus? He didn't recline in a comfy chair with his feet up while his blood was drawn through a (relatively) painless process. He didn't walk away with a tasty snack and drink. He hung from a cross by nails through his hands and feet, an agony that I can't even wrap my head around. His only refreshment was from a sponge soaked in wine vinegar that was held to his cracked and bleeding lips. What did Jesus give up for his efforts? Everything. His very life.

The blood of Jesus isn't just a temporary fix—a temporary transfusion: **"In him we have redemption through his blood, the forgiveness of sins, in accordance with the riches of God's grace that he lavished on us"** (Ephesians 1:7,8).

Jesus died to save the entire world. He died for you. And for me. And for everyone who believes in him from the creation of this world until its very last day. There's everlasting power in that blood.

Before the beginning
Andrea Delwiche

Feeling unsettled? scared? like it all depends on you? like you're powerless to do what needs to be done? Feeling sick of others? tired of the chaos of this world? You're not alone. Chances are that nearly every person reading this in every corner of the globe has had these thoughts. The individual cries of all of us are heard by our God who stands with us and surrounds us.

Our world lacks grounding and certainty. When one problem resolves, another jumps eagerly in to take its place. Overwhelming. Consider the much deeper, sustaining reality of our universe in this one sentence: **"In the beginning was the Word, and the Word was with God, and the Word was God"** (John 1:1).

Before the chaos and tragedy of our modern, news cycle-driven world was the Word, Jesus Christ. One with the Father and the Spirit, our triune God intentionally spoke our world into being. God still sustains it. We are here purposefully as his hands and feet and heart, working with him to love it still.

We're not riding on a careening ball of destruction, alone and without hope. We're planted in a carefully conceived world that's presided over and saturated with the love, care, and attention of the One who gave it life.

God stands before the beginning of the world. He stands with us now. How can you hold on to the reality of God's eternal presence in your walk today?

Go to church
Christine Wentzel

Addicted to something? Go to church.
Have a potty mouth? Go to church.
Workaholic? Go to church.
Parental issues? Go to church.
Hate anyone? Go to church.
Lust struggles? Go to church.
Gossip much? Go to church.
Think you deserve things? Go to church.

These commandments are for believers who know they are saved through Jesus and already alive and active in the body of Christ. Struggling in your sins, dear believer? Go to church. We'll meet you there—the end.

However, going to church doesn't save people. Jesus saves people. Jesus didn't show us how to build a church. He showed us how to build his church.

"In him the whole building is joined together and rises to become a holy temple in the Lord. And in him you too are being built together to become a dwelling in which God lives by his Spirit" (Ephesians 2:21,22).

The next time an unchurched someone gets enough courage to open up, let us love them enough by bringing the church to them. This is a God-given opportunity where nothing will be wasted. May we allow the relationship to unfold with the courage of our conviction in God's love for sinners just like us.

Then invite them to church to receive the means of God's grace. It's a place committed to encouragement and education in the Word and a retreat for nurturing one another in Christ. Go to church together.

You're free
Linda Buxa

I don't love the phrase, "Work Hard, Play Hard." It might be because I like naps, and I'm not sure where those fit in. Mainly though, I think it feels as if the world is telling me that I need to "do this" or "be that" to have a fulfilling life.

Maybe you feel like Christianity sends that same message too. Only sing music we approve of. Only watch "Christian" movies. Go to church three times a week.

You're not alone. About two thousand years ago, a preacher named Paul wrote to a group of believers in a city called Colossae who were hearing some man-made rules. Paul wanted to let them know that because of Jesus' sacrifice, they were freed from rules imposed by others. **"Since you died with Christ to the elemental spiritual forces of this world, why, as though you still belonged to the world, do you submit to its rules: 'Do not handle! Do not taste! Do not touch!'?"** (Colossians 2:20,21).

Jesus obeyed every one of *God's* standards and gives you credit for that. He took the punishment and died for all the mistakes you've made and sins you've committed. And then he defeated death, declaring that you are free from man-made regulations.

You don't have to work hard to get to heaven; he's done it for you. **"Stand firm, then, and do not let yourselves be burdened again by a yoke of slavery"** (Galatians 5:1).

Adjust your speed
Pastor Matt Ewart

"Therefore, as God's chosen people, holy and dearly loved, clothe yourselves with . . . patience" (Colossians 3:12).

I'm a regular consumer of audio podcasts. It's an easy way for me to be filled up spiritually and to grow intellectually. A feature of my podcast app is that I can increase the playback speed. I like to keep it at 150%, which means I can consume lots of content in a short amount of time. It's great.

But what isn't great is when I try to impose my preferred speed on people in my life. I think you do this too. It's called impatience, and it's something that everyone struggles with.

Impatience is when I expect someone else to match my preferred pace. Impatience is when I act like my time is more valuable than the people around me. Impatience is what God should have for people like me and you.

But when the time was fully right, God sent his Son to live in our world at our pace. He came from the timelessness of eternity to enter a life that would now impose limits on his time. Yet what he demonstrated to everyone was a perfect patience that was content to live at the pace of the people around him.

The secret of patience is to live in the appreciation of God's patience for you. His patience is something he wants to clothe you with today.

When life is bleak
Andrea Delwiche

Sometimes everything is laid bare before us. We see clearly the reality of our situation and our neediness. We can assess how our own actions have led to the pain that characterizes our lives.

This seems to be David's state of mind in Psalm 38. He's conducting a reality check with the Lord: **"Your arrows have pierced me . . . there is no soundness in my bones . . . my wounds fester . . . because of my sinful folly"** (verses 2,3,5). He describes himself as feeble, crushed, and in anguish.

He is also humble: **"All my longings lie open before you, Lord; my sighing is not hidden from you"** (verse 9). David's situation is bleak. His own actions have brought painful consequences. He senses that the Lord is letting him sit in the pit that David's own actions have dug.

David is isolated and friendless. Yet in his misery and honesty, lies the way forward. He is confident that God forgives him and will continue to provide the path to wholeness, newness, and life.

It's hard to hold ourselves up for examination, to be brutally honest and vulnerable. Yet as David tells us, our Lord lovingly walks through this process with us, even as we sometimes have to bear the results of our choices. He stands waiting to tread the path with us and lead us to renewal.

"Lord, do not forsake me; do not be far from me, my God. Come quickly to help me, my Lord and my Savior" (verses 21,22).

I want it all
Pastor Matt Ewart

"Whoever loves money never has enough; whoever loves wealth is never satisfied with their income" (Ecclesiastes 5:10).

The verse quoted above makes a direct reference to wealth, but the principle behind it applies to much more than just money. The best way to highlight the principle is to ask you to do a little work.

Think of *something* you love, then fill in the blanks with that thing:

Whoever loves _____ never has enough; whoever loves _____ is never satisfied with it.

There are a lot of things that I can put in those blanks. I can love a lot of things in this life. But no matter what I put in those blanks, the statement is always true. No amount of *anything* will satisfy. I will always want more. The principle is simply this: You want all of whatever it is you love. Our version of love means that we try to take more and more.

But God's version of love is different. His love did not compel him to take. God so loved the world that he gave. He was not satisfied until he gave his *everything*—his one and only Son, whose sacrifice would redeem the entire world to him.

When you find yourself chasing something you love, stop to think about what it means that God loves you. It's God's love that will leave you satisfied.

No filter
Linda Buxa

"For now we see in a mirror dimly, but then face to face. Now I know in part; then I shall know fully, even as I have been fully known" (1 Corinthians 13:12 ESV).

Thanks to technology and its ability to colorize, brighten, enhance, and remove flaws in our photos, people feel the need to post #nofilter when they share beautiful photos that haven't been touched up. They want everyone to realize that *this* is the real deal.

Currently our entire world has a filter, one that causes every single good thing not to look better but to look worse. Every joyful event has some sadness because a loved one isn't there to share the joy. The success we've worked so hard to attain doesn't feel as fulfilling as we hoped it might. The mistakes we've made (intentionally or not) leave us feeling guilty even when we pretend we're fine.

Even our faith is affected by the reality of this tainted, filtered world. We know God forgets and forgives our sins, but other people still bring them up. We know that in heaven there will be no more pain, no more sorrow, no more sadness, but we can't really wrap our minds around what true joy in God's eternal presence will be like. We can read what his Word says, but it may not always make sense to us.

This is why every day Christians look forward to meeting Jesus face-to-face. That's when the filter is not simply removed but completely destroyed. There will truly be #nofilter.

Speed bumps
Christine Wentzel

Ugh! Speed bumps. They're everywhere. It was bad enough when they put them in parking lots. Now they're on the narrow streets of neighborhoods where the speed limit is slow enough to walk instead of drive.

So why are they there? The selfish mind is wired to go at its own speed regardless of warnings for the driver and the other travelers. These undercarriage scrapers serve a purpose.

It is our time of grace to look toward God's Son, Jesus, to learn why life's speed bumps are there. After all, he traveled those roads before us, and he knew of them before they were made.

"Carefully walk a straight path, and all your ways will be secure" (Proverbs 4:26 GW).

So think carefully!

Was I going so fast I missed the signs of heavenly direction?

Was the speed bump for me or ultimately someone else?

Was anyone following me?

Did I slow down to offer help?

When we slam through those speed bumps, there's a cause and effect on all of us. We can learn from our recklessness, warn of the dangers, encourage the weary, and be inspired by the long-distance travelers up ahead.

Slow down! Here comes another speed bump . . .

A meaningful beginning
Andrea Delwiche

"Send out your light and your truth; let them lead me; let them bring me to your holy hill and to your dwelling!" (Psalm 43:3). These words are a request for God's presence. When you pray these words, you are asking God to navigate and direct the path that you take. You ask him to shine his light on each situation and to teach you how to evaluate the circumstances and path of your life to make decisions that are Christ-like—"send out your light and your truth."

When you and I walk by the light of our own version of truth, led by our own desires and fears, we risk lives twisted with the deception of self-interest. Feeding our own desires seems to lighten the burdens of our lives temporarily without providing any real change or hope.

Instead, we ask for God's light and truth to provide the beam of light for our journey. We can be confident that he shows us, step by step, the way forward to a Christ-like life. We can open ourselves up to love and honor others above ourselves and to love and honor God above everything.

Jesus called himself the Light of the world. In the gospels, we see example after example of Christ calling people to change their way of looking at life. As the light of God's truth radiates, it frees us from bondage. Changing our ways and living by God's light and truth is not the *end* of life; it is a meaningful beginning.

How to help the abused (& abusive)
Pastor Mike Novotny

Many years ago, a woman came into my office and confessed to me that her husband was hurting her and her kids physically and verbally. What was more, the husband was also a member of our church, which meant that within days I would sit with him in the same room and address the same issue. God was calling me to help both the abused and the abusive.

Given the widespread numbers on abuse, God will call you to do the same. Maybe your friend shares some concerning details of the fight she had with her boyfriend, and the bruise on her wrist tells the rest of the story. Or your nephew jokes about your brother's parenting in a way that feels . . . off. Or your roommate starts dating a girl who belittles him in public and checks his phone in private. He worries constantly that he might make her angry. In those moments, when abuse is right in front of us, what should God's people do?

In the days to come, I want to explore that question as we meditate on a single verse from Isaiah: **"Learn to do right; seek justice. Defend the oppressed"** (Isaiah 1:17). Some of God's greatest work is using his forgiven children to help and heal the hurting. I pray these words enable us to do just that.

Perhaps today, when this devotion is done, you could pray for wisdom and compassion to do what is right in a world filled with the wrongs of abuse.

Help the abused with truth

Pastor Mike Novotny

If you know someone who's been abused, you need to read and heed Isaiah's words: **"Learn to do right; seek justice. Defend the oppressed"** (Isaiah 1:17). The word *defend* makes me picture an ancient city with towering walls and strong gates, a place built to keep dangerous people outside and to keep people safe inside. So picture yourself standing on top of the wall with people you love huddled inside as an abusive person comes riding up toward the city. How do you protect your loved ones?

With truth. Abuse can only exist when lies get the last word, so when we immerse ourselves in truth, in what God sees, in what God says, we defend the oppressed. For example, an abuser lies to his victim and says, "This is your fault," even though it isn't. "This isn't abuse," even though it is. "You made me do that," even though he/she freely chose to do it. But truth turns up the lights, takes off the makeup, and shows things for what they really are.

More truth leads to less abuse. Therefore, Isaiah is encouraging us to be people whose lips speak the truth that's overflowing out of our hearts. No, the process will not be easy (abusers are good at lying, and the abused are accustomed to being lied to). But, yes, the process will be godly. Because our God loves to defend the oppressed.

So speak up and speak the truth. Then do it again tomorrow. And the next day. Until the Day when Truth himself returns.

Help the abused with grace
Pastor Mike Novotny

I once knew a woman who had been badly abused by her significant other and yet, despite calling the cops, went back to him. In that moment, I realized how complicated abuse is. There are factors—childhood wounds, generational sins, and decades-long habits—that keep us caught up in toxic and oppressive relationships.

The prophet Isaiah once wrote, **"Learn to do right; seek justice. Defend the oppressed"** (Isaiah 1:17). How do we do that? Not simply with truth but also with God's grace.

As your friend fights to believe the abuse really isn't his fault, grace waits. As your daughter goes back to the guy you want to run over with your truck, grace stands by. Grace is being ready whenever they're ready, like the father of the prodigal son who waited until his boy came home.

Grace gives the gospel. If the victim is a Christian, you can say, "You are a child of God. You are precious to our Father. He doesn't think you're worthless or stupid or useless. He smiles when he thinks of you." If the abused isn't a Christian, you can say, "God wants something better for you. Jesus understands what you're going through. He wants you to have the hope of a place where there is no more crying or tears or abuse." Grace defends the abused from an eternity of pain by promising them eternal life through Jesus.

Defend the oppressed with the gospel, giving them Jesus, the best grace of all.

Help abusers with truth
Pastor Mike Novotny

I once accused a man of being a liar. Following a conversation with his wife and daughters, three quiet women who told me about his abusive behavior, I met with the man himself. He swore to me that he was absolutely innocent. May God forgive me if I was wrong, but I was 99% sure he was trying to manipulate me to maintain control in his home, so I told him he was a liar and needed to repent.

In some tough-to-translate Hebrew, my Bible says, **"Defend the oppressed,"** but there's a footnote that suggests this passage might mean, **"Correct the oppressor"** (Isaiah 1:17). Whatever the right translation, that's a biblical idea. People who oppress/hurt/abuse other people need to be corrected strongly and unwaveringly.

What might that correcting sound like? Perhaps like this: "Abuse is your choice. Yours. Even if he . . . even if she . . . you made the choice to threaten your kids. Okay, you were drunk when you spewed those words, but you made the choice to drink. I know you were stressed, but not every stressed person smashes things. This is on you. And you need help. You can't turn off your anger and jealousy and craving for control like a light switch. It's time to humble yourself. Time to give up control, confess your sins, and seek professional help. That's the truth."

Will it work? Maybe, maybe not. But God calls us, for the sake of every soul involved, to correct the oppressor. Is there someone God is calling you to correct today?

Help abusers with grace
Pastor Mike Novotny

Recently 159 members of our church completed a survey to help me prepare for a series of messages on abuse, and one of the themes that came up often was the idea of grace. While our church family recognized the need for repentance, strong boundaries, and real consequences, they didn't want to act as if grace didn't apply to abusers.

God would agree. Just one verse after addressing oppression and abuse, the prophet Isaiah wrote, **"Though your sins are like scarlet, they shall be as white as snow; though they are red as crimson, they shall be like wool"** (Isaiah 1:18). Yes, abuse is a sin that stains us in ways that we can't wash out. But God can make us clean. Jesus was abused on a cross so that even abusers could be saved. So that you could come to him with all of the consequences and end up with no condemnation (Romans 8:1). So that God himself could look at you and see someone who brings him joy, someone who has been rescued by Jesus.

Two thousand years ago, our Savior chose Simon the Zealot (a man associated with a violent group of Jewish rebels) and Saul of Tarsus (a religious man who hurt many people) to repent and follow him, proof that grace isn't reserved for good people.

That grace is for you too. Confess your sins to God and others, and believe the good news that grace is for abusers too.

If you can save just one
Pastor Mike Novotny

As I was preparing to teach a series of messages on abuse, members of our church gave me some honest feedback on a survey about these topics. Many of the responses, comments, and stories gripped my heart, urging me to approach every sermon with humility, truth, and grace. The wounds and trauma and triggers were real, emotional hurts that held on long after the abuse ended.

But one comment caught me more than the others. A woman wrote, "If you can save just one person from the situation they are in, you have done a wonderful thing." Just one person is wonderful.

I wish that our efforts would end every act of abuse once and for all, but this world is too broken for that. Yet Jesus' stories about one lost coin and one lost sheep and one lost son remind us of the celebration in heaven when a single soul is found. When you came to faith in Jesus, the angels didn't mope around in heaven, lamenting the billions of others who hadn't come to faith yet. Instead, they put on their party hats and danced around the throne that you, that "just one," had been saved.

As you seek justice and attempt to help and heal both the abused and the abusers you know, remember this wise woman's words. Just one person matters to God. Just one. **"Learn to do right; seek justice. Defend the oppressed"** (Isaiah 1:17).

May

In him we have redemption through his blood,
the forgiveness of sins, in accordance
with the riches of God's grace.

Ephesians 1:7

Significant to God
Pastor Matt Ewart

In the days of Jesus, disabled people were hardly viewed as people. They were viewed as a burden on society. They were often forgotten and considered insignificant.

One day a blind beggar named Bartimaeus heard that Jesus was passing by. Rather than humbly gesturing for some alms, this blind man did something so bold that it annoyed the people around him. Over and over, he shouted with all his might, "Jesus, Son of David, have mercy on me!"

What happened next shocked everyone. This blind beggar who was just one person in a crowd was significant to God. Jesus called him to come near.

"'What do you want me to do for you?' Jesus asked him. The blind man said, 'Rabbi, I want to see'" (Mark 10:51).

I wonder what would happen in your life today if you were bold like Bartimaeus. What would happen if you lived as if you were significant to God? What problems would you bring to him in prayer? What hopes would you ask him to grant? How boldly would you call out to him in times of need?

While I don't know who is reading this devotion, I do know each reader is significant to God. You are not just an anonymous person in the crowd who has nothing to offer him. He loves you and he makes a big deal about you, as was proven by what Jesus did for you.

Live today as if you are significant to God. Because you are.

Surrounded by his love
Andrea Delwiche

"Show me, LORD, my life's end and the number of my days; let me know how fleeting my life is. But now, Lord, what do I look for? My hope is in you. Save me from all my transgressions; do not make me the scorn of fools" (Psalm 39:4,7,8).

These words come from a place of absolute honesty. David's troubles seem to be from God, a needed life correction. And yet David turns to God. God administers the stinging antiseptic, but he's also the cure, the cooling breeze, the solace.

There's no sin too big for God or surprising to God. There's no question too big for God. Every dilemma, even those of our own making, can be brought to the Lord. There's no one who understands the ways of human beings like God. There's no love that matches God's love.

There's no easy conclusion to this psalm. It ends in pleading and anguish. We too sometimes feel our questions and prayers spoken into a void or echoing in emptiness. This is a sacred space between us and the Lord, where in confusion and even anger we lean into our relationship with him and ask hard questions. Even as we wait for answers, we can know that we are surrounded by his love.

Our questions are heard and answered. Even in darkness God promises: "I have loved you with an everlasting love. . . . I will build you up again. . . . You will . . . go out to dance with the joyful" (Jeremiah 31:3,4).

It's all on you
Pastor Jon Enter

I couldn't do what Moses did. You couldn't either. In Exodus chapter 17 (read the whole chapter; it's a short one!), the Israelites, who were freshly freed from Egyptian slavery, faced the Amalekite army. They were outnumbered, out weaponed, inexperienced, and in certain peril. They were going to die, and they knew it.

Imagine you're Moses. You send your fighting men with no fighting experience to war, and you struggle up a hillside to watch. As long as you keep your hands and staff overhead, the Amalekites' blood flows. When you drop your hands, your Israelite brethren bleed. Try it. You probably won't last ten minutes without your arms burning, begging you to stop. Try it. I'll wait.

Did you drop your arms? Your best friend died. Then your neighbor. Then another. And another.

Moses *had* to keep his arms up. Too much was at stake. What's at stake that's all on you? Are you exhausted, stressed out, burned out? Failure isn't an option, but you just can't keep up, right?

That was Moses. Moses was asked by God to carry that burden. It was rough but worth the payload. Anything worth doing is worth the struggle. It's not easy to struggle to fulfill God's commands. Moses didn't fail because the Lord Almighty was gracing him, guiding him, and giving him what he needed. God does the same for you. You're not alone. With Jesus, you are never alone.

It's all about others
Pastor Jon Enter

In our last devotion, we left Moses on a mountaintop with his arms burning. Each time he lowered them, the Israelites died by the Amalekites' swords. But Exodus chapter 17 reveals, **"His hands remained steady till sunset"** (verse 12). This was a planned battle that likely started in the morning. His hands were raised all day? That's impossible. Or is it? God sent reinforcements. Moses' brother, Aaron, and another man, Hur, sat Moses' tired body upon a rock. **"Aaron and Hur held his hands up—one on one side, one on the other"** (verse 12).

Do you know someone who's struggling? who's crumbling under the load of what they're holding up? Someone likely came right to your mind and heart.

How can you help? How can you be an Aaron or a Hur? Well, it takes two very key components to be a heaven-sent helper. You need *presence*. You need to be willing to step into the drama. Aaron and Hur made themselves visual targets of the Amalekites, but the cause and their care for Moses made it worth it. It's worth it to help the person whose name came across your heart, but that means their mess becomes yours.

And you'll need *persistence*. The devil knows what's working to cause chaos, and he won't give it up easily. But you hold the name of Jesus that makes Satan scatter and demons disperse. You come in the name of Christ, and in his name, victory is won!

Look up!

Pastor Jon Enter

Imagine being an Israelite in the Old Testament. You remember that when Moses' staff hit the Nile River, the river turned to blood (Exodus 7:20). When Moses' staff was held over the Red Sea, the sea peeled apart (Exodus 14:21,22)! And when Moses' staff struck a rock, drinking water flowed (Exodus 17:5,6). The staff was great at water miracles, but now you're against the Amalekite army.

As the battle rages, you look up to see Moses, hands held up with the staff! As long as the staff is raised, your sword slays. When the staff falls, so do Israelites next to you.

It wasn't the staff in Moses' hands that won the battle; it was the power of God that won the victory. Moses prayed for help. We pray with hands folded and heads bowed. The Israelites prayed with hands raised and heads lifted up. As long as Moses and the Israelites looked up to God in prayer and trust, they were safe.

The staff shaped as a cross didn't do a thing; it was the power of Christ dying upon it. When the battle of your life rages, look up. Look up to Christ on the cross. Look up to him who lost his life so that yours isn't lost. Look up in prayer. Look up in trust. Raise up to God the words of Psalm 121:1,2: **"I lift up my eyes. . . . My help comes from the Lord, the Maker of heaven and earth."** Look up, and don't give up because Christ fights for you.

Let nothing move you
Linda Buxa

"But now he has reconciled you by Christ's physical body through death to present you holy in his sight, without blemish and free from accusation—if you continue in your faith, established and firm, and do not move from the hope held out in the gospel" (Colossians 1:22,23).

My son loves football, and he's a stereotypical lineman. Sometimes when I give him a hug, I try to push him over. With barely any effort, he stands there while my sock-covered feet keep slipping out from under me. No matter how hard I try, nothing moves him. Sometimes he even laughs and asks if I'm ever going to start actually pushing. (What a stinker!)

Then one day I realized that his unyielding stance against my feeble attack is the perfect picture of hope for people who believe in Jesus.

Because Jesus died for us, we are holy and perfect in his sight. This gives us the strength to stand against the world and its sadness, accusations, hurts, and lies. Those things keep trying to discourage us, but when they come up against our hope in Jesus, they slip. From multiple angles, they keep trying to push us over, but we are unmovable. Thanks to Jesus, our hope is true and firm—now and forever. And we can laugh at the days to come, not because the world isn't painful but because we are clothed in Christ's strength.

Who touched me?
Pastor Matt Ewart

One day Jesus was walking through a crowd so big that it had the potential to crush him. While plenty of people were bumping up against him, there was one woman who intentionally reached out to touch his cloak.

She had been suffering from a condition that left her subject to bleeding for 12 long years. No doctor could help her. Her only hope was that getting close to Jesus would allow her to be healed. She believed he could help.

And he did.

The moment she touched the edge of his cloak, her bleeding stopped. Jesus also stopped. He wanted to know who had touched him.

Jesus didn't just want to heal her. He wanted to tell her something. But what could he possibly tell her that would add to the blessing of her healing? Here's what he said: **"Daughter, your faith has healed you. Go in peace"** (Luke 8:48).

If you fail to see the significance in what Jesus said, just look at the first word. Jesus wanted her to know that even though nobody noticed her, she was known by God himself. She was his daughter. She was loved by him.

You will have private things in your life that you want to keep that way. Some struggles will go unnoticed by all the people around you, even as you reach out to God for help. What Jesus wants you to know is that you are known and you are loved, even when you go unnoticed.

God guides our healing
Andrea Delwiche

Look at this beautiful request embedded in one little sentence of Psalm 41: **"I said, 'Lord, be merciful to me; Heal my soul, for I have sinned against You'"** (verse 4 NKJV). The psalmist, knowing that he has gone wrong in his relationship with God and others, asks the Lord for healing.

Human beings, by nature separated from the God who made them, have sickly spirits that are curved away from God. By nature, we shun the very One who provides the straightening and healing that we need. But as children of God, we grow in trust, love, and relationship with the Lord, and our situation improves. Our forgiven souls are transformed and healed.

The sin that we inherited and our own misdeeds are forgiven, but the damage done to our spirits by our selfishness toward God and others takes time to heal, as do the scars of sins perpetuated against us. But thanks be to God that we don't need to be our own physician. We have *El Rapha*, the God who heals, as the initiator and sustainer in this work. We are forgiven, loved, and thought beautiful by our Lord. He himself guides our healing process.

Be ready, though; our good God is deliberate. He is capable of instant healing of body and soul, but for our own good growth, he tends to walk alongside us in our healing much as a parent teaching a toddler to walk: slowly, steadily, and patiently. It can be incremental work, and we will sometimes fall. But we will be healed!

Look for fullness
Jason Nelson

I'd like you to think about something I'm wrestling with. How do you see the Bible? Is it half empty, or is it full? Are you a stickler for the rules, or is your favorite commandment, "Love one another"? Do its warnings urge us toward good deeds, or are they a destiny we must fulfill? I suppose we could bring doomsday on ourselves if enough people believe the Bible says it should happen soon. Do you keep the commandments because you are afraid not to or because you really want to? Are you crabby because nothing is perfect, or are you happy to see beauty where you least expect to find it? Do you think being a Christian won't pay off until you die, or are you enjoying yourself now because your faith adorns your walk with good character? Is your life half empty, or is it full?

When you read the Bible, are you looking for the fullness of God? **"For in Christ all the fullness of the Deity lives in bodily form, and in Christ you have been brought to fullness. He is the head over every power and authority"** (Colossians 2:9,10). Jesus is the fullness of God, and he is God's Word brought to vivid life. He is the embodiment of God's love for us. When you're not sure what to focus on in the Bible, focus on Christ. Jesus' life and work and teachings and example make everything in the Bible complete. And he makes us complete.

Be kind to those with special needs
Pastor Daron Lindemann

In ancient times when a king assumed the throne, he killed off all the members of the family that had been in power. Not King David.

David remembered a promise he had made to both his friend Jonathan and also to former King Saul: in Jonathan's absence, David would look after members of Jonathan's family.

Mephibosheth was the son of Jonathan, who was the son of Saul. Mephibosheth wasn't the kind of strong, sexy, and successful person a typical king would want hanging around the palace. He was disabled. Special needs.

David felt kindness toward Mephibosheth, prompting him to remember his promise. **"Is there no one alive from the house of Saul to whom I can show God's kindness?"** (2 Samuel 9:3).

Whose kindness? David, with a worshipful heart, focused on God. He appreciated God's kindness to him so much that it overflowed to a young man with special needs.

Because David had special needs too—spiritual needs, that is. He needed exceptional forgiveness and mercy from God. He trusted in divine guidance and wisdom that he himself couldn't produce. He relied on God's strength to win battles.

David didn't consider himself superior in any way, even as a king.

In what ways have you resisted coming closer to those with special needs or disabilities? Why is it so easy to feel superior to them? Pray today about showing more kindness to them.

New wine needs new skin
Jason Nelson

"Neither is new wine put into old wineskins. If it is, the skins burst and the wine is spilled and the skins are destroyed. But new wine is put into fresh wineskins, and so both are preserved" (Matthew 9:17 ESV).

Every day is new wine and our minds are wineskins. The human brain is one of God's greatest creations. It's where he put his image in us. It's where he creates our faith in Jesus. It's where we regret our failures and understand our potential to do his will. It's where we rise up to meet all the challenges we face in life. It's where we accept who we are and aspire to become what we can be.

Unfortunately, we have the ability to turn a perfectly flexible mind into an old wineskin. If we don't continue to educate ourselves, if we fail to expand our horizons, if we never explore the universe near and far, if we don't try to fathom what's going on in other people's minds, we can become neurologically incapable of expanding our own. The pathways in our brains become so narrow and rigid that when new wine comes at us, we have no capacity to contain it. It blows our minds. We habitually resist anything new. But this is our time of grace. God preserves us by renewing our minds and giving us the mind of Christ.

Heating and pounding
Pastor Jon Enter

Have you ever watched a silversmith work? It's mesmerizing. As a child, I attended a renaissance festival and was captivated by the craftsmanship. The silversmith started with a formless blob of silver. Into the fire it went. He punished it with hammer blows, and back into the fire it went. Back and forth. Heating and pounding until it took the form of something useful. Then came the smaller hammers. More heating and pounding. Not one person yelled, "Hey! I think the silver has had enough!" We watched the mastery of his skill shape the silver.

The Lord declares, **"I will refine them like silver . . . and they will say, 'The Lord is our God'"** (Zechariah 13:9). The Lord is an accomplished silversmith who shapes your life. *Silversmith* is from the old English word *Silver-Smite*, for he is an accomplished smiter. So is God.

Heating and pounding. Strife and stress. Loneliness and layoffs. Heating and pounding. Conflicts and clashes. Disease and death. Heating and pounding. All done to shape you, to form you.

Do you know when a silversmith finishes his work? When he can see his reflection in what he's working on. The heating and pounding you're enduring has a purpose. It's so you see the love of Christ in you. Jesus knows heating and pounding. He went through the fires of hell after nails were pounded into his flesh. He knows what is needed for you to shine, to reflect his love to others, and to be made into something useful. And you are!

Filled with thanks
Pastor Matt Ewart

According to a lot of scientific research, thankfulness is a powerful thing. It has been shown to improve everything from physical health to personal relationships. (Do a quick online search for "benefits of gratitude" to see for yourself.)

I have one question for you: Are you as thankful as you could be?

The biggest thing that can keep you from being full of thanks is discontentment. Even if your life is filled with blessings, discontentment will empty your bucket of thankfulness.

When you are discontent with what you have, it means you are forfeiting the benefits of thankfulness. More than that, it means you are denying God of the thanks that is due him.

Do you want to stop the leak so you can be filled with thanks? The apostle Paul shared the secret to get you there: **"I have learned the secret of being content in any and every situation, whether well fed or hungry, whether living in plenty or in want. I can do all this through him who gives me strength"** (Philippians 4:12,13).

It requires strength to be content with little. It also requires strength to remain content when you have a lot. But the strength doesn't have to come from you. It comes from Jesus, who emptied himself completely to fill you with eternal blessings.

He said, "Yes!"
Christine Wentzel

The news headline read (in part), "Answered prayer!" to the survival story of an accident victim.

Does that well-intentioned declaration really testify to the completely awesome work of God? Or does it lead another to question why his or her prayers "weren't" answered, or even heard?

Christians say it all the time for good reason. We are ecstatic over divine love coming to our rescue. It's fuel for our faith. It's validation to our witness. It's proof of God's personal care in our lives.

But for a fellow Christian who is struggling in their wait (and even the unbelieving public watching us under a microscope), we can testify that the fuel, validation, and proof also come with a closed door or a command for patience. God does his best work behind the scenes of our understanding.

"Then you will call on me and come and pray to me, and I will listen to you" (Jeremiah 29:12).

Let's have the headlines read, "God answers ALL our prayers!"

This is a statement of our sure hope that God hears every single prayer from his children. He answers every one with a yes, no, or wait. It's the yeses we crave, because we think we know what's best for us, especially when in crisis mode. But if we truly trust that only God knows best, that he is passionately invested in our well-being, then we will rest in his "silence" with the support of our family.

Today is the day
Linda Buxa

Usually joy comes pretty easily to me. My go-to passage in the Bible mentions it twice. But then 2020 came along, and I had to put much more thought and effort into being joyful.

See, I kept looking ahead and thinking joy would come as soon as I got what I wanted. Once we got through safer-at-home, then I'd be fine. But that got extended. Instead, I hoped the kids could do track or the mission trip or the sports camps. Nope. Nope. Nope. Okay, joy would come as long as my oldest could do her study abroad. (You might guess how that one turned out.) Well, I would be fine as long as school started in person and fall sports could happen. (That one did get a yes, with a bunch of caveats!)

I'm not sure when it happened, but finally the Holy Spirit reminded me that **"*this* is the day that the Lord has made; let us rejoice and be glad in it"** (Psalm 118:24 ESV). I was so busy looking forward that I was forgetting to look right in front of me.

What's your "I'll be joyful when . . ."? Is it finishing the house project? Is it when the promotion takes place? Is it finally getting pregnant? Maybe it's something else.

I think we all need the reminder that *today* is the day the Lord has made. *Tomorrow* will be the day the Lord has made too, but *this* is the day to rejoice and be glad.

Strong tree
Pastor Daron Lindemann

Ancient shipbuilders would prepare the masts for their ships long before installing them.

They would go to the forest and find an appropriate tree. Then they would clear out all the surrounding trees and leave that one standing, exposed to the wind and storms and total sunlight.

As the tree continued to mature, it would gain strength, the kind of strength it would need to be able to stand up in the storms at sea while holding a large sail.

Peter says that the Bible is **"completely reliable, and you will do well to pay attention to it, as to a light shining in a dark place, until the day dawns and the morning star rises in your hearts"** (2 Peter 1:19).

The light of God that he shined on the Bible writers, unique in all of history, makes the Bible stand alone as special. It is a supernatural and miraculous work of God.

The Bible stands alone and stands strong like a tall, strong mast of a ship. Because the Bible stands alone, you never will. You'll never stand alone. You'll never be helpless or lost.

Forged through storm and by the light of God shining on the writers, the Bible stands taller and stronger than any other media or information you could ever consume.

It will take you through storms and through darkness, and the clouds will break and the light of God will shine in your heart.

God is close to the abused
Pastor Mike Novotny

While abuse is not a comfortable topic to talk about, we need to. If the Centers for Disease Control and Prevention's statistics are correct, 59,000 people who watch *Time of Grace* on TV each week have suffered some type of abuse in their lives. By "abuse" I mean a pattern of behavior that uses fear or force to maintain power and control.

Maybe that description hits home. Your dad was aggressive in his physical discipline. Your mom degraded you with her words. Your boyfriend isolated you from your friends, pushed until he got his way, or gave you an allowance as a grown woman. Your wife twisted Scripture ("You have to forgive me!") and swore she would hurt herself if you talked to the pastor. Your husband abused the Word ("You have to submit to me!") and threatened to take the kids if you didn't do exactly what he wanted.

There are many things that God says in response to the tragedy of abuse, but here is the place we must start: **"The Lord is close to the brokenhearted and saves those who are crushed in spirit"** (Psalm 34:18). When fear or force breaks our hearts and crushes our spirits, God is near. He is close to us, grieving the sins committed against us and promising to heal our wounds.

Given the statistics and our experiences, we pray that Jesus would come and save us soon. But until that day arrives, may you always remember that the Lord is close. God is here.

God hates abuse
Pastor Mike Novotny

A man came to my office and confessed to me that he had been abusive with his girlfriend. After expressing my grave concern for his behavior, I told the man what I would tell any seemingly repentant sinner—Jesus forgives you. Although there would be consequences for his actions, Jesus had taken away his eternal condemnation. I even texted him a Bible passage so the guilt wouldn't overwhelm him. (FYI—I also consulted law enforcement to see what I could do to keep this woman safe from future abuse.)

A while later, however, his girlfriend stopped by my office and told me what had happened next. The man had taken my text, shoved it in her face, and boasted, "See! Even the pastor is on my side!" My heart slumped as she repeated his words, and I came to hate abuse more than I ever had in my life.

"Those who love violence, [the Lord] **hates with a passion"** (Psalm 11:5). That passage is a terrifying reminder that God hates not just abuse but abusers themselves. So if you're using fear or force to maintain control in a relationship, repent! Before you stand before the God who "hates" you, change your heart and your life. You might fool the pastor or the judge, but you can't fool God.

And if you've endured abuse, let these stark words remind you that God is on your side, close to the brokenhearted. As the psalm goes on to say, **"[The Lord] loves justice; the upright will see his face"** (verse 7).

Abuse is not your fault
Pastor Mike Novotny

As I prepared a series of messages on the topic of abuse, I sent my first drafts to a woman I knew who specialized in domestic violence, hoping to speak more accurately and helpfully to those who had suffered trauma in their lives.

Her feedback was priceless. In particular, I remember her saying that one of the most important things for victims to hear is, "It's not your fault." Abusive people have a way of finger-pointing and blame shifting, convincing us that if only we hadn't _____, they wouldn't have hurt us. It's sick, but it's common. And it's a key way that abuse continues for months or years on end.

So let me be as clear as my colleague encouraged me to be—*It's not your fault.* Your sin is your fault, but their sin is not your fault. It's their fault. Read that last sentence again. Say it out loud until you believe it in your heart. *It's not your fault.*

When Jesus taught, **"If anyone causes one of these little ones—those who believe in me—to stumble,"** he didn't go on to blame the little children for the grown-ups' sins (Matthew 18:6). Why not? Because the sin wasn't their fault.

Healing from abuse is hard enough. So please believe the voice of the One who loves you. Abuse is not your fault.

God loves the abused
Pastor Mike Novotny

A few years back, a pastor told me about the funny way our minds do math. He had just read a study that said when one person says something to you ten times and ten people say something to you one time, our brains feel about the same. In other words, $1x10=1+1+1+1+1+1+1+1+1+1$. So if your mom or your boyfriend constantly says, "You're so dumb. You're an idiot. You're useless and fat and stupid and worthless," your brain finds it very hard to remember that only one person said that. Only one. But it feels like the truth.

I wonder if that's why the one true God calls you so many names. Throughout the New Testament, there are over 680 names that God calls those who believe in Jesus. Guess how many are positive, names like Holy or Beloved or Blameless or Pure? Not 1 or 2 or 10, but 610! Despite all our struggles and sins, God himself has 610 names to lift us up and give us hope.

If you are one of the many people who carry the wounds of abuse, turn your ear toward Jesus. Through his death and resurrection, he wants to overwhelm your mind with love and set you free. As Jesus himself said, **"**[God] **has sent me to proclaim freedom for the prisoners . . . to set the oppressed free"** (Luke 4:18).

God gets your abuse
Pastor Mike Novotny

Have you ever been going through something in life and had a conversation with someone who truly understood what you were going through? Maybe you were dealing with daily anxiety or divorce court or a family member who was walking away from church, but God gave you a person who had walked in your shoes and could relate to your pain. Isn't there something powerful about such moments? Even if your situation doesn't change, there's something about knowing that other people understand.

Maybe that's why Jesus was abused. An old prophecy about his suffering predicted, **"He was oppressed and afflicted"** (Isaiah 53:7), which Jesus felt in the soldiers' fists, their verbal taunts, and the crown of thorns they pressed onto his head. Our Savior was physically, verbally, and emotionally shamed behind closed doors and on a hill outside of Jerusalem for everyone to see.

Jesus' experience on earth means that he gets what it's like to be abused. When you call out to him in your prayers, Jesus doesn't wrinkle his forehead in confusion, unable to relate to your situation. Instead, his head slowly nods and his eyes brim with compassion. He knows what that's like. He has felt that pain. He has carried those wounds.

One day, Jesus will come back and end abuse once and for all. Until that day comes, however, he walks by our sides and listens to our prayers as the Son of God who gets it. Jesus gets you.

Jesus lights the dark corners
Andrea Delwiche

"The light shines in the darkness, and the darkness has not overcome it" (John 1:5).

We could return to these 13 words every day and find new ways to apply them in our own lives, but sometimes they may seem too abstract to understand. Here's an image that may bring comfort, courage, and hope as we live in a world that can be pretty dark.

Picture a room. It's nighttime, and the blinds are closed. No ambient light can be seen. It's completely dark. But into that darkness someone carries a lit candle with its warming glow of flame. As the candle is brought into the room and set on a table, the darkness must disappear. It has no choice. Darkness cannot stand in the presence of light. Light wins. Our lives can be pitch black with bitter daily circumstances, binding fears, or addictions of many kinds. Day and night, Jesus the Light brings light and wants to bring more light into our dark rooms.

Would a symbol help you remember the truth of God's power over darkness in this world and in your own life? Consider lighting a candle in your home each day to remind yourself that "the light shines in the darkness" and that still, even today, "the darkness has not overcome it."

In what area of your life do you need to remember that Christ is light and *has* the light of life to shine and rid your life of darkness? Ask for his bright presence to illuminate every dark corner. May you be blessed.

One thing to do before you die
Ann Jahns

Nothing evokes panic in me more than books like *1,000 Places to See Before You Die*. The authors of books like this must not be the rule-following, checklist maker that I am. Unless all those spectacular places are within a reasonable driving distance of my home, I won't be able to check them all off of my bucket list.

So let's boil it down to something a little more attainable for ourselves, like *One Thing to Do Before You Die*. What would that one thing be?

Take a look at your relationships. Is there one person you want to reconcile with while you still can? Someone who harmed you or someone you harmed? Perhaps you need to forgive—or ask for forgiveness.

And how about that one person in your life who doesn't yet know Jesus? You know who that person is, and you want that person to spend eternity in heaven.

Our time on this earth is short, and we don't know when Jesus will return on the final day. The apostle Paul cautions us, **"Now, brothers and sisters, about times and dates we do not need to write to you, for you know very well that the day of the Lord will come like a thief in the night"** (1 Thessalonians 5:1,2).

If you're a checklist person, add that *one thing* to your list right now: Today I am going to reach out to _____. Or, today I am going to share Jesus with _____.

Spurs and bull riding

Pastor Daron Lindemann

I see lots of spurs at the Austin rodeo that kicks off every spring. One of the most popular competitions is bull riding.

In bull riding, spurs are dulled and mostly help the bull rider hold on to the one-ton bull with their legs and feet. And what happens then? A wild ride. Getting bucked around and off. Broken ribs. Mental toughness. The cheers of the crowd. Telling your grandkids someday that you rode a bull named Fumanchu. Growth. Strength.

Now listen to what the Bible says about Christian community: **"Let us hold unswervingly to the hope we profess, for he who promised is faithful"** (Hebrews 10:23).

"Hold unswervingly" are Greek words in the original Bible that literally mean "hold on tight!" The Bible calls us to be spurs that help each other hold on tight and not let go. Let go of what? "The hope we profess."

We don't let go of each other. We hang in there with each other. Why? Because we have this agreement that we profess. This body of teaching we believe. That's the Bible that reveals Jesus Christ. The Bible and Jesus define our fellowship as a church.

Hold on to Jesus and his church! Be like spurs and help others hold on to Jesus and his church too. It might result in a wild ride. It might cause pain but will also result in spiritual growth.

And remember, Jesus—who believes in his church— is holding on to you. "He who promised is faithful."

Don't be stupid
Linda Buxa

A little boy once asked me if a lot of people read the things I write. When I told him that sometimes my words reach hundreds (and occasionally thousands) of people, he was impressed. Then another little boy piped up, "Yeah, but there's like seven billion people in the world."

I laughed. Honesty is cute when it comes from kids, who really do say things bluntly. Do we take correction so well, however, when it comes from those close to us who have the courage to confront us about far more serious things? When they point out that our life choices are having a negative impact on our lives? Not so much.

I really don't want to hear that my quick tongue and sarcastic words hurt you. Nobody wants to hear that their drinking is starting to affect relationships. We don't want someone to tell us that our interest in politics might be taking the place of our relationship with our eternal King Jesus. I don't like hearing someone say, "That's gossip; let's not go there."

But these are exactly the kinds of things the people closest to us need to be free to say. Before we get defensive, let's take a deep breath and remember the time when a really wise man named Solomon wrote, **"Whoever loves discipline loves knowledge, but whoever hates correction is stupid"** (Proverbs 12:1).

Gift formula
Pastor Matt Ewart

There's a piece of artwork on my desk that's quite valuable—at least to me.

One of my kids took some crayons and drew a picture of a house and five stick people. I *think* it's a picture of our family. (The dad in this picture is much taller than I am. ☺)

The artwork is valuable to me, not because of the cost of materials that were required in its making but because of who gave it. For those who see things mathematically, here's the formula: VALUE = (GIVER) x (GIFT).

The more you love the giver, the more you will value their gift. The more you despise the giver, the more you will despise their gift.

One day a sinful woman (GIVER) poured out some perfume (GIFT) on Jesus. The people who witnessed this took offense because in their minds, the identity of the giver negated the value of the gift. Jesus should have rejected both, but instead he highly valued both. He even explained why: **"Therefore, I tell you, her many sins have been forgiven—as her great love has shown"** (Luke 7:47).

Her gift was valuable, not because of its intrinsic value but because of who she was. She was a loved daughter of God who overflowed with thankfulness.

Today you will have the opportunity to show great love for God through the gifts you extend to others. He is pleased with them because of who you are: a child of God himself.

The teacher's focus
Jason Nelson

Jesus was an amazing teacher. He was willing to teach anyone, anytime, anyplace. **"Now when Jesus saw the crowds, he went up on a mountainside and sat down. His disciples came to him, and he began to teach them"** (Matthew 5:1,2).

Jesus never lost his focus. He knew that teachers don't teach texts. They don't teach information. They don't teach traditions. Teachers teach students. With every lesson, teachers ask themselves: "What do my students need to think? What do my students need to feel? What do my students need to do? What do my students need to believe?"

"When Jesus had finished saying these things, the crowds were amazed at his teaching, because he taught as one who had authority, and not as their teachers of the law" (Matthew 7:28,29). Jesus amazed his students. He could do it seminar style on a mountain and hold a crowd's attention with powerful ideas. Mary got what she needed, and Martha got what she needed from the same family devotion. Jesus didn't pull punches in a one-on-one conversation with a naive young man and let him walk away. He made a follower out of a foreign woman fetching water by getting inside her head. Jesus gave a cautious old man a new lease on life when he told him he was born again because God so loved him. Jesus left lesser teachers scratching their heads.

Jesus is still an amazing teacher; he is focused on you.

God said no

Ann Jahns

I begged God to take my friend's cancer away. She was a force of nature with a larger-than-life personality. If anyone could beat cancer, I knew she could.

So I reasoned with God, offering very logical points: Her husband and kids need her. Her friends and students need her. She can still be a gospel witness while she is here. But God said no. Despite the prayers, tearful pleas, and sound arguments, he took my friend to her real home, leaving her devastated family and friends behind.

In the Garden of Gethsemane, an agonized Jesus pleaded with his father—twice—to take the cup of suffering away from him. God said no. So Jesus said, **"May your will be done"** (Matthew 26:42) and turned to the cross, where he would die and triumph over death for us.

The apostle Paul pleaded with God to take away his "thorn in the flesh." He asked God—three times—to take it away. God said no. So Paul carried on with his gospel work, saying, **"I will boast all the more gladly about my weaknesses, so that Christ's power may rest on me"** (2 Corinthians 12:9).

Sometimes *no* is God's answer, even though we hate it. We fight against it, kicking and screaming like toddlers, pounding our fists and yelling to get our way. But like a wise and patient parent who knows what's best for their child, God sometimes says no.

Lord, may we accept your no, knowing it's a part of your perfect plan for our lives. Amen.

On second thought . . .
Christine Wentzel

Can you relate to second-guessing? Do you doubt your decisions habitually? If you do, then you have some work to do on strengthening your trust in God. Here are some confidence-building tips to help get you started:

- More often than not, second-guessed conclusions are not based on solid facts. It's guessing—anticipating an outcome that's usually based on fear.
- Ask yourself why you doubt a particular decision. Do you have all the facts? If not, then find them. It's the same as studying for a test in school. You can't get the best passing grade without it.
- Is it a decision you wouldn't mind letting God know about? You know he knows already, but you can fool yourself with this through self-justification. If you're not sure, ask someone who is spiritually mature and knowledgeable in Scripture. Look up Matthew 18:20, and you will know why.
- While your Bible is open, read the entire chapter of Proverbs 3. It was written for such a time as this!

Speaking from firsthand experience, prayer, time, and practice increase confidence and trust. And you know what? It's stress relieving.

"His divine power has given us everything we need for a godly life through our knowledge of him who called us by his own glory and goodness" (2 Peter 1:3).

All glory to God that growing in his wisdom with a Christ-like humility means getting off the "what if" train of thought once and for all!

Jesus' sacrifice
Linda Buxa

I can't get through the national anthem without tearing up. It started long ago when I watched Dan Jansen on the podium. Yes, I had a crush on my hometown's speed skating hero, but it was more about his journey to the gold.

Now that I'm older, my reasons are less schoolgirlish. I know people who have died while serving, and I think of those left behind. I see children singing the anthem and wonder which of them might volunteer their life for the rest of us. I cry because I realize that my nation's flag has draped countless caskets of those who sacrificed so my nation would be free.

I cry at Easter hymns for many of the same reasons. My Savior Jesus tells me that he is my (and your) Good Shepherd who **"lays down his life for the sheep"** (John 10:11). He came as a servant, sacrificing his life so that we can all be free for all eternity.

The United States has set aside a day to honor those who died while securing our country's freedom. After a moment of respect for them, the best thing you can do with the freedom they've gained for you is to share the good news about the One who laid down his life for them. They gain nothing if they sacrifice their lives for our country but don't know that Jesus sacrificed his life for theirs.

This is not normal
Pastor Mike Novotny

A pastor friend of mine often says about our ministry: "This is not normal." Recently, we have been blessed with some noticeable (and abnormal) gifts—a new church property, lots of new faces, and some shockingly generous people. When we look at the blessings, in spite of all our sins, weakness, and flaws, my colleague shakes his head and repeats, "This is not normal."

That phrase is a good way to describe the Christian faith, isn't it? When God is willing to listen to run-of-the-mill men and women like us—that's not normal. When the God who needs nothing to be happy wants us to be with him in his happiness—that's not normal. When taking care of sin is something Jesus did and not something we do—that's not normal. When salvation is a gift by grace and through faith and not something we work for—that's not normal.

Jesus, who knows all your sins, loves you. He likes being with you. He sees you as holy, washed pure by the sacrifice he made on a cross. None of this is normal. But it is so, so good, isn't it?

"Now to him who is able to do immeasurably more than all we ask or imagine, according to his power that is at work within us, to him be glory in the church and in Christ Jesus throughout all generations, for ever and ever! Amen" (Ephesians 3:20,21).

June

As Scripture says, "Anyone who believes in him will never be put to shame."

Romans 10:11

Will God provide?
Pastor Matt Ewart

For the longest time, I was sure there was a biblical promise that God would provide everything I need for my life—that I would always have food on the table, clothes on my back, and a roof over my head. But the more I looked for that promise, the more I realized it wasn't there.

Yes, God is the provider of all your physical needs. But nowhere does he guarantee that all your physical needs will always be met.

Paul acknowledged that in Romans 8:35. We may go through **"trouble or hardship or persecution or famine or nakedness or danger or sword."** Ultimately your life will end because one or more physical needs are no longer being met. If you merely look to God as a provider, you will eventually be let down.

But he is more than that. Because of what Jesus did, God is not just the provider. God already provided. Jesus removed the gap between you and the Lord Almighty. Jesus connects with you by faith to bring you into an inheritance that is so much bigger than anything this world can contain.

You don't have a guarantee that your physical needs will be provided on this side of heaven. But Jesus is the guarantee that even in times of trouble or hardship or famine, **"in all these things we are more than conquerors through him who loved us"** (Romans 8:37).

Today as you marvel at all that God provides, be thankful that in Jesus, eternal life has already been provided.

Broken bones
Pastor Daron Lindemann

A few years ago, I broke the first bone I've ever broken in my body: the tip of my finger. Man, that hurt! I crushed the little fingertip bone and split it in half.

I remember thinking, "If I'm in this much pain with a broken fingertip bone, what about all those people who break the big stuff?" Yowza! Respect.

For months, I'd bump it or even just rub it along something and, "Ouch!" The nerve endings were so sensitive to the touch.

So it was an incredible joy when it finally healed. The bone that I crushed rejoiced!

"Let me hear joy and gladness; let the bones you have crushed rejoice. Hide your face from my sins and blot out all my iniquity" (Psalm 51:8,9).

Imagine if every one of your 206 bones was broken. Crushed. Ouch! That would hurt for months, but then would come healing and rejoicing! They probably wouldn't all heal at the exact same time though, so you'd experience multiple moments of joy.

Instead of just saying, "I forgive you" one time and telling you that you better remember it or you'll miss out, God says, "I forgive you" for each one of your sins. He says it often. He says it in different ways.

Every broken bone rejoices. Every one of your sins every day is fully forgiven: specifically, individually, again and again. Now be careful and take care of those bones in the joy of forgiveness.

Never give up
Christine Wentzel

Irene came of age during the Great Depression—a young mother before WWII. Her marriage was fraught with neglect and abuse as she raised her seven children through four decades of monumental societal changes. She was a warrior, wrangling family order through the chaos. The "look" turned her hellions into statues.

In reality, it was her faith in Christ that was on full display. In all opposition, she made sure her children were baptized into God's family and educated in God's wisdom. She believed Jesus would work the messes and mistakes into something that would bless her family members' lives sooner or later. As each of us walked away from all her efforts, her fervent prayers for our prodigal return dogged us.

In her final years, while in my care, I listened to her speak of living her life in Jesus. I compared it privately to mine without him. I realized she didn't force her children into "useless" religious and secular routines. She gratefully made it a mandate to live a life that reflected her trust in a personal God that it might win over her children to Christ. That's when the Holy Spirit woke me from my spiritual slumber.

"Let us not become weary in doing good, for at the proper time we will reap a harvest if we do not give up" (Galatians 6:9).

The Lord took my mother to heaven. And Jesus has opened the door of my heart. He leads me in protected pastures like he led my mother.

Mom, until we meet again—thank you.

Put it all together
Jason Nelson

Athletes become superstars when they can put it all together. The fundamentals of the game are in them. They hit the shot consistently. They don't have to think about it anymore. They can feel it. They just do it. Singers become rock stars when they can put it all together. The music is in them. They nail the note consistently. They don't have to think about it anymore. They can feel it. They just do it. Mastery of anything is a synthesis of God-given abilities that have been honed by lots of rehearsal until it all becomes second nature. The performer is one with the performance.

That is the level of Christianity God wants for us. He wants us to put it all together on a consistent basis. We will still miss some opportunities and sound some sour notes. We can learn from them, but we can't dwell on them. God wants us to shake them off. He tells us to pull ourselves together in him. He sent his Son in the flesh so we know what love is. We have received God's love. We live in God's love. We can express God's love to others. Love makes us one with God. **"Whoever lives in love lives in God, and God in them"** (1 John 4:16). Loving others is not something we need to think about. Loving others is not something to hesitate over. It's our new nature. We can just do it.

Shine the light on your words and thoughts
Andrea Delwiche

"Whoever lives by the truth comes into the light, so that it may be seen plainly that what they have done has been done in the sight of God" (John 3:21).

Do you ever think about the motivation behind words and ideas that you might throw out to others? Do you wonder if the thoughts that *lead* to those words are of God? Sometimes our words can take on a veneer of Christianity, but in actuality they stand in opposition to Jesus' teachings.

It can certainly happen these days. Words and ideas come to us prepackaged. They trigger emotions in us—fear, hatred, self-preservation. We receive them, and to ease our own anxiety, we pass them on to others. They may even *sound like* Christianity as we've heard it represented by people whom we love and respect but, in actuality, may have nothing to do with Christ and his love.

How can we guard against this false religion? We can take time to hold thoughts and words up to the light of Christ. Prayerfully read through the gospels—Matthew, Mark, Luke, and John—to see what was important to Jesus. How did he live? What did he prioritize? Ask the Spirit to help sort out longings and fears, to separate what is of Christ and what is a construct of human hatred masquerading as Christ.

Lord Jesus, let your light shine among us. Give us courage to hold every thought and action up to the light of your goodness and truth. Help us change where we need to change. Amen.

The issue regarding abortion
Pastor Mike Novotny

Given how frequent, emotional, and personal abortions are, we need a God-given foundation for what we believe and why we believe it. Since many will either have an abortion, consider an abortion, or know someone who is considering/has gotten an abortion, it's vital for us to be full of grace and truth, imitating the heart of our Father in heaven.

I want to dig deep into what I consider to be *the* issue regarding abortion—personhood. Personhood answers questions like, When does a person become a person? Is that a *who* or a *what* within the womb? How do we know?

Why is that *the* issue? Because most people, both pro-life and pro-choice, know exactly how to treat a person. We would agree a preschooler's life can't be ended for the reasons people choose an abortion, even if those reasons are heartbreakingly complicated. Even if the timing was terrible, the was mother poor, the father was abusive, the parents weren't a good fit, the genetics were abnormal, the conception was tragic, or the world was unstable, we would protect that preschooler from danger or death because that preschooler is . . . a person. In light of God's command to **"defend the oppressed"** (Isaiah 1:17), we would know exactly what to do.

So when does life begin? at birth? when the parents desire a child? when a child can live outside the womb? when it looks like a baby? at conception? In the days ahead, let's explore these five top answers to the personhood question with open minds and open Bibles.

Does life begin at birth?
Pastor Mike Novotny

One of the top five answers to, When does life begin? is "At birth." Once out of the womb, we're no longer looking at a part of the mother but instead at a separate human being.

Does the Bible agree with that view? Jesus' birth offers a fascinating answer. In Luke chapter 1, Mary is pregnant and goes to see her relative Elizabeth, who is six months along with the soon-to-be-named John. When Mary shows up at Elizabeth's home, John, in the womb, starts to jump around like preteen girls at a middle school dance. The Scripture says, **"When Elizabeth heard Mary's greeting, the baby leaped in her womb"** (Luke 1:41). The Greek word used here for *baby* is *brephos.* What was in the womb was a *brephos.*

Jump ahead to Luke chapter 2. Mary makes it to Bethlehem, gives birth to Jesus, and lays him in a manger before an angel shows up to some shepherds and says, **"This will be a sign to you: You will find a baby wrapped in cloths and lying in a manger"** (verse 12). Want to guess what Greek word is used for *baby? Brephos.* So Jesus out of the womb and John in the womb are the same thing in the Bible's eyes. A *brephos.* A baby.

This detail helps us consider when life begins. Based on God's view, our Father creates life sometime before Mom's final push and the child's first breath. Is that all the Bible says? Or does it offer other truths to help us answer the vital question of personhood? . . .

Does life begin at desire?
Pastor Mike Novotny

In exploring people's answers to, When does life begin? I discovered that some say, "When the mother wants a baby." Since every child should be a wanted child, the thinking goes, then children come into existence when they are wanted.

In *Shout Your Abortion*, a collection of stories from women who are unashamed of their choice to abort, one author declared, "The simple truth is this: if a sperm and egg come together when a child is desired, a human being is born. But if a sperm and egg come together when a woman knows in her bones that it is not the right time for her to be a mother, then perhaps what is born is her own confident agency over her life" (p. 54). That's a poetic way of saying that a woman who doesn't want a child doesn't have a child within her.

Does the Bible agree? In Psalm 139, a classic text for discussing abortion, King David writes, **"You created my inmost being; you knit me together in my mother's womb"** (verse 13). Notice the "you" that David mentions—God. God creates life in the womb. God knits children together within their mothers. God is the author—the starter—of human existence.

God's confident agency, his desire to bring forth life, gets the deciding vote over what a woman may feel about her pregnancy. That doesn't end the debate, nor does it address all the issues why a woman might not want a child, but it takes us one step closer to figuring out when exactly life begins.

Does life begin when babies can survive?
Pastor Mike Novotny

Dr. Willie Parker doesn't believe that performing abortions conflicts with his faith in God. Why? In describing abortion, he writes, "Before twenty-two weeks, a fetus is not in any way equal to 'a baby.' . . . This is organic matter that does not add up to anything that can live on its own" (*Life's Work: A Moral Argument for Choice*, p. 12). In his thinking, an 18-week fetus can't live outside of the womb, which means it must not be a human life.

Like Paul **"reasoned with"** (Acts 17:2) the people of his day, let's examine this belief. Dr. Parker said his belief applies to "before twenty-two weeks." Why that number? Because, as of the writing of his book, First World NICU technology has been able to sustain the life of a child born that early. But imagine if a pregnant woman flew to a Third World country without the advanced technology to save a 22-week-old. Would her change in location change the fact that her child is a child? Or imagine if that same pregnant woman lived in the 19th century instead of the 21st. Would changing her birthday change the fact that her child is a child?

Dr. Parker's reasoning falls short not only of biblical standards, since John the Baptist was called a baby (*brephos*) despite being six months along in a world that lacked our technology. But this argument also falls short of reason. Something as vital as human life isn't measured based on the year or location of your birth. This is why we need to open our Bibles and ask deeper questions about when life actually begins.

Does life begin at recognition?

Pastor Mike Novotny

Last night my daughters and I got into an unexpected discussion about when life begins. Without tipping my hand, I asked the girls when a baby becomes a baby, a question that led them to scratch their heads a bit. One of them commented, "When you can see that little heart beating."

Without knowing it, my daughter offered one of the top answers to abortion's biggest question—When does life begin? Her answer was recognition. When we can recognize, through an ultrasound, that the mother is carrying a fingered, toed, spinal-corded, heart-beating baby, then we can be sure that it is a baby.

Does the Bible agree with that view? Psalm 139 offers a helpful hint when King David says to his Creator, **"Your eyes saw my unformed body"** (verse 16). Unformed. Without a definite form. Without a clear shape. Even at that early stage of development, what did God's eyes see? My body. That was David's body and not just a part of his mother's body.

Advances in technology have turned our ultrasounds into breathtaking images of curled-up cuties whose heartbeats bring tears to their parents' eyes. But, once again, the Bible pushes us back even further, claiming that life began even before we could identify the images confidently, even when our bodies were yet to be formed.

So is it true? Does the Bible really claim that life begins at conception? Let's explore that question next.

Does life begin at conception?
Pastor Mike Novotny

"Is our couch sinful?" I asked my daughters as we discussed the issue of abortion during a family devotion. "No," my youngest said, "unless it grows arms and starts to punch us!"

The more I think about her goofy comment, the more I see the logic behind it. She knows instinctively that things (couches, chairs, pillows) are not sinful because they are not people. But if those things were more like people (with arms that could punch you!), then *sinful* might be the right word to describe them.

What does all this have to do with abortion? Back in Psalm 51, King David wrote, **"Surely I was sinful at birth, sinful from the time my mother conceived me"** (verse 5). David confessed that he was sinful from the moment of his conception. If only people are sinful, as opposed to things like couches (or clumps of cells), then God is telling us a massive truth that must shape our views of the womb. God is declaring that human life begins at conception.

If that passage wasn't enough proof, consider the unique DNA formed once a sperm fertilizes an egg. Unlike the mother's cells around it, that zygote has its own genetic code. Perhaps God was winking at us, reminding us when created life truly begins.

So what does this mean for us? For those of us who have had or have encouraged an abortion? I hope and pray that you come back tomorrow for God's answer to that question.

The cross and your abortion
Pastor Mike Novotny

"It's kind of an emergency," a woman from church insisted as she handed me her phone. That's when I heard the confession of her friend who had an abortion 20 years ago. Abortion seemed like the best choice at the time, yet she still carried the guilt of having ended a life that began at conception.

Maybe you feel that way too. Maybe long ago or just this week you ended a pregnancy. Maybe you're the guy who pushed it, paid for it, or who didn't say anything and let her do it. Maybe you're the mom or dad who didn't want the pregnancy to prove you weren't that perfect after all. Maybe you had some good reasons. Maybe not. But maybe now, with an open Bible, you realize God's perspective.

If so, listen—Jesus came to forgive and save you. Jesus came from the line of David, once appeared on a mountaintop with Moses, and personally called Paul to be his apostle. What did these three men have in common? They all ended human lives, proving that Jesus forgives the worst things we have done. **"If we confess our sins, he is faithful and just and will forgive us our sins and purify us from *all unrighteousness*"** (1 John 1:9).

Abortion doesn't have to be the end of your story. One woman with two abortions in her past recently said, "*Good Friday has never been the same for me since.*" Look to the cross and see Jesus dying for sins. For everyone's sins. For all your sins. All of them.

His pants are not on fire
Linda Buxa

When my children were little, my husband said I should write a book called *How to Lie to Your Kids*, because I'd say stuff like, "Oh, bummer, I was going to give you ice cream, but because you're fighting that's not going to happen." I didn't have ice cream. Or I'd suggest we'd go to the neighbor's pool but not follow through because I was tired.

So when I read that our heavenly Father **"does not lie or change his mind; for he is not a human being, that he should change his mind"** (1 Samuel 15:29), I'm a little baffled—and humbled.

I'm in awe that the God who made me not only doesn't lie but also can't lie, because it's not in his nature. (Satan, on the other hand, is called the father of lies, so it's pretty clear whose pants are on fire.)

Plus, God keeps his promises, every single one. He knows what's good for us in both the short and long term, and he sticks to that plan. His Son, Jesus, could have come to earth and changed his mind when he saw just how painful a death on a cross would be, but he didn't. He endured the pain, never wavering in his commitment to us. When he promises heaven, heaven is actually there waiting for us. When he tells us we're going there, we know he'll follow through.

The key to great prayer

Pastor Mike Novotny

A few weeks ago, I asked our church a dangerous question: "What grade would you give your prayer life?" About 160 people gave their mostly uninspiring answers: C+, D, B, D-. "My prayer life lacks intentionality." "My mind is always distracted." Most people longed to be better at prayer.

I can relate to that. Over the years, I've preached on prayer, read books on prayer, and set goals around prayer, but I'm not there with prayer. Not close to where I want to be in my daily conversations with my Father.

But recently, God showed me the key to a great prayer life. It happened while I was studying Jesus' words: **"Whoever takes the lowly position of this child is the greatest in the kingdom of heaven"** (Matthew 18:4). What is it about children that makes them so great in Jesus' eyes? Answer—They know they are helpless. The reason little kids cry, "Mommy!" a hundred times a day is because they don't have the skills to cook lunch, the money to buy toys, or the height to see over the grown-ups. Their helplessness forces them to ask for help.

Light. Bulb. Moment. When we remember that we are helpless without God, it forces us to pray humbly. "God, without you I can't love my brother. Or raise this daughter. Or forgive my ex. Or make my friend a Christian. Or escape this shame. Or say no to this sin. Or trust you in this tragedy. I need you, God. Every day, I need you."

Remembering our lowly position—as helpless humans—will keep us talking to God in prayer.

Not forgotten
Linda Buxa

On September 12, 2001, many people in remote areas of Alaska hadn't heard the news that shook the world (9/11). Hunters were stranded, waiting for their small planes to pick them up. They had no communication because cell phones were still fairly new and didn't work out there anyway. Eventually an Alaskan senator got special permission for the planes to fly, worried that people would panic and start to hike their way out or die from lack of supplies.

Knowing the kind of anger and irritation they would face when they landed, bush pilots carried newspapers to explain the enormity of the situation and why they were late. Fear and anger turned to understanding because the stranded people saw the truth.

Enormous heartache and sadness and problems on this earth leave you feeling like those hunters. You have no idea what's going on. Why aren't the plans you made being carried out? Where is the person who's supposed to help you? How will this all turn out?

It's easy to ask the same questions that King David asked: **"How long, Lord? Will you forget me forever? How long will you hide your face from me?"** (Psalm 13:1).

You might not get the answers you're looking for now, but when angels come flying in to take you home to heaven, it will all make sense. Until then, remind yourself of this: **"But I trust in [God's] unfailing love; my heart rejoices in your salvation. I will sing the Lord's praise, for he has been good to me"** (Psalm 13:5,6).

Embracing the quiet
Andrea Delwiche

Take a moment to slowly read these verses: **"As the deer pants for streams of water, so my soul pants for you, my God. My soul thirsts for God, for the living God. When can I go and meet with God?"** (Psalm 42:1,2).

Do you see the deer? Do you see yourself? Can you picture your Lord with his arms open, asking you to sit with him and breathe in his peace so that you are refreshed by his perspective?

We live in a raucous world. Noise can become a security blanket of sorts to protect, distract, and entertain us—day and night. Silence becomes uncomfortable. But immersed in sound, we won't hear what the noise drowns out—the call to enter into the quiet to be refreshed by God.

In another section of Scripture, we hear God's tremendous invitation: **"Come, all you who are thirsty, come to the waters; and you who have no money, come, buy and eat! Come, buy wine and milk without money and without cost. Why spend money on what is not bread, and your labor on what does not satisfy? Listen, listen to me, and eat what is good, and you will delight in the richest of fare. Give ear and come to me; listen, that you may live"** (Isaiah 55:1-3).

Father, thank you for the invitation to rest. By your Spirit, help us see where noise needs to be supplanted by quiet. Give us grace to change our ways. Amen.

Therefore, we have hope
Ann Jahns

If you've ever read the book of Lamentations in the Old Testament, let's just say its name says it all. It overflows with sorrow and despair. God's people, the Israelites who had been living in Jerusalem, were exiled in Babylon. Time and time again they had rejected and turned their backs on God, resulting in the destruction of their beloved Jerusalem by the Babylonians. Now they were living as strangers in a strange land, taken there against their will. They didn't fit in there. They didn't belong.

But in the middle of the darkness and desperation, there it is in Lamentations chapter 3, almost leaping off the page: **"Therefore I have hope: because of the LORD's great love we are not consumed, for his compassions never fail. They are new every morning; great is your faithfulness"** (verses 21-23).

Do you ever feel like God's Old Testament people, exiled in a land where everything is foreign to you? Do you ever feel like you don't quite belong in this world? That's because your heart longs to be reunited with your Creator. You and I long to be in our true home: heaven. The author and theologian C. S. Lewis said, "If we find ourselves with a desire that nothing in this world can satisfy, the most probable explanation is that we were made for another world." We are longing for more. We were made for more.

Therefore, we have hope. Jesus died to give us that hope. Because of him, soon we will be home.

Battle your thoughts
Pastor Matt Ewart

It's true that there can be many things in this world that influence you, but the biggest influence comes from inside of you. It's the influence of your thoughts.

The person who talks to you the most is yourself. Your thoughts are always there, providing self-praise or self-criticism in response to the things you do. The way you think determines the way your life goes. But your thoughts are anything but trustworthy.

It's easy when the enemy is outside of you. You can flee from the devil. You can separate from the world. But you can't flee from your thoughts or separate yourself from them.

What you have to do is take them captive. Here's what the apostle Paul said: **"We take captive every thought to make it obedient to Christ"** (2 Corinthians 10:5).

Thoughts must be redirected and retrained so that they conform to the truth that Jesus Christ has declared to you. When your thoughts convict you and lead you to guilt, make them obedient to Christ, who declared that you are forgiven. When your thoughts lead you to doubt your purpose, subject them to Christ, whose Spirit bears fruit in you for specific purposes. When your thoughts deceive you to look inwardly for your hope, redirect them to the cross, where you were given a hope that's greater than this life.

Sometime soon you might have to do battle with your own thoughts. Make them obedient to Jesus, who is full of grace and truth.

Spurs and barrel racing
Pastor Daron Lindemann

One of the most popular competitions in the Austin rodeo is barrel racing, where the fastest time wins.

The rider and horse bust out into a full gallop, kicking up dirt and gaining speed. Then they maneuver through three barrels in a cloverleaf pattern.

Spurs in this event aren't meant for hanging on but for getting going. "Yeeehaaaw! Giddyup!"

That's the Christian community of the church, described by the Bible in this way: **"And let us consider how we may spur one another on toward love and good deeds"** (Hebrews 10:24).

This means you might get kicked in the ribs by other church members because you're sitting around instead of volunteering. Because you're sleeping in at home on Sunday instead of singing God's praises in church. Because you're separating yourself instead of staying on course.

The words "spur one another on" here in Greek literally mean "agitate" or "provoke to discomfort." Yes, church can be a pain. A good pain that helps win the race.

So spur each other on! Don't let each other slack!

"Ouch! Leave me alone! Ouch! Get away! Ouch!" Spur. Love. Good deeds.

Like barrel racing. You maneuver through obstacles you thought you'd never be able to face. Your church achieves a mission goal nobody imagined would ever be possible. A strained relationship with a fellow church member—after hard work and prayer—is reconciled.

God is at work. Through spurs.

Light becomes hope
Jason Nelson

When darkness was so thick you could wear it, God had an idea. **"Let there be light"** (Genesis 1:3). In a flash, he knew he could get photons excited enough to glow. He made them glow in the direction of his magnetism. He dialed in different intensities so he could create day and night, dusk and dawn. He sourced light in suns, moons, stars, and on his own face. He figured out that light across a spectrum would make for a very colorful existence. He put all the physics in place in the blink of an eye. There it was. Light. And he wanted others to enjoy the beauty of light as much as he did. He willed for people to see the light and reflect the light. To be the image of light.

Darkness didn't surrender. It never does. It's powerful too. It always threatens to snuff out any little bit of light. But God is light. He will not let evil take us back to only darkness. God is there in every ray of hope for a happy ending. His face lit up with pleasure in his one and only Son who is the Light of the world. Christ's love for us brightens our mood.

When you feel darkness creeping in, may the light of the Lord bless you and keep you. May his face shine on you and show you his grace. May he look you right in the eye and give you peace. Amen.

Four phrases to help you witness
Pastor Daron Lindemann

These four phrases are all in Psalm 66. Here we go . . .
Isn't God awesome?

The more you recognize God's work in your life and give him credit for it, the better you will witness. **"Say to God, 'How awesome are your deeds!'"** (verse 3). When people give you a compliment, give credit to God.

Can I share something?

Ask a person that question before you witness. It anticipates something important. Then follow up with, **"Come and see what God has done, his awesome deeds for mankind"** (verse 5). Questions invite interest.

God will work it out.

One of the strongest moments to witness is when you are in trouble. **"For you, God, tested us; you refined us like silver. You brought us into prison and laid burdens on our backs. You let people ride over our heads; we went through fire and water, but you brought us to a place of abundance"** (verses 10-12). How you handle suffering will say a lot to those unsure about God and his goodness.

That's an answer to prayer!

Stay tuned in to God by remembering what you have asked in prayer. Is he opening a new door? closing one? Are you crossing paths with new people? Acknowledge God's hand. **"Let me tell you what he has done for me. . . . God has surely listened and has heard my prayer"** (verses 16,19).

These four phrases will help your witnessing. Which will you use today?

Fathers matter!
Linda Buxa

Father's Day is a little less sentimental than Mother's Day, and people seem more prone to laugh at Dad's foibles than praise him for his presence. In 2014, Paul Raeburn wanted to show just how vital dads are, so he published *Do Fathers Matter? What Science Is Telling Us About the Parent We've Overlooked.*

He shared that fathers have more influence on children's language development than mothers do, which leads to better performance in school. He showed that the father's genes inside a developing baby pass along crucial signals that allow a baby to raise the mother's blood pressure to get more nutrients and allow the baby to thrive. Raeburn also pointed out that when fathers are absent, daughters enter puberty up to a year earlier and are more likely to engage in risky sexual behavior. Just by being present, fathers increase the odds of protecting their daughters.

For as much as earthly fathers matter, there is a Father who matters even more. You can read about him in the Bible. There you'll read about the Father who sacrificed his Son so you can be his child too. He's the one who, thanks to his great love, motivates you to live a life of integrity. He's the Father who provides for you so you thrive. He's the Father who promises that you matter to him too: **"As a father has compassion on his children, so the Lord has compassion on those who fear him"** (Psalm 103:13).

The first Christians loved life
Pastor Mike Novotny

The Romans, as you may have heard, did not love children. Not only did they often abort them; they also "exposed" them, meaning that during the first days after birth, people took their little ones and left them outside to die. If the children were sick or disabled or the "wrong" gender (women were tragically under-valued), their parents frequently exposed them to the elements and to the animals, a historical fact that is grim to envision for even a second.

But guess who showed up to change that tragedy? Christians. Christians picked up the babies, adopted them, and raised them as their own. In fact, this was so common that churches quickly became the places where the pagans abandoned their infants. "Leave those little lives with the church," the pagan people started to say. "The Christians will love them. The Christians will care for them."

Today, we can do the same. While much has changed in the past two millennia, the opportunity to impress our world by our sacrificial love has stayed the same. Consider the needs around you, especially the needs surrounding unplanned pregnancies, as you ponder Paul's epic words: **"For Christ's love compels us, because we are convinced that one died for all, and therefore all died. And he died for all, that those who live should no longer live for themselves but for him who died for them and was raised again"** (2 Corinthians 5:14,15).

God is near
Ann Jahns

Have you ever felt defeated, deflated, and bone weary?

King David of Israel felt this same soul-crushing weariness. Despite God's promise that the Savior would be one of his descendants and despite the fact that he was called "a man after God's own heart," David struggled with his faith and his faithfulness to God. He had a man murdered rather than admit that he slept with that man's wife. His own son Absalom coveted his throne with a zeal born of hatred. Another precious son died as a consequence of David's sin. Deceit. Betrayal. Sorrow.

In Psalm 22:1,2, David groans, **"My God, why have you forsaken me? Why are you so far from saving me, so far from my cries of anguish? My God, I cry out by day, but you do not answer, by night, but I find no rest."**

How often do we feel like David? When we spin in a slow circle and all we see are the steep walls of the valley we are in? When God seems so far away?

But God is near. The same David who at times felt light-years away from God later exults in the same psalm, **"He has not despised or scorned the suffering of the afflicted one; he has not hidden his face from him but has listened to his cry for help"** (verse 24).

Take heart, weary one. God hears your cries and sees your tears. He has not left you. He is there in every valley, in every circumstance, holding you close.

Regrets
Pastor Matt Ewart

A regret is when something from your past weighs you down in the present. How many regrets are you carrying with you today?

The impact they have is never good. Regrets can fill you with negative self-talk. They can take away your appetite. They can rob you of confidence. If left unaddressed, they can have a profound impact on your future.

But they don't have to.

Jesus has taken away the power that your regrets had over you. I love how Paul put it in Titus 3:7: **"So that, having been justified by his grace, we might become heirs having the hope of eternal life."**

By grace your past has been settled. Whether the regret you have is from an intentional sin or an honest mistake, it no longer has any legal power over you. You have been justified by grace. That means that even though your mind is telling you that you are guilty for something in your past, God's gift is that he has declared you to be innocent.

And that has a profound impact on your future. You have ahead of you an inheritance that is so big it can only be quantified with the words *eternal life*.

In this life it is unavoidable to get your fair share of regrets. But what is avoidable is how much they weigh you down. Today when you are tempted to let something from your past weigh you down, let Jesus carry that weight for you.

Finding a place
Andrea Delwiche

"As the deer pants for streams of water, so my soul pants for you, my God. My soul thirsts for God, for the living God. When can I go and meet with God?" (Psalm 42:1,2).

Have you asked the psalmist's question lately? Perhaps your daily routine is disturbed, and your habitual time with God no longer happens; life feels haphazard without an extended time of God's loving guidance and presence. Maybe you've *thought* about deepening your practice of quiet time and have been searching for a way to make it happen. In all these things, you can ask, "Where (or when) can I go and meet with God?"

Susanna Wesley, the mother of hymn writers Charles and John Wesley, was a busy woman. Her husband, a minister, was in and out of debtor's prison. She schooled her ten children at home and had a vibrant Christian ministry to the people of her community. If anyone could ask, "When can I go and meet with God?" it was Susanna. But Susanna's time of solitude and renewal with the Lord traveled *with* her. Her family knew that when she threw her work apron up over her face, she was in prayer; they respected her sanctuary.

An *apron* may not be the answer to your time-with-God dilemma, but there is an answer for each of us. Maybe it's a room set aside. Maybe it's your morning bus ride. Maybe it's the kitchen table before everyone's awake. The Lord longs to spend time with you—each day. He is comfortable anywhere.

How to be a man
Pastor Daron Lindemann

I have this black leather vest that I wear when I ride my motorcycle. It's weathered with rain, sweat, sunscreen, and the remains of a few dozen bugs.

When I wear it, I feel like a tough guy. And they call me Revvv. Get it?

But much better than that, I feel like a real man because a patch on that vest reads, "Real Men Love Jesus."

Men, you'll be the best dads, father figures, husbands, male spiritual leaders, business owners, or alpha males in the room when you act not like you're the king of the hill but as you actually are. A child of the King.

Jesus says, **"Truly I tell you, anyone who will not receive the kingdom of God like a little child will never enter it"** (Mark 10:15).

Don't let maturity cause you to lose the innocent trust of a child who believes God, even if it's not logical and analytically resolved.

Put down your tough-as-leather self-reliance, and let Jesus' death be your life. Let Jesus' foolish-sounding, impossible promises be your money-in-the-bank reality. Let Jesus' high expectations be your purpose. Let Jesus' weakness be your strength. Let Jesus' words be your truth. Let Jesus' cross that made him nothing be your everything.

That's how to be a man. Be a child. Trust everything Jesus says. Follow Jesus everywhere he leads you. Sing "Jesus Loves Me," and really believe it.

The last runner
Ann Jahns

My son ran on his high school cross country team. At his first meet, we saw the most remarkable thing at the finish line. Of course, the first runners finished to an explosion of cheers. But if you stuck around until the bitter end, the very last runner also received applause and shouts of encouragement from the spectators who remained. It was a beautiful thing.

Jesus once told a story to his followers to explain something about the kingdom of heaven. In the story, a vineyard owner hires a group of workers at daybreak. They toil for hours in the blazing sun. As the story progresses, the owner hires a final group of workers at 5:00 P.M. who end up working only one hour.

When it comes time to pay the workers, they all receive the same amount—no matter how long they have worked. Those hired first complain bitterly to the landowner. He responds, **"I want to give the one who was hired last the same as I gave you. Don't I have the right to do what I want with my own money? Or are you envious because I am generous?"** (Matthew 20:14,15).

Unfair, right? But Jesus was making a point about something far greater. There will be as much rejoicing in heaven over the one who confesses Jesus on their deathbed as there is for the lifelong believer.

Do you know someone who needs to hear about Jesus while there's still time? Cheer for that last runner. Share God's love with that person while they still draw breath.

25 weeks 'til Christmas!

Linda Buxa

It's time to start planning for Christmas. Not for decorations and presents, but about which friend, coworker, neighbor, or family member you and I are going to invite to church.

You see, Christmas is one of two times (Easter is the other) when some people are open to the idea of walking into a church. So start strategizing! However, as you think about which person (which people) you'll invite, make sure that your actions and attitude make it easier for an invitation to be well-received.

If you don't talk to your neighbors for ten months and then hand them an invitation, they might question your sincerity. If you're crabby at work, a sudden, "Hey! Want to come to church with me?" might make it seem like Jesus hasn't made a difference in your life. If you're quick to judge, they may think God doesn't want them in his house either.

However, when you're full of compassion, kindness, and can speak the truth in love, you offer a respite from the world. When you share that even when you are weak, you are strong, you are testifying to the power of Jesus in your life. When you open your home, make meals, and genuinely celebrate or mourn with them, you **"make the teaching about God our Savior attractive"** (Titus 2:10).

Time to start planning.

Legacy
Jason Nelson

I've done lots of different things in my life. My resume tops out as a writer for Time of Grace. It's been an extraordinary privilege to be part of this ministry. If I have a legacy, it's in bits and pieces in a few hundred Grace Moments devotions. Each was a sincere attempt to put my faith, my education, my experiences, and my philosophy of life to work in a way that might be meaningful to you.

It could take a while before I know if it was worth it. For all of us who follow Jesus, the final assessment of our work won't occur in this life. We'll hear it when God reads out the celestial biography he is writing about each of us. **"Then I heard a voice from heaven say, 'Write this: Blessed are the dead who die in the Lord from now on.' 'Yes,' says the Spirit, 'they will rest from their labor, for their deeds will follow them'"** (Revelation 14:13). Somehow, someway, God will give us eternal glory and allow us to drag our earthly accomplishments with us. His grace makes our less-than-perfect efforts worth remembering forever.

I was startled when someone I didn't know asked me if I was that guy who writes devotions. In heaven we'll recognize each other immediately because of our glowing reputations. See you then. In the meantime, I hope I made you think, and I hope I made you smile.

July

The Lord replied, "My Presence will go with you,
and I will give you rest."

Exodus 33:14

The (second) longest sentence in the Bible

Pastor Mike Novotny

The second-longest sentence in the Bible is one of my favorites. The longest sentence, technically, is the genealogy of Jesus from Luke chapter 3, a run-on sentence of "the son of . . . the son of . . . the son of . . ." that spans 16 verses and includes dozens of names you probably can't pronounce. The second-longest sentence, at least in the original Greek of the New Testament, is Paul's epic praise party in Ephesians 1:3-14.

The English version of the Bible that I use breaks up this sentence into eight separate sentences to avoid the red pens of English teachers everywhere, the ones who cringe when authors add too many commas and subordinate clauses. But the apostle Paul wasn't ashamed to go on and on about all the good things he had to say about God.

Since these devotions, unfortunately, have a word limit, I literally can't fit Paul's words into the rest of this message. However, I can give you a glimpse of how it starts: **"Praise be to the God and Father of our Lord Jesus Christ, who has blessed us in the heavenly realms with every spiritual blessing in Christ"** (Ephesians 1:3).

If you want to learn more about "every spiritual blessing"—how you are chosen, holy, blameless, predestined, adopted, graced, redeemed, forgiven, included, saved, marked, filled, and more—find a Bible. See what inspired the man who saw the risen Jesus to ignore the conventions of grammar and run on in praise of his God.

Jesus prayed for you
Ann Jahns

Sometimes I'm envious of Jesus' disciples. For three years, they got to talk with him, eat with him, laugh with him, weep with him. They saw him heal the sick and raise the dead. They witnessed his transforming mercy on people who were drowning in sin and despair. His disciples even got to walk and talk and eat with him after he conquered sin and death and burst out of the tomb, victorious. Can you even imagine how their short time with him changed their lives?

The night before Jesus went to the cross, he shared a final precious Passover meal with his best friends, those beloved disciples. You can almost feel the weight of sorrow in his words as he poured out his final instructions, cautions, and comfort on them. Their time with their teacher was almost at an end. He then prayed to God, his Father, for them: **"Holy Father, protect them by the power of your name"** (John 17:11).

It's almost unbelievable who Jesus prayed for next: **"My prayer is not for** [my disciples] **alone,"** he continued. **"I pray also for those who will believe in me through their message, that all of them may be one, Father, just as you are in me and I am in you"** (verses 20,21).

Even with the cross looming, Jesus prayed for you. Specifically. Personally. You are the believer whose life has been impacted by the disciples' message and witness. In his final hours, Jesus had you on his mind, dear believer. That's true love.

Depression is real
Pastor Clark Schultz

Today I'm depressed.

Did you read that first statement and immediately look up to see who wrote this devotion? If you know me, you might say, "Depressed? Come on. I see his photos on Facebook and his YouTube videos. There's no way he can be depressed."

Depression is real. It's estimated that 16.2 million adults in the United States, or 6.7% of American adults, have had at least one major depressive episode in a given year. Would it shock you to hear these statistics are from a pre-COVID world?

Where or what can we do to cope? (Insert run to Jesus line here, and say, "Amen.") Friends, that's just it. I know I'm loved. I know I'm forgiven. It still doesn't take away the depression instantly. I do not have a magic pill to give you, but what I do have is empathy for you and advice. Diet, exercise, and talking openly to you and to others has helped my depression. Will it ever go away this side of heaven? Probably not, but you do not have to go it alone.

Like Peter taking that first step out of the boat to meet Jesus on the water, it defies logic, but it literally was a leap of faith. Pick up the phone, seek counsel— yes from God but also from a professional. It doesn't make you weak, as Paul reminds us: **"But he said to me, 'My grace is sufficient for you, for my power is made perfect in weakness'"** (2 Corinthians 12:9).

A better country
Sarah Habben

As many as 400,000 Central American migrants try to enter the U.S. every year. By the time they reach the Mexico-U.S. border, they've made a perilous journey, enduring a constant threat of assault, rape, robbery, or kidnapping by criminal gangs and corrupt police.

Why risk that journey? They're running from hopelessness, from violence. They're longing for a better life. A future. A home.

Those of us with no reason to run sometimes forget that we're nomads too. The Bible describes believers as **"strangers on earth . . . longing for a better country—a heavenly one. Therefore God is not ashamed to be called their God, for he has prepared a city for them"** (Hebrews 11:13,16).

Maybe we're too comfortable. Every morning we should long for *heaven*, not just our first cup of coffee. We should willingly endure our hardships—after all, we know our suffering will one day be swallowed up by joy. We should help our fellow travelers; instead, we check our watches and wallets and decide we don't have help to spare. We shouldn't fear to cross death's border . . . but our hearts still cling to earth's brief pleasures.

God is ashamed of us. And yet, he loved us by sending his Son. Jesus left his throne to join our pilgrimage. A stranger to sin, he carried ours. Wrapped in shame and pain, he crossed death's border. He won for us a heavenly country. He teaches us to serve our fellow travelers. He equips us to one day bid a cheerful farewell to this world because a better home awaits.

Anointed with oil
Pastor Jon Enter

In the Old Testament, Israelite kings were anointed with oil, marking them as new leaders of the people. In Psalm 23:5, King David wrote, **"You anoint my head with oil."** That actually happened. David was anointed king of God's people. Remember, though, this psalm is packed full of pictures of shepherd and sheep. There's another meaning here connected to shepherding and to you.

In the arid landscape of the Middle East, grass doesn't grow in abundance. The tufts of grass are quickly snatched up by sheep. Some of the choicest grass is found beneath thorns and thistles. It grows long as it's untouched by other grazing animals, and the thick cover of the thorny bush keeps the refreshing dew on the grass longer into the day. Sheep cannot resist the temptation. When the thorns and thistles rip into the sheep's heads, flies feast on the open wounds. It's painful. It brings infection. The shepherd—after seeing the wounds from the sheep's waywardness—applies oil to the animals' heads generously. Oil protects sheep from the attack of flies and soothes pain.

Jesus anoints you with oil. Jesus sees the wounds you carry from being drawn into the devil's temptations. He knows you're in pain because you're infected by the consequences of wrongdoing. So he comes to you. He calms you. He anoints you with his loving mercy and soothes your pain. You are forgiven. In that forgiveness, he keeps away the devil from pestering you and paining you. Oh, how he loves you!

The eternal answer to troubles
Pastor David Scharf

What's troubling your heart today? Is it a particular thing that you did wrong long ago, but it's not long forgotten? Is it a temptation that's currently nagging at you, tripping you up time after time? Is it a health, job, or financial situation? Listen to the words of your Savior:

"Do not let your hearts be troubled. . . . My Father's house has many rooms; if that were not so, would I have told you that I am going there to prepare a place for you? And if I go and prepare a place for you, I will come back and take you to be with me that you also may be where I am" (John 14:1-3).

Jesus says, "Do not let your heart be troubled." Why not? Because there is a place for you in heaven! You may protest, "But that's just pie-in-the-sky thinking. I have to live in the here and now!" True. But who's with you right now? The same Jesus who told his disciples not to let their hearts be troubled is the same Jesus who is with you. He is the One who died for you, rose for you, and even now is preparing a home for you in heaven.

No, that doesn't mean this life will be easy, pleasant, or even successful outwardly. It does mean you know where you're going. It means you know where your life will end up, at Jesus' side in heaven. No more troubles, forever!

You are the problem—and the solution
Linda Buxa

A friend asked on Facebook, "Quick question for everyone: why do you think things are so messed up right now?"

I skimmed through every one of the 158 comments, and they ranged from politics to social media, from division to pandemics, from fear to history. You know what I noticed? No one said, "*I am.*"

My concern is that when we think everybody else is the problem, then it's easy to believe everybody else is responsible for the solution. When "they" change, act better, are more loving, and make better decisions, then the world will get better.

I think we'd be better off if we did three things.

First, recognize we're part of the problem—we're all sinful, short with others, quick to be harsh. Second, thank God that Jesus came to solve our biggest problem—our sins separate us from God. Jesus' payment brought us back to God.

Third, recognize that God has put us in this exact time and place in the world to spread his love. **"You are the light of the world. A town built on a hill cannot be hidden. Neither do people light a lamp and put it under a bowl. Instead they put it on its stand, and it gives light to everyone in the house. In the same way, let your light shine before others, that they may see your good deeds and glorify your Father in heaven"** (Matthew 5:14-16).

Abusers at church?

Pastor Mike Novotny

There's a man in prison who watches *Time of Grace* and writes me grateful, encouraging, and faith-filled letters. One day, however, I came across his legal history online, and the words *assault of a minor, repeated,* and *felony* grabbed my attention and broke my heart. I thought about this man's potential release and the possibility he would show up on Sunday to worship next to my family. As I considered the glory of his forgiveness and the reality that his sin could happen again, I agonized over the question, What would Jesus do?

If a man with an abusive history was in the crowd in the first century, what would Jesus do? And what should we do today? Should we lock the church doors when certain types of sinners get out of their cars? warn the parents? "forgive and forget"? Saying, "Everyone is welcome" is easy, but when everyone includes *everyone*, what then?

In the days to come, I want to wrestle with that question by speaking directly to people who have committed the sin of abuse. This description of Jesus will guide my words: "[The Son] **came from the Father, full of grace and truth**" (John 1:14). To do what Jesus did means to be full of grace and truth. It means being Christians who care about "the least of these" without watering down undeserved love and while also holding to the highest standards of truth and healthy boundaries.

Keep reading to find the four things I would say to our friend in prison and anyone who comes to church with abuse in their past.

Look at you
Pastor Mike Novotny

Depending on how you grew up, how your dad treated your mom, how your mom spoke to your dad, or how the adults in your life treated you, you might not know what abuse looks like.

Here are some glimpses of what abuse is: Do you have a pattern of getting angry when your partner or children don't do what you want? Do you express anger by name-calling, threatening looks, physical threats, or physical acts like breaking things or hurting pets? Do you blame those outbursts on alcohol, drugs, or someone else? Do you ever use the Bible to get what you want, telling him he has to forgive you no matter how much you belittle him and she has to submit because you are the head of the household? If that happens often, that's abuse. (And if you don't want others to read these words, it's likely you are abusive.)

I need you to know how much God hates abuse. **"Those who love violence,** [the Lord] **hates with a passion"** (Psalm 11:5). The biggest issue with your behavior isn't that it might get you in legal trouble or cost you control at home. The biggest issue is that it makes God hate you. No one who continues living in this sin, hurting people God loves, will end up loved by God. So before you have to stand before our Father holding a history of hurting his children, look at yourself.

And before the guilt of your sin overwhelms you, please run to Jesus. There is hope in his name for every sinner, even for you.

Look at him
Pastor Mike Novotny

If you've ever used fear or force to maintain control in a relationship, I want you to look at Jesus. Psalm 11 says that the Lord hates those who love violence, a blunt fact that I hope leads you to repent and cry out to God for forgiveness.

Because there's hope even for abusive people. The apostle Paul is the proof. **"Even though I was once a blasphemer and a persecutor and a violent man, I was shown mercy because I acted in ignorance and unbelief. The grace of our Lord was poured out on me abundantly, along with the faith and love that are in Christ Jesus"** (1 Timothy 1:13,14). Paul was, by his own admission, a violent man, yet when God opened his eyes to the depth of his sin, Paul found mercy, grace, and love through Jesus.

God wants to open your eyes to see his mercy, grace, and love. Jesus forgave your sins of abuse. After being slapped and spit on, mocked and nailed to a cross, Jesus cried out, **"Father, forgive them"** (Luke 23:34). He still says that, and every sinner who is truly sorry receives that. Abuse is ugly, but Jesus took that ugliness to the cross. When you look at Jesus, when you change your mind about who is in control, God stops hating you and starts calling you his own dear child. So look at Jesus. With me, with us, look at Jesus. There will still be consequences, but when you look at Jesus, there is no condemnation (Romans 8:1).

Look at them
Pastor Mike Novotny

Abuse often has generational roots. As the saying goes, "Hurt people hurt people." If you were raised by a father who physically threatened you or a mother who degraded you daily with her words, you might have ended up in a fog about how relationships are supposed to work. The abused can easily turn into abusers.

This is why it's essential for us to look around at the people God has placed in our path who are able to help us heal. Jesus' half brother James wrote, **"Therefore confess your sins to each other and pray for each other so that you may be healed. The prayer of a righteous person is powerful and effective"** (James 5:16). There's healing power in the people of God. When you confess your sins to others and they, in turn, pray for you, you can heal wounds and change behaviors far faster than if you were on your own.

Today, I'm asking you to look at them. At your pastor, if you have one. At Christian counselors in your area who specialize in abuse. At friends who know you, love Jesus, and have healthy relationships. Yes, it will be humbling to confess your sins and your story to them. Yes, there might be consequences to the truth coming out. But it's the best step in the world to take.

If you come from a long line of hurting people, the cycle can stop. Your family tree can change. Please look at them. It's how God will help and heal us.

Look at me

Pastor Mike Novotny

If I knew that one hundred abusive people showed up at our church on a Sunday, I would say, "I'm happy you're here. This is a Christian church where sinners are welcome. In Jesus' day, the worst people in town were tax collectors and prostitutes, but Jesus called them to follow him. We want to be like Jesus, so you are welcome to follow Jesus here too."

And then, with all the compassion in my heart, I would continue: "And we welcome you with wisdom. We don't tempt alcoholics by having them buy the wine for Lord's Supper. And we don't let abusive people alone in situations where abuse can happen. So, yes, we require background checks for our children's ministry. Yes, we will communicate with parole officers and craft a personal plan that meets and, perhaps, exceeds the requirements of the law. Because we care about you and about everyone else."

I'm not sure how that message would be received, but I know what the Bible says about those who are truly repentant: **"See what this godly sorrow has produced in you: what earnestness, what eagerness to clear yourselves, what indignation, what alarm, what longing, what concern, what readiness to see justice done"** (2 Corinthians 7:11). People who are truly sorry will take steps to prove it, submitting to the leadership of the church.

If you have a history of abusive behavior and want to change, go to church. Even if there are consequences for your past, a Christian church can help you walk with Jesus for your eternal future.

God exalts the humble
Pastor Mike Novotny

Around 2014, I met a man who had committed a felony against a minor. When the man was released from jail, he wondered if he would be welcome as a part of our church family. Our church leaders discussed it for a long time, working with his parole officer and pouring over the issue in prayer, thinking of this precious soul craving a Christian community and thinking of our own children at the church we loved. Eventually, we said we'd love to have him here, but there would be boundaries, restrictions, other people who would need to know.

This guy—to his immense credit—said, "The more people who know, the better. I will stand in front of church and tell everyone if that's what you want. It will only make me more accountable." So that's what we did. And I am ecstatic to tell you that years later, this brother in Christ is still an active member of our church family, hearing about God's unending grace Sunday after Sunday in our midst.

Jesus once promised, **"Those who humble themselves will be exalted"** (Luke 18:14). You might have a complicated story or sins serious enough to come with legal consequences. But by the blood of Christ, that doesn't have to stop you from being a child of God, equal in status to every other Christian. Cry out in humility to Jesus, and you will be exalted.

No quick fix
Jan Gompper

I come from a family of solvers. Whenever we face a problem, we dig in to try to fix it quickly.

Sometimes we approach people that way too. We see something wrong in the way they're living, and we want to "fix" them. The reality is people can only be fixed if they *recognize* they need fixing and *want* to be fixed.

None of us wants a doctor who prescribes a remedy before listening to our ailments. Perhaps that's why Jesus is known as the Great Physician. Yes, he healed people, but, more important, he took time with them. He listened to the physical and spiritual pains they shared and helped them *discover* that they needed a cure. The placard on his office door did not read, "For a quick fix, come on in!" It read, **"Come to me, all you who are weary and burdened, and I will give you rest"** (Matthew 11:28).

This kind of problem-solving takes time. There are no quick fixes for broken or obstinate people who may not realize they need help and often don't want it. It can be uncomfortable for us to listen to their ailments, but offering them a "place of rest" to unburden their minds and hearts without the fear of us trying to fix them might put them on a path toward lasting spiritual wellness.

We are merely Christ's interns. Often, the most powerful prescription we can provide is a ready ear to listen and a follow-up prayer to our Great Physician to do the healing.

Time pressure
Pastor David Scharf

You and I are busy. Time is precious. Do you ever say, "But I don't have time!"? These are some of the things we might spend time on today: 2 minutes to read this devotion, 15 minutes for breakfast, 30 minutes for the news (21 if you DVR it first), 8-10 hours for work, 2 hours for family, etc. But how much time will we spend with our Creator, Savior, and Sustainer, the One who brings meaning to everything we do today?

The apostle Paul encourages us, **"Be very careful, then, how you live—not as unwise but as wise, making the most of every opportunity"** (Ephesians 5:15,16).

Let's be wise. Let's recognize that when we say, "I don't have time," what we're really saying is, "I don't have time for *that*." We all have 24 hours in each day. The real question is, What do you want to use your time for? This is a priority question. Ask, What is really important to me? As you look at your life, you might realize why you feel so busy. Take time to rest in God's Word and in prayer to find real rest in him. There you will find his promises, his forgiveness, his peace, his providence, and his protection. When you focus on what's most important, you will find you're not so busy after all. And you'll be able to make the most of every opportunity to serve your Savior!

Where's the Shepherd?
Pastor Jon Enter

In Psalm 23:1 God proclaims his protection in full measure! **"The Lord is my shepherd, I lack nothing."** But what about when you're stuck in peril, in pain, with no rescue in sight? Where's the Shepherd?

An American journalist traveled overseas to observe a shepherd in Palestine. The writer watched in amazement as the shepherd provided for all the needs of his beloved sheep. Suddenly, one sheep wandered off. The shepherd searched hurriedly, only to discover it had fallen off a cliff and landed on a small section of rock about 6 feet down. The outcropping was narrow, with the valley floor 40 feet below.

The shepherd backed up calmly from the cliff and sat down to eat his lunch while the sheep bellowed below.

Eventually the journalist asked through an interpreter what the shepherd was doing. "That sheep is so scared," he replied. "If I go rescue it now, it will slip off the edge to its death. I'm protecting it from predators who also hear its cries. When the sheep is exhausted, I will rescue it."

The Lord is your Shepherd. You might be wondering where his rescue is. You have not been forgotten. Jesus is protecting you from the attack of Satan, who is prowling around you. When the timing is right, the rescue will come. It comes on God's timetable, in God's way, but always for your good.

Better than 7,700,000,000 likes
Pastor Mike Novotny

It feels pretty good to be liked. Whether you're a social media user or not, you've probably felt the rush of having someone notice your outfit, approve of your work project, or be impressed by your efforts on the field. That desire for approval exists in every human heart.

But it can be dangerous. Jesus said, **"And when you pray, do not be like the hypocrites, for they love to pray standing in the synagogues and on the street corners to be seen by others"** (Matthew 6:5). Why do some people love to pray in church and in public? "To be seen by others." In other words, they might look like they really love to talk to God, but what they really love is being liked by people.

Don't do that. Instead, remember what's better than being liked by all 7.7 billion people on earth—God. **"But when you pray, go into your room, close the door and pray to your Father, who is unseen. Then your Father, who sees what is done in secret, will reward you"** (Matthew 6:6). Jesus promises that our Father sees our private prayers. No, we might not impress people at church or on the street, but we will be rewarded by the full attention of our Father in heaven.

Do the math: 1 God > 7,700,000,000 people. So pray privately, quietly, humbly, and trust that your heart will find everything it needs in God.

The best-laid plans
Ann Jahns

Thousands of years ago in Israel, a king was given a choice. God invited King Solomon: "Ask for whatever you want. Anything." And Solomon humbly responded, *"Wisdom."* God gave it to him. As if that weren't enough, God also showered him with wealth and honor. The world bowed at Solomon's feet. He amassed wealth and possessions and more wives than he could count.

But then this king, the one who had been given everything, let the treasures and the wives and the accolades go to his head. He stumbled and made plans that didn't include the God who had given him everything. He walked down a narrow road that didn't make room for his heavenly Father.

At some point in his life, a humbled Solomon admitted, **"In their hearts humans plan their course, but the Lord establishes their steps"** (Proverbs 16:9). What a wake-up call for him. And what a wake-up call for us.

Have you ever made plans that didn't turn out? Despite your preparation and plotting, things headed in a completely different direction? Did you have big plans for 2020, for example, then a global pandemic turned life on its head and control slipped through your fingers like grains of sand? You aren't alone.

It's good to plan—God wants us to use our time and our blessings wisely. But let's not hold on too tightly. God's plans might not be our plans. And that's good, because he loves us and knows better than we do. Father, may your will be done.

Better than Broadway

Pastor Mike Novotny

My musical-loving daughter wrote letters to some famous Broadway actors and actresses. One day, a reply letter showed up in our mailbox from New York City. Guess who wrote it? The guy who played Alexander Hamilton himself in the smash hit *Hamilton*! Lin-Manuel Miranda, a stunningly gifted actor and writer, wrote my baby girl a personal letter, answering her questions, cracking a few jokes, and giving her a smile wider than a Broadway stage. No wonder she immediately framed the letter and set it on her bedroom dresser!

As happy as that letter made her, Brooklyn didn't set that frame underneath her bedside lamp as the last thing she would see each night. Instead, that spot is occupied by a small wooden block that reads, **"Let the morning bring me word of your unfailing love"** (Psalm 143:8). Every morning, as she turns off her alarm, that passage reminds her that unfailing love is hers through Jesus. She might not know what the future will hold, but she does know, in Jesus, that she will be loved.

That's true for you too. Today might be a day when good news shows up in your mailbox (or inbox). Or it might be another bill or doctor's appointment. But whatever is going on in your physical and financial life, your spiritual life is going to be okay. Why? Because every morning the gospel brings the good news that God's love lasts forever.

Smile, Christian. You are loved. Now and forever.

Burden bearer
Sarah Habben

Are you an anxious Christian? Your anxiety is no surprise to God. The fact that the Bible addresses anxiety so often shows that God knew his beloved children would struggle with it.

Maybe you think if you believed hard enough, you could turn down anxiety's boil. But faith is sometimes big and sometimes small. It doesn't cure anxiety any more than it can mend a broken bone.

Instead of examining your faith, examine God's faithfulness. Picture a father backpacking with his little girl. She isn't built for the kind of effort it takes to carry a backpack and climb a hill. Her father knows this. So he takes her bag. What does his child learn? Her dad is compassionate. Her weakness doesn't disappoint him. He wants her to make it, to share the experience, to be in his company. The father's faithfulness gets the child up the hill.

Your Savior demonstrated his faithfulness at the cross. He did what you could not—he carried the burden and penalty of your sin. He did it so you could be with him forever. No hill of grief or guilt or worry is too steep for your faithful God. You might start each day at the bottom of anxiety's hill, but you aren't alone. You are with your heavenly Father. He daily bears your burdens so you can make it to tomorrow, to next year, to your heavenly home.

"Praise be to the Lord, to God our Savior, who daily bears our burdens" (Psalm 68:19).

Is your God dead?
Jan Gompper

Early church reformer Martin Luther sometimes fell into periods of depression that could last for days. During one of these periods, his wife, Katie, decided to dress in black mourning clothes. Luther finally noticed and asked, "Are you going to a funeral?" She replied, "No, but since you act as though God is dead, I wanted to join you in the mourning."

Is your God dead? Are you living like you are in mourning because of a pandemic or the political and racial tensions in our country? Worse yet, have you become cynical and angry because you believe America is going down the toilet—our political systems broken, our elections rigged, our country without hope?

Katie Luther taught her husband an important lesson that day. She taught him that hope and optimism are a choice, not a feeling. She was confident that no matter what happened in the world, her God was still in control.

We can have this same confidence, for **"the LORD Almighty has sworn, 'Surely, as I have planned, so it will be, and as I have purposed, so it will happen'"** (Isaiah 14:24). Furthermore, **"We know that in all things God works for the good of those who love him"** (Romans 8:28).

Katie Luther's God was not dead, and neither is ours. So turn off your political news channels and stop listening to social media fearmongers. Your God is very much alive and well and **"works out everything to its proper end"** (Proverbs 16:4).

You must be in the front row!
Linda Buxa

One night my daughters and I went to a concert. On our way in, we saw friends who had front-row seats. We stopped by to hug them—and then went to our seats on the third level.

Though we heard the exact same concert, we experienced it differently. They had a far more personal experience with the performers. We could barely see faces, but we loved the concert anyway.

Some friends and I joke that, kind of like the concert, we'll be sitting in the back row of heaven. The front seats are reserved for the good people, the more valuable people. We will still enjoy heaven, but probably not have the same experience.

While we may joke about it, deep down it's easy for us to worry this might be a reality. Maybe you don't have the right past or maybe you keep falling into the same sin over and over again so you don't feel like you really qualify.

In reality, because Jesus took the punishment you deserved, God isn't pushing you to the back row. **"He will take great delight in you; in his love he will no longer rebuke you, but will rejoice over you with singing"** (Zephaniah 3:17).

As he's rejoicing, he invites you to the front row, saying, **"Well done, good and faithful servant! . . . Come and share your master's happiness!"** (Matthew 25:23).

You will be in the front row!

You'll never walk alone
Pastor Clark Schultz

When the world of sports was on lockdown during the COVID pandemic, there wasn't much to do other than walk. Walk with my family, my wife, or just take a stroll to think. Destinations often included a park, an ice cream shop, around the block, and . . . did I mention another ice cream stop? :)

Two men walking a seven-mile, two-hour trip had a walk they would never forget. **"Jesus himself came up and walked along with them"** (Luke 24:15). The two were sad because they had hoped to confirm the reports that Jesus was alive. No dice. In this particular case, **"they were kept from recognizing him"** (verse 16). The duo was having a pity party.

Jesus did what we can do in times of trouble. He pointed these two back to Scripture. He connected the dots of all the prophecies that spelled out who and what the mission of the Savior was to be.

As you read this, maybe things are going your way. Or maybe they aren't so good right now. Friend, you're not walking alone. Jesus is with you. You may not recognize him, but he reminds us in his Word that he is ALWAYS with us. Preacher Charles Spurgeon was quoted as saying, "A Bible that's falling apart usually belongs to someone who isn't." Your walk will not always be trouble free, but the assurance of sins forgiven and a place in heaven is sweeter than any flavor of the day.

Don't forget to celebrate
Andrea Delwiche

"My heart bursts its banks, spilling beauty and goodness. I pour it out in a poem to the king, shaping the river into words. . . . (Her wedding dress is dazzling, lined with gold by the weavers. . . . She is led to the king. . . . A procession of joy and laughter! a grand entrance to the king's palace!)" (Psalm 45:1-3,13-15 MSG).

Psalm 45 recounts a celebration in poetic language: the good character of the bridegroom, the blessed life of the bride, and the joy of being in company with those who celebrate God's goodness.

How well do you celebrate? If someone spoke of you, would they say as it was said of Ebenezer Scrooge at the *end of his life*, "And it was always said of him, that he knew how to keep Christmas well, if any man alive possessed the knowledge."

Did you know celebration is written into Old Testament guidelines? Did you know Jesus himself was welcome at celebrations in part because he enjoyed times of hospitality and friendship with a variety of people?

Sometimes we forget that our God is a God of delight, hospitality, and goodness. He wants us to celebrate beauty and goodness as well.

Have you considered Jesus' life and other Bible stories and made note of the joy and celebration? What would happen if we who follow Christ did so through hospitality and daily celebration of all the beauty of this world? What if we saw others through the hospitable heart of Christ? How would we impact others with God's love?

A picture of God
Pastor David Scharf

A child draws diligently with crayons. His teacher asks, "What are you drawing?"

"I'm drawing a picture of God."

"Honey," the teacher corrects, "no one knows what God looks like."

The boy responds without looking up, "Of course not, my picture isn't done yet!"

We laugh at the boy's boldness to show the world God's face. Then we turn back to continue creating our own picture of what we think God is like. Sometimes we think he's like this: "I know what I'm doing is wrong, but God will understand because there are really good reasons why I do it." It's as if we think God sits in heaven with a huge rug that he uses to sweep our wrongdoings under. What does God actually look like? **"May the grace of the Lord Jesus Christ, and the love of God, and the fellowship of the Holy Spirit be with you all"** (2 Corinthians 13:14).

He is our Father, whose love caused him to create our world. He was brokenhearted when we rejected his love and insisted on living life on our own terms. He is the Son, whose mercy wouldn't allow him to see us get what we deserved. He cared more for giving us the joys of heaven than keeping his own life. He is the Holy Spirit, whose desire for fellowship with us caused him to work faith in our hearts. We now live in the warm glow of God's forgiveness. In this picture, a self-portrait by God, there is no rug. There's only a bloodstained cross, shining with his love.

Avoid the pitfalls of prayer
Pastor Mike Novotny

Have you ever driven up a mountain? On one side of your car is a cliff with a drop that would plummet your car to certain disaster. On the other side of your car, however, are all the other cars that are trying not to crash into the mountain and are sneaking over into your lane as they come around that blind turn. When my wife and I drove up the Smoky Mountains recently, we rarely relaxed. Instead, we stressed, gasped, yelled, and, at one point, switched drivers!

Prayer can feel like that. On one hand, we can worry about what other people are thinking about us while we pray. At a restaurant, we might hesitate to bow our heads as we wonder what the waiter or the folks in the next booth might think. On the other hand, we can crash into the feeling of unworthiness, wondering what right we have to pray to a holy God just hours (or minutes . . . or seconds) after our last sin.

So how do you avoid those pitfalls? You remember your Father. In Matthew 6:4-8, Jesus used the title **"Father"** four times in four verses. Prayer is leveraging the chance to talk to our Father, not impressing the folks at Applebee's. And if he is our forgiving Father, we never have to wonder or worry if we are worthy to pray. Through Jesus, the door has been opened and the invitation has been extended, so pray with confidence and joy today—our Father can't wait to hear from you!

The shadow of death
Pastor Jon Enter

Every funeral I've attended has included Psalm 23. This psalm pours on comfort with its opening words: **"The Lord is my Shepherd"** (verse 1). The Lord with all capital letters is a special name for God, revealing the abundance of his mercy. God then ties his unstoppable, unending grace to the picture of a shepherd constantly there for his sheep. The hearts of the hurting at funerals relax in the comfort of this grace.

But then verse 4 sucker punches everyone in the heart: **"Even though I walk through the valley of the shadow of death"** (ESV). Death. It becomes the focus. How could it not at a funeral? But death is NOT the focus of this sentence grammatically or spiritually. "Of death." The word *death* is in a prepositional phrase, so it's not the focus. God calls death nothing but a shadow! A shadow can't hurt you. A shadow has no substance. It can scare you if you let it, but it can't hurt you. Death is a shadow for you, for those who believe Jesus destroyed the power of death.

Make no mistake. The devil is a prowling lion who's looking for someone to devour; he's looking for you. Let him roar. Let him growl. His roar is empty. It's powerless. Why? Jesus' tomb was empty on Easter Sunday, giving power to these words: **"Then you, my people, will know that I am the Lord when I open your graves and bring you up from them"** (Ezekiel 37:13). Death cannot hold you!

There *is* such a thing as a free lunch
Ann Jahns

There's something about free stuff that we just love, right? It causes our hearts to speed up a little bit. It compels us to hit the brakes to examine the ramshackle item on the curb bearing the raggedy piece of cardboard with "Free" scrawled across it. We happily accept things that are free—even if we don't need them or even really want them.

So why are we sometimes so reluctant to accept the fact that the greatest, most amazing, most wonderful gift of all time is free—the gift of salvation through Jesus? Maybe because it seems way too good to be true. Maybe because its rewards are completely disproportionate to what it will cost us. Maybe because we can't do a single thing to earn it or pay for it. Ephesians 2:8,9 declares, **"For it is by grace you have been saved, through faith—and this is not from yourselves, it is the gift of God—not by works, so that no one can boast."**

You've probably heard that there's no such thing as a free lunch. Or is there? There is such a thing as free grace. And it's way better than that saggy, avocado green couch on the side of the road that calls your name as you drive by. God's marvelous and miraculous grace is totally and completely free for all believers because it has already been paid for. Jesus paid for it with his blood, shed on a cross on Calvary. Salvation is ours through faith—no strings attached.

Brighter days
Jan Gompper

When I was younger and going through a rough patch, my mother would always (and I mean *always*) tell me, "There are brighter days tomorrow." I would generally respond by rolling my eyes, as if to say, "Yeah right, Mom."

Perhaps you are rolling your eyes also. It's hard to believe that brighter days could lie ahead when you are struggling with something. Some of you may have lost jobs or, worse yet, loved ones. Some of you may be experiencing loneliness or depression. Some of you may be wondering if God has taken a vacation.

My mom's catchphrase wasn't based on wishful thinking or a "glass half full" outlook on her part. Truth be told, she experienced many dark days in her own life—poverty, the Great Depression, a challenging marriage to a husband who struggled with mental illness. No, her maxim had far deeper roots. It was rooted in her unwavering belief in her Savior's promise that **"neither death nor life, neither angels nor demons, neither the present nor the future, nor any powers, neither height nor depth, nor anything else in all creation, will be able to separate us from the love of God that is in Christ Jesus our Lord"** (Romans 8:38,39).

When I think about my mother's words, I no longer roll my eyes. Instead, I glance upward, knowing that she is now sharing "brighter days" with her Savior and that one day I will too.

I am not ashamed
Ann Jahns

Have you heard of Alfred Paul Seckel? An American raised in a Jewish household, Seckel wrote multiple books about optical illusions. He was also the founder of a group called the Southern California Skeptics.

You may never have heard of Mr. Seckel, but you are probably familiar with one of his creations. In 1983 he cocreated the Darwin fish symbol—a parody of the ancient Christian fish symbol, the *ichthus.* Seckel's version has "evolved" legs and feet that protrude from the fish, with the name Darwin replacing that of Jesus.

The Darwin fish has been cast into sticky plastic and slapped on countless vehicles. There's even a website devoted entirely to its purchase in various forms.

Seckel created the symbol in response to the proliferation of the Christian fish symbol. As a proponent of reason and free thought, he wanted to promote alternatives to belief in God, the Creator of the universe. Seckel was an avowed atheist.

Do you have a Jesus fish on your vehicle? Display it proudly. Take courage from the example of the apostle Paul, a former persecutor of Christians whose heart was changed by Jesus: **"I am not ashamed of the gospel, because it is the power of God that brings salvation to everyone who believes"** (Romans 1:16).

Maybe that little fish symbol will start a conversation about Christ. You might be ridiculed or mocked. That's okay. So was Jesus. He endured that—and even death—for you. He loves you that much.

Meditate on God's unfailing love
Andrea Delwiche

The Bible is chocked full of recommendations for the people of God to spend time contemplating our relationship with him. In Psalm 48:9,10, the psalmist meditates on God's unfailing love: **"Within your temple, O God, we meditate on your unfailing love. Like your name, O God, your praise reaches to the ends of the earth; your right hand is filled with righteousness."**

How can we do like the psalmist?

Different followers of Jesus have different habits when it comes to focusing on God's love and the work we have to do together and how God has revealed himself in Scripture. The apostle Paul encourages us in Colossians 3:2: **"Set your minds on things above, not on earthly things."**

If you or I meditate on God's unfailing love, we might sit with no television in the background, with phones silenced and away from us. We might take a walk, focusing on the many manifestations of God's love in the world around us. By the working of the Holy Spirit, we can dwell in the examples of God's unfailing love that dominate the pages of the Bible and in our personal lives as well. Like a well-loved family story, handed down through the generations, the actuality of God's love will become familiar to us and provide comfort, confidence, and motivation. Even as we go to sleep at night, meditating on God's love and goodness brings peace: **"On my bed I remember you; I think of you through the watches of the night"** (Psalm 63:6).

August

Let the morning bring me word of your unfailing love,
for I have put my trust in you. Show me the way
I should go, for to you I entrust my life.

Psalm 143:8

August 1

The bigger picture of abortion
Pastor Mike Novotny

During middle school, my church showed me a video of what happens during a late-term abortion. It was, as you can imagine, graphic enough to make an impression on my views on the subject. But since that seventh-grade day, I have learned a lot about the reasons why people choose that irreversible act.

Imagine a pregnancy when you barely know each other. When there are red flags with the father's anger. When birth will bind you together with a verbally abusive monster. When you're already depressed or currently addicted or can't afford the kids you presently have. When your parents are demanding an abortion or your boyfriend is already out the door or your church has a history of judging single mothers. Or imagine—God forbid—that the pregnancy isn't the result of a sin committed by the mother but a sin committed against the mother.

So, fellow follower of Jesus, what can we do? Here's God's answer—*Be pro (every) life*. Many Christians speak, post, and pray for life inside the womb. Today, God wants to encourage us not to just care about that life but about all the lives involved when someone is pregnant and didn't plan it.

"Dear friends, since God so loved us, we also ought to love one another" (1 John 4:11). It was the love of God that found us, saved us, and provided us eternal life at the cross of Jesus. May that same love inspire us to love every life involved in every pregnancy.

Pro (every) life meets spiritual needs
Pastor Mike Novotny

When considering an abortion, what people need, more than anything else, is truth and grace.

Planned Parenthood tells us that one of the top reasons that women have abortions is convenience—"I'm not ready for a baby." "I want to finish grad school." "I don't want to do the infant thing again." Such desires need to be challenged by biblical truth. But the Bible says it would be murder to end a life that God himself created. Improving your life does not justify ending someone else's.

For others, however, their spiritual need is grace. Since sexual immorality is a sin that sometimes "shows," you might wonder what the church people will say, how they'll look, how they'll judge, even if you are repentant as Peter was after denying Jesus.

Friends, these fears are real. So you and I need to show love. Evident, obvious, impossible-to-miss love. Smiles. Hellos. You-belong-here love. I'm-glad-you-came love. I-thank-God-that-you're-considering-other-options love. Jesus-forgives love. Jesus is pro-me-and-pro-you-by-grace love.

One of my favorite descriptions of Jesus is when John writes that he **"came from the Father, full of grace and truth"** (John 1:14). Jesus knew when to speak truth and when to show love, without watering down either one.

God, help us do the same as we deal with the unplanned pregnancies in our lives. Amen.

Pro (every) life meets eternal needs
Pastor Mike Novotny

Earlier this year, I met a man who worked for a pro-life ministry who, along with his wife, invited a young woman to stay in their guest bedroom while she got back on her feet. However, the girl was drawn to the party scene and found herself pregnant. She knew her hosts were church people and very much pro-life. Since she had grown up with a strict religious father, she assumed her sin meant she was no longer welcome in their home. "I'll leave," she mumbled abruptly one morning. But this man—thank God—saw her spiritual need and met it. He gave her grace. He spoke to her of Jesus' love.

That story reminds me of the reputation that many Christians have on the issue of abortion. For various reasons, many of our neighbors assume we are all truth and no grace, that we only care about life in the womb, that we have no place for people who have sinned and fallen short of biblical standards. This is why showing and speaking grace is so essential in our day and age.

"Where sin increased," Paul wrote, **"grace increased all the more"** (Romans 5:20). When you see/hear the confessions of those who have disobeyed God's desires for sex, marriage, and pregnancy, be quick to give them Jesus. You might assume they know about forgiveness and the cross, but many don't. It's our privilege to give grace.

While you're at it, preach a bit to yourself. Let grace convince you to forgive yourself as God has first forgiven you.

Pro (every) life meets financial needs
Pastor Mike Novotny

According to a 2004 Planned Parenthood survey, 23% of abortions happen for financial reasons. Medical bills, then diapers, then formula, then two decades of unending expenses. No wonder so many people, especially those who are already poor, are tempted to end life soon after it begins.

Which is where Christians come in. Would you sell your cabin to save a kid? Would you drive your car into the ground to convince a young couple to keep their baby girl? Would you put off your retirement, skip a vacation, or say to a worried niece, "We've got you. Whatever it costs, we've got you"? Could we, like the earliest Christians, create a culture where no one has to starve or shiver or abort because they're broke? James wrote, **"Religion that God our Father accepts as pure and faultless is this: to look after orphans and widows in their distress"** (James 1:27). Pure religion meets the vulnerable right where they're at.

The Christian religion cares about people's needs because it is built upon the Christ who cared about our needs. When he saw our need for grace, he met it. And when we prayed for daily bread, he gave it. Despite the immense sacrifice required, love drove Jesus to do everything in his power to meet our deepest and most important needs.

With eyes fixed on him, let's do the same for others.

Pro (every) life meets relational needs
Pastor Mike Novotny

If the Christian church is passionate about protecting every life, then we will need to learn how to meet relational needs. When an unplanned pregnancy happens, the baby's parents often have massive needs to help them grow as people and, perhaps, as a couple. Could you be God's way of meeting such needs?

Moms, that scared young woman might need to learn how to be a mom, because she hasn't had years to plan and research and read *What to Expect When You're Expecting*. Guys, that wide-eyed dude might need to learn how to step up, how to grow up, and how real men put down the Xbox controller and pick up a box of wipes. That couple might need mentors, babysitters, or counselors to help them figure out their lives together.

Or, if there's not a dad in the picture, that child will need some men to model the faith for him, to take him under his wing, to remind him who he is and whose he is. Or, if the couple chooses adoption (a great option!), they will need support, love, prayers, and resources. They might even need you to step forward and personally open your own arms and home to their developing baby.

Paul wrote, **"Therefore, as we have opportunity, let us do good to all people, especially to those who belong to the family of believers"** (Galatians 6:10). Unplanned pregnancies give the church plenty of "opportunity" to do good to others. With God's help and strength, let's do it!

Jesus was pro (every) life
Pastor Mike Novotny

Have you ever considered how shockingly pro (every) life our Savior was?

Think back two thousand years about whom and how and how much Jesus loved. Jesus loved the lives of lepers and adulterers and prostitutes and Pharisees. Despite their messiness, he didn't abort his mission to die on a cross for their sins.

Thankfully, Jesus hasn't changed one bit. Jesus knows all the reasons why we sin, the something-to-them reasons and the senseless ones, yet he loves us all the way to eternal life. When Jesus died on a cross and rose from the dead, he made a promise that, through faith in him, God would adopt us as his own children, that our Father would set the table with a place for us. He promised that he would leave the light on and the door unlocked so we could always come back, always have a room to rest, and always have grace to come home to.

The sexually immoral and the selfish, the abortionist and the apathetic, all of us can come to Jesus and have every need met, every sin erased, every mistake covered so that God would be for us. The apostle Paul promises, **"Anyone who believes in him will never be put to shame"** (Romans 10:11). Anyone—that's you—who believes in him—that's Jesus—will never—never, ever, ever—be put to shame. We will always belong.

Because Jesus was pro (you and God together forever) life.

Becoming childlike again
Andrea Delwiche

"Clap your hands, all you nations; shout to God with cries of joy. Sing praises to God, sing praises; sing praises to our King, sing praises. For God is the King of all the earth; sing to him a psalm of praise" (Psalm 47:1,6,7).

Do you read encouragements like the one above and feel slightly awkward? *Clap my hands?* There was a time when clapping, praising, and excitement over life came easily to most of us—childhood.

What would it look like to return to the childlike faith that Jesus himself recommends to his serious adult followers: **"He called a little child to him and placed the child among them. And he said: 'Truly I tell you, unless you change and become like little children, you will never enter the kingdom of heaven'"** (Matthew 18:2,3).

There are many good truths to be taken from Jesus' words; one of them is an encouragement to leave adult pridefulness and cynicism behind. These postures are not worshipful and relegate the beautiful work of God to being unimportant. Rather, as children do, we can turn our eyes in appreciation to the One who gives good things and clap our hands with joy.

Take a walk or sit outside and see things with childlike appreciation. Notice shapes and colors, flowers and leaves, birds, insects; these were all made by our Creator-God. As you are able, begin to celebrate. God has made it, and it is good!

A good kind of jealousy
Jan Gompper

Merriam-Webster Dictionary defines the word *jealous* as "hostile toward a rival or one believed to enjoy an advantage: envious." Jealousy is considered a negative attribute (aka, a jealous boyfriend or coworker), and Scripture calls it a sin.

Yet God describes himself as being a **"jealous God"** (Exodus 20:5). And Paul told his church in Corinth, **"I am jealous for you with a godly jealousy"** (2 Corinthians 11:2). Can jealousy also be good?

Note that Paul uses the word *for*, not *of*. God is not jealous of us; he is jealous for us. He is hostile toward any rival who wants to destroy our relationship with him. He loves us and wants our love in return *so much* that he will go to the utmost lengths to keep us in a relationship with him. In fact, he already did. He sent his Son to the depths of hell on our behalf to make certain that no one (including Satan) could ever snatch us from his hand (John 10:29).

The David Crowder Band poetically describes the amazing goodness of God's jealousy with the lyrics of their song "How He Loves." Check it out on YouTube!

Lord, how I thank you . . . for being jealous for me. Amen.

Watch what you take in
Linda Buxa

The other day we had appetizers for dinner. I'm usually pretty consistent about making sure our meals have vegetables or fruits, protein, and healthy fats.

But that night everything came out of a box—from taquitos to mozzarella sticks, from chicken nuggets to deep-fried cheese curds. As the "food" was served, everybody commented how it was all a shade of light brown—no rainbow of colors, no nutritional value.

An hour later the digestive complaints started. What tasted so good left the kids sick to their stomachs. Well, my son didn't seem to have any complaints, but my girls swore off that kind of food for quite a while.

That got me thinking about what we put into our hearts and our minds. We know what's healthy for us, but occasionally we feed ourselves garbage. I know it isn't good for me to spend too much time on social media or watching the news, but in the name of "being informed" or "keeping in touch," I spend too much time watching or clicking—and then I end up worried, angry, frustrated, and (sometimes literally) sick to my stomach. I know I shouldn't hang on to past hurts, but I let my mind stew about things I thought I had let go.

Maybe you do too. So today, maybe you want to join me in "eating healthy" and swearing off the garbage.

"Whatever is true, whatever is noble, whatever is right, whatever is pure, whatever is lovely, whatever is admirable—if anything is excellent or praiseworthy—think about such things" (Philippians 4:8).

Protected pasture
Pastor Jon Enter

It used to be that whenever I read Psalm 23:2 (**"He makes me lie down in green pastures"**), I was confused why God would need to *make me* lie down in green pastures. Make me? It's not that God forces you and me against our will to lie down and rest. What God, our Good Shepherd, is promising is that his protection will surround us so we can pasture, so we can rest even in this broken life.

Without a shepherd watching the sheep, they are basically gigantic balls of cotton candy with slow-moving legs. Sheep have zero natural defenses against animals who eat them. No quills. No sharp claws. No shell. No antlers. No stinky skunk smell. In fact, when sheep get really scared, their legs freeze up; they fall over and become lunch.

Because of their lack of defense systems, sheep will not lie down unless they are free from all fear (friction with other sheep, pesky flies and parasites, predators, and free from hunger). When these needs are met, they lie down peacefully.

It is nearly impossible to rest when you have friction with others or are pestered by problems and hungry for contentment. If that's you, if you aren't resting, refocus your relying. In order to lie down in peace, don't count sheep but count on your Shepherd, Jesus. He protects you from evil. He provides grace and guidance so you can rest.

Continually refocus yourself on Jesus and rest well in the pasture of his protection.

But you promised
Sarah Habben

When I'm overwhelmed, I sometimes wish God would pull up a chair and advise me.

Jacob had reason to feel that way too. He was following God's command to head home to Canaan after 20 years in exile. But Jacob's estranged twin, Esau, who had sworn to kill Jacob, was now coming to meet him. *With 400 men.* Jacob figured this wasn't a welcoming party.

So Jacob began a sleepless night, wrestling with God in prayer. But he didn't pray, "God, please tell me what to do!" Instead, he prayed, **"I am afraid . . . but you have promised"** (Genesis 32:11,12 paraphrase).

When I fear what tomorrow will bring, I need God's promises. They break through the dark cloud of the future like rays of sunshine: promises to forgive, to provide, to bless.

In the middle of Jacob's internal struggle, God suddenly appeared. But he didn't pull up a chair—he pulled Jacob into a headlock! They wrestled all night, until finally God dislocated Jacob's hip. Jacob hung on, saying, **"I will not let you go unless you bless me"** (Genesis 32:26). God blessed him. And Jacob limped off to meet his brother, weaker in body but stronger in faith.

When my fears grapple with God's promises, the process can hurt. But I learn God is not hiding. He speaks to me in his Word, feeds me with his Holy Supper, washes me in Baptism. He wrestles down my doubts, teaching me that hardship is not a reason to let go of God. Sometimes God allows me to limp so that my faith can grow.

My God can turn water into wine
Pastor David Scharf

Wedding feasts in Jesus' day could be huge events that lasted for a week. The host provided everything. In fact, if the family was wealthy enough, they would even provide clothing for the guests! For a family to run out of wine was simply unthinkable . . . but Jesus was at a wedding in Cana where the family ran out of wine. Jesus could have left them to fend for themselves. Instead, he provided at least 120 gallons of the best wine! **"The master of the banquet tasted the water that had been turned into wine. He did not realize where it had come from, though the servants who had drawn the water knew"** (John 2:9).

God continues to provide for you and me today. Just look at the clothes you wear, savor the food you eat, consider the house you live in. Most of us have heat, electricity, running water—we often take it all for granted! Some of us even have more than one vehicle, not to mention computers, televisions, and "toys." How richly God has provided for us! Just as for that family in Cana, it is all undeserved. Jesus has not changed. The same powerful Jesus who turned water into wine has promised to care for you. No, he may not give you all you want, and you will at times have struggles, but he has promised to provide. And if he can turn water into wine, then he can and will provide for all your needs!

I will survive!
Pastor Clark Schultz

A highlight from my tour of Israel involved no light. Some friends encouraged me to go with them through King Hezekiah's tunnel. To give you a dark visual, this tunnel is about 5½ football fields long, 3.28 feet deep with water in some areas, and as narrow as 1.9 feet. Oh, and did I mention I'm extremely claustrophobic? Halfway through the tunnel, the batteries on all three of our flashlights went dead. Yup, heavy breathing and gasping for air took over, and I was in the darkest place I have ever been.

"'Neither this man nor his parents sinned,' said Jesus, 'but this happened so that the works of God might be displayed in him'" (John 9:3). With this text, Jesus is helping his disciples see that it is Jesus alone who can open the eyes of the blind. The listening Pharisees didn't think they needed saving because their good works alone could save them. WRONG—and blind. It's God's grace and faith in Jesus alone that save. The disciples saw the man's blindness as a punishment from God. WRONG—and blind. Man's critical need is God's opportunity.

What got us through that tunnel in Israel was listening to each other's voices. As you travel the tunnel of life, listen to the One who traveled and kept the path of the law for you and whose voice and saliva can cure any blindness. Better than an "I survived King Hezekiah's tunnel" T-shirt is the statement: I will survive death because of the GREAT KING JESUS.

Choices, choices
Ann Jahns

We love choices, right? We love the freedom to choose things that make us happy or make our lives better. Regular or curly fries with that? Paper or plastic? We could stand in the salad dressing aisle in the grocery store for an hour in an agony of indecision. So many choices!

Joshua, the leader who took over for Moses and guided God's people into the promised land of Canaan, also needed to make a choice. Nearing the end of his life, he gathered the people to deliver a mini history lesson. He reminded them about how God had taken them out of slavery in Egypt to a land filled with blessings. He reminded them how God had again and again remained faithful to them, even though they, in turn, had again and again rejected their God in favor of the false, disgusting gods of the nations living around them.

Joshua told the people they had to now make a life-or-death choice: **"Choose for yourselves this day whom you will serve, whether the gods your ancestors served beyond the Euphrates, or the gods of the Amorites, in whose land you are living. But as for me and my household, we will serve the Lord"** (Joshua 24:15).

Joshua's choice was a whole lot more crucial than which two sides he wanted with his entrée. Our choice is crucial also. Each day this world tells us to choose false gods like money and possessions and substances and beauty. Don't be fooled. There's only one God. Who will you serve today?

A word for younger Christians
Pastor Mike Novotny

After purchasing a 150-foot rope, I hung one end so it dangled at eye level as you walked through the front doors of our building. Then I stretched the rope across the wide lobby before tying it off near the other wall. Finally, I wrapped a piece of black tape around the dangling end so every worshiper would see 1 inch of tape followed by 1,799 inches of rope.

Why? In part, because I wanted everyone to see life from God's perspective. In our teens, 20s, and 30s, we're given dozens of opportunities to prioritize something other than God. It might be college, dating, friends, or starting a family. These are all good gifts from God . . . unless they subtly replace God. Unless they rob us of the time and energy required for church, meditation on the Word, and connection with God's people. While we'd all love to believe we can prioritize both, the truth is we can only seek one thing first.

If you're there (or know someone who is), remember the rope. This life, from heaven's point of view, is like that tiny stretch of black tape, less than .1% of your eternal existence. Resist the urge of your generation to forget heaven's math; fix your eyes on the eternal happiness that Jesus lived, died, and rose to give you; and organize your life accordingly. You won't regret it.

"We fix our eyes not on what is seen, but on what is unseen, since what is seen is temporary, but what is unseen is eternal" (2 Corinthians 4:18).

A word for older Christians
Pastor Mike Novotny

Any gray-haired people of God out there? After passing the 40-year mark recently, I'm realizing that getting older has its frustrations. I'm finding that it's harder to remember people's names, more challenging to memorize God's words, and near impossible to feel great about the wrinklier, droopier body that's reflected in the mirror each morning. (Some of you are thinking, *Pastor, just wait until 50! or 60! or 80! You have no idea . . .*)

It's easy to give in to grumbling as our bodies start to break down. But the apostle Paul had a different perspective that kept his faith young and fresh. He wrote, **"Though outwardly we are wasting away, yet inwardly we are being renewed day by day"** (2 Corinthians 4:16).

You 60-somethings can have a faith that is faster and fresher than an all-conference freshman. How? By fixing your eyes on what is unseen and eternal (see verse 18). I know many of your friends gather together to grumble about medication, doctor's appointments, and surgeries, reminiscing about the glory days of their youthful past. But you can focus on the glory days to come, when Jesus returns to make all things new. On that day, the first of an endless streak, Jesus will raise your body, transformed to be as glorious as his own, and present you in the Father's presence once and for all.

Ah, the millennials should envy the elderly who have their eyes fixed on forever! So whatever your age, fix your eyes on Jesus and thank God for forever.

Beware the bully
Jan Gompper

Most of us grew up with a bully in our schoolyard. You used to be able to see him or her coming. Today, it's not as easy. They hide on social media platforms, sit behind newsroom microphones, or stand behind political podiums. Sometimes they incite others to bully with them.

Jesus had experience with bully mobs. He stopped one from stoning a woman who had committed adultery. He watched another release a malicious criminal named Barabbas so they could, instead, crucify him.

How did Jesus respond to these two bully mobs? To the first, he said, **"Let the one who has never sinned throw the first stone!"** (John 8:7 NLT). For the second, he prayed, **"Father, forgive them, for they don't know what they are doing"** (Luke 23:34 NLT). And when Peter wanted to start his own insurrection, Jesus laid his hand on Peter's arm and whispered, **"Put away your sword. . . . Those who use the sword will die by the sword"** (Matthew 26:52 NLT).

Peter took Jesus' words to heart and later encouraged: **"Don't repay evil for evil. Don't retaliate with insults when people insult you. Instead, pay them back with a blessing. That is what God has called you to do. . . . For the Scriptures say, 'If you want to enjoy life and see many happy days, keep your tongue from speaking evil and your lips from telling lies. Turn away from evil and do good. Search for peace, and work to maintain it'"** (1 Peter 3:9-11 NLT).

May we also take these words to heart!

Every day is a jubilee for you
Pastor David Scharf

In the Old Testament, God wanted his people to celebrate a year of Jubilee. It was to take place every 50 years. In that year, all debts were canceled, and all slaves were released to return to their own families. Just imagine what a joyful event the year of Jubilee must have been for the people of Israel!

"Consecrate the fiftieth year and proclaim liberty throughout the land to all its inhabitants. It shall be a jubilee for you; each of you is to return to your family property and to your own clan" (Leviticus 25:10).

You see, sometimes it happened that an Israelite had to sell himself into slavery to pay off debts. However, that Israelite knew he was not going to be a slave forever. He knew freedom was coming. What a day to look forward to, the day he would be set free!

We no longer need to look forward to that day. We are living that day, every day. We have been set free from our slavery to sin. When Jesus said, "It is finished," he was proclaiming your freedom. Sin is no longer your master. You and I can now live our lives in freedom, serving our Savior! We have that freedom today, right now. It will get even better when we go to heaven and live in perfect, eternal freedom with our Savior Jesus. Jubilee is a time for rejoicing. In Jesus, every day is a Jubilee for you.

Many rooms
Sarah Habben

Three-year-old Ellis loves to talk about heaven and who will be with her there.

My mom and dad believe in Jesus. Will they be in heaven?
Yes, Ellis, they will.

My grandma and papa believe too. Will they be in heaven?
Yup!

And my friends who believe in Jesus . . . will they be there too?
Yes! It'll be SO great.

But suddenly Ellis looks a little worried.

How can there be room for everyone?

Maybe you wonder that too. Not for yourself, a law-abiding citizen, decent friend, and frequent churchgoer. No, you wonder how there could be room for that guy who comes to church smelling like Saturday's bender or that teen who admitted she's struggling with her sexual orientation. How can there be room—for *them*?

Or maybe you *are* that guy or girl, struggling with powerful temptations that keep getting the upper hand: "How can there be room—for *me*?"

Jesus pushes away any doubt about who will fit in heaven. His death paid for our holier-than-thou hypocrisy. It paid for the times we let temptation win. His resurrection assures us that our repentant faith in him is not a dead end but a door. And it leads to a mansion with room for everyone who clings to Jesus as their Savior.

"Do not let your hearts be troubled. . . . My Father's house has many rooms; if that were not so, would I have told you that I am going there to prepare a place for you?" (John 14:1,2).

My cup overflows
Pastor Jon Enter

I remember reading Psalm 23:5 as a child and wondering why God would promise to make my cup overflow. If I poured a glass too full and spilled it, I got in trouble for being careless. I knew God meant it as a good thing, a blessing, but I didn't understand how.

In biblical times, wedding celebrations would last up to a week, sometimes more. When guests arrived, they received a cup that would be filled continually by servants throughout the party, even for days. If your cup continued to be filled, that revealed the host wanted you to stay longer. If your cup ran dry, it was a polite way to tell you it was time for you to go without having to embarrass you verbally in front of others.

Your cup overflows! Do you know what that means? The Almighty Lord, the Creator of the universe, the One who spoke and mountains grew and the seafloor fell, who spoke and the sun shone and the bee buzzed and the gorilla grunted. That God. The only God. The true God wants continual presence with you. Your cup overflows. He pours his mercy continually into your heart and out through your life. **"God's love has been poured out into our hearts through the Holy Spirit, who has been given to us"** (Romans 5:5).

It's incredible to know that Jesus' heartfelt desire is to spend eternity with you, and he already is!

Thorns are good?
Pastor David Scharf

"Why did this happen to me? Why is life always such a struggle? I'm tired of the battles with myself and with everyone else. God, just take the bad things away!"

The apostle Paul could relate. God had allowed Paul to suffer a "thorn in the flesh." Paul called it a "messenger of Satan." Understand that when a thorn comes in life, there are always two messages attached to it, one from Satan and one from God. You will either be discouraged or strengthened, depending on which one you listen to. Sometimes, like Paul, we beg God to take it away, but God allows it to remain.

Maybe your suffering or weakness has lingered. Perhaps it weighs heavily on you. If so, listen to the message God attaches to your thorn: **"My grace is sufficient for you, for my power is made perfect in weakness."** It's why Paul went on to say, **"Therefore I will boast all the more gladly about my weaknesses, so that Christ's power may rest on me . . . for when I am weak, then I am strong"** (2 Corinthians 12:9,10).

Do you see? Your struggle doesn't mean God has abandoned you or he doesn't love you. Instead, the struggle leads you to lean on the strength of God instead of your own. It forces you to rely on the love of Jesus, who saved you by his cross. Because they lead us to our real strength, even thorns are good!

And who knows but . . .
Linda Buxa

Queen Esther lived about 2,500 years ago. She was Jewish and (unknown to him) the king had said it would be okay to destroy all the Jews. Tragedy was about to strike, and her Uncle Mordecai told her, **"And who knows but that you have come to royal position for such a time as this?"** (Esther 4:14).

Even though he had no idea how the story would end, Mordecai said, "And who knows but . . ." He trusted that his God had a plan and possibly Esther was a vital part of it. And she was. (Read the whole book of Esther to find out. It's pretty short.)

None of us knows how our days, much less our lives, will end. Tragedy can strike us too, bringing more questions than answers. We lie awake at night wondering *why?* Like Mordecai, when we face dark days, we cling—sometimes desperately, sometimes boldly—to God's promises to be with us, comfort us, and use us, even in our grief, to bring hope to a hurting world.

"Praise be to the God and Father of our Lord Jesus Christ, the Father of compassion and the God of all comfort, who comforts us in all our troubles, so that we can comfort those in any trouble with the comfort we ourselves receive from God. For just as we share abundantly in the sufferings of Christ, so also our comfort abounds through Christ" (2 Corinthians 1:3-5).

Are you all in?
Jan Gompper

Have you ever done the Hokey Pokey? "Put your right foot in, put your right foot out, put your right foot in, and shake it all about." It ends with, "Put your whole self in." When you're doing it, you feel rather silly—maybe that's why it's called the *Hokey* Pokey.

But have you ever really put your whole self into something? I did when I went to graduate school. I worked three part-time jobs, ate a lot of mac 'n' cheese, and averaged three to four hours of sleep per night—I was "all in" because I was 100% committed to getting my degree.

We are likely to put our whole selves in when we really want or believe in something. So have I ever been all in for Jesus? I believe in him, and I want to do his will here on earth. But have I ever worked as hard doing his work as I did when I was trying to attain other goals in my life? Sadly, I confess I haven't. Perhaps you confess the same.

Fortunately, however, we have a Savior who went all in for us. He sacrificed everything—his rightful place in heaven, his comfort on this earth, his very life—so we could be assured that we would be all in in his heavenly kingdom. And because of what Jesus did, God views even our meager attempts on his behalf as **"spiritual sacrifices acceptable to God through Jesus Christ"** (1 Peter 2:5).

And there's nothing hokey about that.

Daily bread

Sarah Habben

A good friend invites you over for dinner. He uncorks a bottle of wine and pours you a glass. You notice the label on the bottle. This isn't a $15 bottle of wine. It's a $1,500 bottle of wine!

Your host grins, "Just wait and see what's next."

You're pretty sure it's not leftover pizza.

Like a fine wine, God poured out the life of his only Son on a cross. It's a staggering gift, but it's just the beginning. **"He who did not spare his own Son, but gave him up for us all—how will he not also, along with him, graciously give us all things?"** (Romans 8:32).

If our heavenly Father loves us enough to pour out his best and brightest treasure, can't we trust whatever else he provides?

Yet when we pray, "Give us this day our daily bread," we're often wishing for someone else's daily banquet—our buddy's European vacations or our neighbor's new cars. But that's like sipping our friend's costly wine and then ordering fast-food takeout. God has already given us his best. He will meet all our needs out of his rich grace and wisdom.

When we pray for our daily bread, we aren't making an Amazon wish list. We're placing ourselves in the hands of our Provider. When we hunger, Jesus feeds us. When we fall, he forgives. When we weep, his Word comforts us. As we age, he sustains us. When our earthly life disappoints, God points us to the cross. He smiles and says, "Just wait and see what's next."

What's in a name?
Ann Jahns

One of the most exciting parts of getting ready to welcome a child into the world is choosing a name. Names are a big deal! Names stick with you for the rest of your life. Expectant parents pore over baby name lists or think about family members they'd like to honor.

And how about the Bible for name inspiration? There are so many fantastic names that are rich in spiritual meaning and history.

For example, check out the "heroes of faith" in Hebrews chapter 11. How about the name Jacob? Oh, wait. He overtly favored one of his sons, sowing the bitter seeds of jealousy in the others. Okay, what about David? *Hmm.* He impregnated the wife of one of his soldiers and then had that soldier killed to cover it up. Or maybe the name Rahab? Oh, boy. Rahab was a prostitute with a checkered past.

But that's the beauty of God's grace, isn't it? He used tragically flawed human beings to carry out his salvation plan. Yes, they often failed, and some in quite spectacular ways. But he used them anyway. Just like he uses you, just like he uses me. And just like he will use that newborn believer with the name of Samuel or Sarah or Noah.

God assures you, **"I have called you by name, you are mine"** (Isaiah 43:1 ESV). No matter the name on your birth certificate, by God's grace your real name is Child of God. That's the only name that matters.

Jesus hates hypocrisy
Pastor Mike Novotny

A few years ago, I heard a pastor confess his struggle with hypocrisy. As his congregation was preparing to host a midweek conference, the pastor noticed a bunch of bulletins left behind from the previous Sunday. So he began to go back and forth through the aisles, picking up the stray papers, a job the church janitor or a volunteer might do. But he confessed that, almost instantly, this thought popped into his mind: *I hope someone sees this.* He hoped that someone would just happen to walk by and say, "Pastor? Is that you picking up bulletins? How kind of you!"

Ever been there? Doing the right thing—serving selflessly at church, giving generously to a charity, loving sacrificially in your family—is hard. But doing the right thing for the right reason—for God's glory, for others' good, and not for attention or praise—is even harder. Yet despite the difficulty, we must fight the desire to put on a show, because Jesus hates hypocrisy.

How do we resist that temptation? By remembering the God who sees. Jesus taught, **"But when you pray, go into your room, close the door and pray to your Father, who is unseen. Then your Father, who sees what is done in secret, will reward you"** (Matthew 6:6).

God will see you and reward you with his full attention. And that is the greatest gift of all.

Color-blind
Linda Buxa

A man had been color-blind for 66 years. For his birthday, his family gave him a pair of glasses that allow people with color blindness to see true-to-life colors. He stood there, obviously overwhelmed, switching between his old vision and his new and not knowing what to do with all his emotion.

I couldn't help but wonder if this is how I'll react when I get to heaven? Maybe I'll tackle-hug my Savior with tears in my eyes because I'm so happy. Or maybe I'll stand there, as if I can't believe my eyes.

For everyone who believes in Jesus, we live on earth seeing but not seeing it all. We know we're saved by Jesus, but we still feel the effects of our sin, earth's sadness, and Satan's attacks. We forget that troubles are light and momentary, which is easy to do when we're discouraged, anxious, tired, and lonely. That's why every day we take a few moments to remember that we aren't seeing everything clearly right now. **"For now we see only a reflection as in a mirror; then we shall see face to face. Now I know in part; then I shall know fully, even as I am fully known"** (1 Corinthians 13:12).

Heaven is a real place where our real heavenly Father is preparing a real room for us. When the time is right, real angels will come to carry us to our real home. That's the day when, in the twinkling of a color-blinded-by-sin eye, you will see your Savior—and you'll finally, fully get it.

Quiet waters
Pastor Jon Enter

"He leads me beside quiet waters" (Psalm 23:2). Our Good Shepherd, Jesus, promises he will lead us beside quiet waters. Water is necessary for life. The body can only last a few days without water. It's essential to survival for humans and animals.

Sheep would not survive without their shepherd leading them to water. They lack the ability to remember where their water source is. Even if a sheep hears streams nearby, it can't find the refreshing waters. Sheep get lost easily. They need to be led to water. If they aren't, they will drink anything, even water filled with feces and foul contaminants. Their desperate search to quench their thirst leads them into danger.

When have you been so thirsty for fulfillment and acceptance in life that you drank the polluted, poisoned water of temptation? No matter how you answer, no matter what you did, there is one truth. It's because you acted like a sheep and wandered from your Shepherd. In Christ you have refreshment. In him you receive the living water of his grace that washes away every sin and every failure.

When you start to thirst for unhealthy, unholy waters, realize you've wandered. There's safety and purity waiting for you in Jesus. The amazing truth of grace is that Christ knows you've wandered. Because he loves you, he runs after you. He rescues you. He leads you beside quiet waters. Stay close to Jesus, and you will be refreshed continually.

An antidote for sin

Pastor David Scharf

Read about God bringing Israel out of slavery in Egypt and you'll notice a frustrating refrain: *"Israel grumbled against the LORD."* How could they grumble against the God who saved them from slavery, you ask? Part of the reason you and I get frustrated with the refrain is that it is a familiar one in our lives.

Once, God sent snakes to bite the people to wake them from their grumbling. Moses prayed for them, and God said, **"Make a snake and put it up on a pole; anyone who is bitten can look at it and live"** (Numbers 21:8). It may seem crazy that looking at a snake led to healing, but it worked because God had promised it. God did not take away the poisonous snakes; instead, he dealt with the poison.

God has done the same for us. The poisonous snake I'm referring to is sin. Has that snake bitten you today? Okay, that's a dumb question. Here's a better question. How badly has it bitten you today? That's more accurate, isn't it? Sin is horrible. Sin is deadly. Sin hurts.

God has given us the answer to sin's poison. When Jesus died and rose, he paid for our sins in full. Jesus said, **"Just as Moses lifted up the snake in the wilderness, so the Son of Man must be lifted up, that everyone who believes may have eternal life in him"** (John 3:14,15). Keep looking to Jesus, your antidote for sin!

Grow in God's wisdom
Andrea Delwiche

"Hear this, all you peoples; listen, all who live in this world, both low and high, rich and poor alike: My mouth will speak words of wisdom; the meditation of my heart will give you understanding. People who have wealth but lack understanding are like the beasts that perish" (Psalm 49:1-3,20).

Notice the opening words of this psalm: "Hear this, *all* you peoples." This word is for all of us. Whether we have little social status or are highly influential, whether we are well-off or living day-to-day, this psalm insists that if we lack the understanding that comes from God, whatever else we gain does not profit us. Our first priority is seeking the kingdom wisdom and life that only God himself can give.

How can we start to grow in God's wisdom? We can sit at the feet of Jesus, our Lord and Teacher, as did those who followed him when he walked the earth. We can marinate ourselves in the gospel and apply it to our own walk of faith.

During Jesus' ministry, he astounded people with his life-giving teaching **"because he spoke as one who had authority, and not as their teachers of the law"** (Matthew 7:29). Jesus' teaching is just as relevant today as it was two thousand years ago.

Each day we have an opportunity to let the words of God penetrate our hearts and bring us understanding. Out of that good beginning, we are equipped to invest ourselves in the work of his kingdom, whatever that work may be.

Always something
Pastor Mike Novotny

In life there's always something to grumble about and always something to be grateful for. Always. If God miraculously doubled your wealth, halved your stress, or increased your success, there would still be something. If you could time travel back to your 16th birthday or fast-forward to your 96th, you would, without a doubt, find something. That means grumbling will always be a temptation and gratitude will always be an option. So how do you resist the former and choose the latter?

The apostle Paul knows: **"All this is for your benefit, so that the grace that is reaching more and more people may cause thanksgiving to overflow to the glory of God"** (2 Corinthians 4:15). Notice what caused Paul's "thanksgiving to overflow"—grace. When God's undeserved love reaches people, it transforms them into grateful people.

Grace is the "something" God's people always have going for them. I know your back might hurt, your sister's cancer might be back, or your family might not be as functional as the neighbors, but you do have grace. You have a God who loves you despite your sin. You have a Savior who died and rose so that you would always have something to thank God for—a better tomorrow.

When you're facing another frustrating something, think about grace. You just might find yourself grateful to God.

September

Therefore I tell you, whatever you ask for in prayer,
believe that you have received it, and it will be yours.

Mark 11:24

Jesus is worth it
Pastor Mike Novotny

Do you know what happens the first day a new Chick-fil-A restaurant opens? Dozens of locals leave their warm beds behind, bring their tents, and camp out in the parking lot, sometimes in grumble-worthy temperatures. Sounds less than wonderful, doesn't it?

Before you answer, I should tell you two things. First, Chick-fil-A has a tradition of giving a year of free food to the first one hundred customers in line on an opening day. In other words, if you can make it through a rough night of sleep, you are rewarded with 365 days of delicious chicken! Second, Chick-fil-A's CEO flies around the country for these events, sleeping among the customers and rising at 6 A.M. to welcome them to the day of their great reward.

Sounds a bit like Christianity, doesn't it? Following Jesus isn't always easy. Like sleeping on concrete on a rainy night, denying ourselves the pleasure of an extra drink, forgiving those who hurt us, and putting other people first can be extremely uncomfortable. Yet Jesus has promised us a great reward—a front-row seat to the Father that endures forever, a sight that will instantly and eternally make us happier than anything in this life (even good chicken!). If that wasn't enough, Jesus promised to be with us until the Last Day arrives. Right by your side. Close enough to hear your prayers. Near enough to help you out.

So, Christian, believe that your faith is worth it, even when Jesus costs you. Your Savior promised, **"Surely I will be with you always"** (Matthew 28:20).

A place for me!
Pastor David Scharf

Have you ever seen the movie *The Passion of the Christ*? One scene sticks out for me. When Jesus died, there were two thieves crucified with him.

What sort of person got crucified? Nice guys didn't get crucified. Instead, people who were, by our standards, horrible were executed. You wouldn't have wanted these thieves in your neighborhood, much less your home. Yet one of them had the audacity to ask Jesus to take him to heaven!

From a logical standpoint, you might expect Jesus to answer, "Are you kidding? Take you to heaven? Look at what sort of person you are! You deserve to be hanging on that cross!"

But listen to what Jesus says: **"Truly I tell you, today you will be with me in paradise"** (Luke 23:43). How can that be? Jesus came to seek and to save what was lost. He came for the sick. He came for sinners. Jesus came because we needed a Savior who could die for us. By dying and rising, Jesus paid for the sins of the whole world! He paid for your sins, for my sins, and yes, that even includes that thief's sins.

That's why we can look at that thief with joy. If there was room in heaven for him, then there is room in heaven for me and you too. And knowing that gives us the confidence to live today and tomorrow and the day after that and . . .

Don't be a navel gazer
Pastor Clark Schultz

Both my father and wife love the challenge of putting together 1,000+ piece puzzles. I, on the other hand, like to stick to the ones my kids hand me that have 8-12 pieces tops. But 1,000 or 8 pieces, nothing is more frustrating then when there's a piece or pieces missing. The puzzle is incomplete. You could try to jam other pieces in there, but it wouldn't look right or complete the picture properly.

Life can be like a puzzle with missing pieces. Every day we wage war with ourselves to fill the missing pieces with items that are me-centric: money, me, possessions, me, sports, me, etc. The trouble is these pieces don't fit, nor do they complete the picture God intends for our lives.

The apostle Paul gives us some practical advice in Colossians 3:1,2: **"Set your hearts on things above, where Christ is, seated at the right hand of God. Set your minds on things above, not on earthly things."** Instead of being navel gazers, look to Jesus who says to you, "My head is filled with the requirements God has for you, and I kept those in your place." He also says, "My heart bleeds nothing but love for you . . . enough to die for you. The trial is over. Stop trying to go back into the courtroom. The puzzle of salvation is complete; you are saved."

So enjoy the blessings God showers on you while letting your head and heart put the pieces together of God's love for you. And be at peace.

Short prayers work
Pastor Mike Novotny

According to Jesus, the power of prayer isn't in the number of words that you pray. Our Savior taught, **"And when you pray, do not keep on babbling like pagans, for they think they will be heard because of their many words. Do not be like them"** (Matthew 6:7,8). That's pretty straightforward, isn't it? Don't be like people who think they will be heard because they pray for a long time. That's not how talking to our Father in heaven works.

Just in case you thought Jesus was joking, he went on to teach the most famous prayer of all time, the Lord's Prayer. Guess how many words it has? In Matthew's original Greek version, Jesus' prayer has only 57 words, less than you use when ordering at the McDonald's drive-thru. Even more eye-opening is Luke's version of the Lord's Prayer, which cuts the word count down to a mere 38 words. 38! Even if you take your time to meditate on each line, that's a lightning-fast prayer.

Why do short prayers work? Because God is both the all-knowing King who knows what you need and the compassionate Father who loves to meet your needs. So don't be afraid to have a short conversation with God about your faith, your family, or your pain. While long prayers can be a blessing too, you don't *need* to spend all day, because short prayers in Jesus' name work.

September 5

He restores my soul
Pastor Jon Enter

Did you know that sheep have flat backs? If one stumbles, falls, and accidentally rolls onto its back, it can't right itself. Blood drains from its legs. Its muscles freeze. Its body starts to go into shock. A shepherd knows not to pick up the sheep abruptly. He gently rolls the sheep over, and blood returns to its limbs. Pain follows, so the shepherd lovingly massages its legs. He then rolls the sheep to its other side, repeating the process—gently, slowly, lovingly restoring the sheep. If the shepherd rushed in and abruptly picked up the sheep, the pain would be immense. The sheep would fight from the shepherd's arms only to fall and possibly break a leg. The shepherd restores the sheep slowly.

Jesus, your loving Good Shepherd, knows the pain you're in. He saw you stumble. He knows you fell and that you're stuck. Like that sheep on its back, you've tried and cried and screamed and dreamed of getting your life righted again. But nothing has changed. Nothing has worked.

It's so easy to charge the Good Shepherd with not restoring you fast enough. It's so easy to accuse Christ of not caring. But he does! **"He restores my soul"** (Psalm 23:3 ESV). Jesus knows. He knows what pain is because he endured a cross for you. Jesus knows. He knows what abandonment feels like because he was forsaken by the Father on a cross. Jesus knows. He knows what you can endure. He knows how best to gently, slowly, lovingly restore you.

See me
Sarah Habben

When my daughter was a toddler, I caught her sitting on the kitchen counter, stuffing marshmallow Peeps in her mouth.

She squeezed her eyes shut and yelled, "Don't see me!"

God has a nickname in the Old Testament: *El Roi*—the God who sees. That should trouble us when we do or say stuff we'd rather hide. God sees. No matter how well we lick the wrongdoing off our fingers, God sees. No matter how we justify our sinful cravings, God sees. No matter how tightly we squeeze our eyes shut, God's are open.

The woman who addressed God as *El Roi* wasn't trying to hide. Hagar was desperate to be seen. She was Sarai and Abram's servant. Neither of them call her by name in the Bible account. Desperate for a child, barren Sarai offered Hagar to her husband as a surrogate. Hagar taunted Sarai with her pregnancy. Sarai retaliated with abuse. Abram turned a blind eye, so Hagar fled.

God found her in the desert, without a plan, alone, afraid, unloved. And he called her *by name*. He gave her a promise and a way to right her wrongs. Hagar marveled, **"You are the God who sees me"** (Genesis 16:13).

When God sees our wrongdoing, he doesn't recoil. He approaches with his Word and promises. He calls us by name. He knows every hair on our heads; he certainly knows our struggles. And he shows us the way out at the cross. There, sinless Jesus became our sinful surrogate—so that we could become his holy heirs.

Where does your trust reside?
Andrea Delwiche

"God is our refuge and strength, an ever-present help in trouble. Therefore we will not fear, though the earth give way and the mountains fall into the heart of the sea, though its waters roar and foam and the mountains quake with their surging" (Psalm 46:1-3).

How motivated are you by fear? You and I may excuse our fear as "just facing the facts" or "just being realistic." Fear of this type means that even though we *say* we trust in Christ, we use earthly means to provide a layer of protection from our fellow human beings. We protect ourselves by where we live, how we spend our time and money, perhaps even how we vote or in the provisions we make for the future. We say, "It makes good sense." But actually, we are afraid.

In these cases, we are not living in the reality of *God* as our refuge and strength. Instead, our faith and trust lie in our wealth, our social standing or ethnicity, the location of our home, our politics, our mental toughness.

How we spend our time and resources and what we put our weight behind are good indicators of where our trust actually resides.

Each of us can examine ourselves with the Holy Spirit and ask, "Lord, reveal to me the deep fears that I have. Give me grace to be able to see the ways that I try to protect myself rather than throwing myself on you for refuge. Show me how to live in an openhearted way toward other people whom you love so very much."

God is our protection
Andrea Delwiche

A city built alongside a river tends to have opportunities for growth and prosperity. In Psalm 46:4,5, we learn of a river **"whose streams make glad the city of God, the holy place where the Most High dwells. God is within her, she will not fall; God will help her at break of day."**

This is a river of God's protection and blessing for those who dwell in his kingdom.

The reality of God's protection gave the psalmist the confidence to say earlier in this psalm: **"God is our refuge and strength, an ever-present help in trouble. Therefore we will not fear"** (verses 1,2).

When the Lord makes plain to us that we are depending on ourselves for protection, we are called to change. God himself is the source and substance of that change. Rather than being fed by fear, we can be fed by the Lord and his goodness and love. Everything that God is and does flows in the water of this river: **"Every good and perfect gift is from above, coming down from the Father of the heavenly lights, who does not change like shifting shadows"** (James 1:17).

These unchanging waters of God's love redeem every area of our lives. We have opportunities to grow and flourish.

This is what God does for us when he is our source. When we are well-satisfied and protected by God's love, it allows us to reach out to others with openhearted love, wanting them to flourish and be filled as well.

Be still; our God reigns
Andrea Delwiche

"Come and see what the Lord has done, the desolations he has brought on the earth. He makes wars cease to the ends of the earth. He breaks the bow and shatters the spear; he burns the shields with fire. He says, 'Be still, and know that I am God; I will be exalted among the nations, I will be exalted in the earth'" (Psalm 46:8-10).

In yesterday's devotion, the psalmist reminded us that freedom from our deep fears is possible because God himself feeds us with the river of his sustaining love. Now the psalmist asks us to look out over the world and see God's power. While weather-related disasters and human-wrought disasters abound, God does not allow the full fruition of evil to take place. Many times he stops evil all together. He "breaks the bow and shatters the spear."

God calls out definitively as we, in our minds, spin tales of disaster and contemplate our own resources: "Be still and know that I am God."

God calls us to stop our anxious fluttering. Stop fanning fears. Stop feeding anxieties. Stop doom scrolling on cell phones and spreading the misdeeds of others. Stop. Be still and know that God is God.

We can dwell instead in this reality: *Our God reigns.* Take five minutes and ask the Holy Spirit to guide you in the way of lasting peace. How is God your refuge? How is God your fortress? Picture yourself abiding, *living* along the river of his sustaining love. Lord, help us change and live in you!

Jerry & Jesus
Pastor Mike Novotny

One of the most content men I've ever met lived in one of the smallest apartments I've ever seen. His name was Jerry, a longtime member of the first church I served as a pastor. As time passed and Jerry and I got to know each other, he invited me to visit him in his home, an apartment a few miles from our church. When I walked through the doors, I was immediately struck by the size of the place, a studio setup where bedroom, kitchen, and living room all squeezed into a few square feet no bigger than a couple of parking spots. Yet the entire time we talked, I didn't sense any frustration or anger over Jerry's simple lifestyle. Instead, I saw genuine joy.

Then Jerry showed me the secret of his contentment. He pulled out a file that was aged and worn from use, a file that contained the personal Bible studies he had completed over the past years. Word by word, Jerry meditated on key concepts in the Scriptures, finding all the uses of *saved* or *grace* and hand copying them into his notes. Nothing brought Jerry more joy than what he had discovered in the Word, truths that led him closer and closer to the loving heart of his Father.

Friend, you don't need a big house, a new car, or another trip to be content. Just a long look at the unfailing love of your Father in heaven. Just like Jerry.

"But godliness with contentment is great gain" (1 Timothy 6:6).

Never forget
Linda Buxa

After planes crashed into buildings on September 11, 2001, people vowed they would never forget. Same with Pearl Harbor, the Holocaust, and the *Challenger* explosion. Today, with any tragic event, people use the hashtag #neverforget on social media.

Each time I see that, there's a little part of me that thinks we say that because we know we just might forget. Actually, we absolutely will forget. Because that's what people do.

A king named David who lived about 3,000 years ago knew it too. Instead of reminding himself not to forget the tragic events in this life, he reminded himself to #neverforget the good things.

"Praise the LORD, my soul, and forget not all his benefits—who forgives all your sins and heals all your diseases, who redeems your life from the pit and crowns you with love and compassion, who satisfies your desires with good things so that your youth is renewed like the eagle's" (Psalm 103:2-5).

Forgetting the blessings God gives is our human tendency, especially in the hard and tragic times. We forget God is faithful and his love endures forever. We forget he promises never to leave us. We forget he puts his love and compassion on us. We forget he told us that even though bad things happen in this world, Jesus has overcome the world. And we forget this hard world is temporary and our eternal home is coming soon.

Praise the Lord. Remember his benefits. #neverforget

I have loved you as my own
Ann Jahns

A young couple I know recently adopted a child from overseas. To say that it was a struggle is an understatement. Pair the moving parts and red tape of an international adoption with the curveballs of COVID-19 and you get a frustrating, drawn-out adoption process that was a true test of faith.

So why did this young couple choose to adopt? Because they had love to give. They were saying to their adopted child, "We love you as our own. We choose to love you forever."

Sometimes it's easy to forget that love isn't just a feeling—love is also a choice. And even before he called the universe into being, God chose to love us. He assures us, **"I have loved you with an everlasting love"** (Jeremiah 31:3).

Sometimes it's hard to understand why God chooses to love us, because we aren't very lovable, are we? On a daily—hourly—minute-by-minute basis we fail him. We stomp on his love. We deliberately do things we know we shouldn't, like the defiant toddler who scribbles all over freshly painted walls with a permanent Sharpie.

But instead of seeing the dark scribbles of wrongdoing that cover our hearts, God sees only our whitewashed souls—souls made pristine through the cleansing blood of Jesus. You see, **"in love he predestined us for adoption to sonship through Jesus Christ"** (Ephesians 1:4,5). He chooses you, friend. You are his adored child through eternity.

Thank God for forever!
Pastor Mike Novotny

The other day I bought a 150-foot rope from Amazon. After it arrived, I wrapped 1 inch of black tape around an end of that rope and piled it next to the pulpit for the following Sunday. Because I wanted to calculate the math of our eternal happiness.

When our church family gets together for worship, we bring all kinds of baggage, issues, and drama. She is trying to forgive her husband for his infidelity. He is struggling to find a job he can see himself doing for the next decade. They are coping with the news of liver cancer. We all are regretting our sinful choices from the past seven days. Collectively, we have thousands of reasons to grumble and give in to the brokenness of this world, including the brokenness of our own hearts.

But the rope reminds them to thank God for forever! All our struggles, compared to eternity, are like that tiny inch of black tape. You might feel like the drama drags on forever, but it doesn't. It will all be over so soon, and then there is only the unending rope of the glory to come! Only smiles. Only relief. Only unity. Only love. Only God and his people, purified by the blood of the Lamb. Thank God for forever!

This is how the apostle Paul kept his spirits up (and how you can too): **"We do not lose heart. . . . We fix our eyes not on what is seen, but on what is unseen, since what is seen is temporary, but what is unseen is eternal"** (2 Corinthians 4:16,18).

What will I look like?
Pastor David Scharf

Do you remember when you were a child and saw a present under the Christmas tree and tried to figure out what was in it? You could take some guesses based on the box's size and shape, but finally you didn't know until you opened the gift. But even before you opened it, you knew one thing: it would be good! How? Because the gift came from someone who loved you.

We know some of God's gifts, like forgiveness and peace, but others we'll have to wait until the Last Day to realize fully. **"So will it be with the resurrection of the dead. The body that is sown is perishable, it is raised imperishable; it is sown in dishonor, it is raised in glory; it is sown in weakness, it is raised in power"** (1 Corinthians 15:42,43).

God is referring to the bodies we will have when he raises us from the dead. What will those bodies be like? They will be "imperishable," "in glory," and "in power." What does that mean? Frankly, I don't know. I haven't experienced a glorified body. It's like that wrapped present under the Christmas tree.

You can know this for sure though: it WILL be good! You can know that because your resurrected body comes from someone who loves you dearly. It comes from your God who loved you to death on a cross. That truth helps you trust God's plan for each day.

Your pain plan: Dial 5-1-1

Pastor Mike Novotny

The next time you're in pain, I would advise you to dial 5-1-1. That's my shorthand way of reminding you to open your Bible to Romans 5, James 1, and 1 Peter 1, three essential passages that have been helping Christians get through pain for the past two thousand years.

Romans 5: **"We also glory in our sufferings, because we know that suffering produces perseverance; perseverance, character; and character, hope. And hope does not put us to shame, because God's love has been poured out into our hearts through the Holy Spirit, who has been given to us"** (verses 3-5).

James 1: **"Consider it pure joy, my brothers and sisters, whenever you face trials of many kinds, because you know that the testing of your faith produces perseverance. Let perseverance finish its work so that you may be mature and complete, not lacking anything"** (verses 2-4).

1 Peter 1: **"These** [trials] **have come so that the proven genuineness of your faith—of greater worth than gold, which perishes even though refined by fire—may result in praise, glory and honor when Jesus Christ is revealed"** (verse 7).

Pain is always more bearable if you have a plan to persevere through it. So the next time you are suffering, grab your Bible and dial 5-1-1. I bet the Holy Spirit will help you bear your pain and remember the blessings of being a child of God.

Love that follows
Pastor Jon Enter

Sheep are helpless creatures. They have no defense mechanism against predators. Their only defense is to watch that no animal is stalking them, following them. As a human with a sinful nature and a flawed free will, you are helpless like a sheep against that prowling lion, the devil. He stalks you, follows you, to kill and destroy.

One of the most effective ways the devil attacks Christians is with guilt. When you look in your past, when you remember that awful act, that sexual sin, that eruptive anger, that intentional lie, that anger-filled exchange, guilt follows. Guilt consumes. Guilt crushes. Guilt wins. When you look in your past, you feel guilty, terrible, worthless.

Guilty means you are liable for punishment. The judge slams the gavel declaring, "Guilty!" That means the person will be punished. But Jesus was punished in your place! Jesus paid the price. Jesus erased your past. There is no reason to look in your past and feel guilty; instead, look in your past and see grace! See the goodness and love of Jesus.

So often Christians are haunted by their past. Don't be. You're not a failure; you're forgiven! That truth is the final promise God gives to you in Psalm 23: **"Surely your goodness and love will follow me all the days of my life"** (verse 6). Guilt doesn't follow you. Your past is gone. Goodness and love follow you, so live in confidence. Jesus' mercy is with you. Always. Forever.

The comfort in the Lord's Supper
Jan Gompper

There are differing beliefs when it comes to celebrating the Lord's Supper. Some Christians believe that the bread and wine "represent" the body and blood of Christ and that when they partake of it, they are honoring Jesus' death and resurrection and his directive to **"do this in remembrance of me"** (Luke 22:19).

Other Christians believe that "in, with, and under the bread and wine" believers also receive the body and blood of Jesus. They base this belief on St. Paul's reminder to his church in Corinth: **"Is not the cup of thanksgiving for which we give thanks a *participation* in the blood of Christ? And is not the bread that we break a *participation* in the body of Christ?"** (1 Corinthians 10:16).

Both views come from a place of heartfelt reverence. The "representational" view, however, seems to leave out the *comfort* that the Lord's Supper offers. It focuses on what we are doing for God more so than on what God is doing for us.

Paul's letter to the Corinthians implies that Christ's body and blood are integrally linked to the bread and wine. This seems to suggest that every time we take Lord's Supper we aren't just "remembering" Jesus, but we are participants (or recipients) of something more.

I don't know about you, but I find great comfort in believing that every time I go to his table (even when my mind is elsewhere, which it sometimes is), Christ still comes to me, giving me a spiritual booster shot, if you will, to strengthen my faith and draw me closer to him.

The grumble/gratitude zone

Pastor Mike Novotny

I have a theory about why we sometimes grumble and why we're sometimes grateful. My theory is that our attitudes are based almost entirely on our expectations.

For example, you step outside of your house and experience a 66-degree day. Do you grumble, or are you grateful? Depends on what you expected. If it's your summer vacation and you expected 86 degrees, grumble. If it's January in Wisconsin and you expected 6 degrees, SO grateful! Get my point? Your gratitude is not based so much on what you experience but on what you expected.

I wonder if this isn't the key to a grateful soul. When we believe we're good people who deserve a good life from God, we expect more than we experience and grumble when hard times happen. But when we believe we're sinful people who deserve nothing good from God, we overflow with gratitude toward the God who forgives us, saves us, and gives even the smallest physical blessing to us.

Paul, a man who experienced incredible pain in his life, wrote, **"Grace . . . may cause thanksgiving to overflow to the glory of God"** (2 Corinthians 4:15). The Bible has a simple equation for gratitude: Remember what you deserve (God's wrath). Remember what you experience because of grace (God's love). React accordingly (thank you, Jesus!).

That's how you resist a grumbling spirit and embrace a grateful one.

When we stop practicing
Jan Gompper

Years ago, a student who had graduated from the Christian high school where I taught shared that she was struggling with her faith. "Don't you ever wonder if it's all a hoax?" she asked. "I've gone to Christian schools my whole life, but I haven't been to church in three months, and I rarely pray anymore. I just don't feel very close to God."

This student had been a basketball all-star during high school, so I inquired as to what had made her such a good player. In addition to having natural talent, she mentioned that she practiced hard. In fact, she practiced her basketball skills pretty much every day to keep them intact.

"Maybe you're just getting spiritually flabby," I proffered.

We've all probably experienced feelings like my student at times. And the first thing we often want to do is to stop practicing—skip church, put our Bibles in a drawer, stop praying. But just like we can't stay physically fit without regularly working out, the same holds true for our spiritual fitness. And we all know that the longer we stay away from Gold's Gym or from God's gym, the harder it gets to go back.

Part of my student's success was due to her coach, who knew her potential and encouraged her relentlessly. **"In the same way, the Spirit helps us in our weakness. We do not know what we ought to pray for, but the Spirit himself intercedes for us through wordless groans"** (Romans 8:26).

I love my job
Ann Jahns

How do you feel about your job? Do you spring out of bed each morning, thinking, *It's another workday! I can't believe I get paid to do what I love!*

Or do you hit the snooze button, dreading the day to come? Maybe you feel underappreciated and overwhelmed. If so, you're not alone. Joseph knew how you felt. Sold into slavery by his spiteful brothers, he later spent 13 years in an Egyptian prison, victim of the lies of a scorned woman.

But while in prison, Joseph thrived: **"The warden put Joseph in charge of all those held in the prison, and he was made responsible for all that was done there"** (Genesis 39:22). Later Joseph interpreted Pharaoh's troubling dreams, giving all credit to our all-powerful God.

Because of Joseph's faithful work for a godless king, he became second in command of the mighty nation of Egypt. Quite a promotion for a Hebrew nobody. And that Hebrew nobody would orchestrate a plan to save the known world from a devastating famine, preserving the family line that Jesus would come from.

Now, in your job, will you work quietly and diligently like Joseph and be plucked from obscurity to become the vice president of the United States? Likely not. But you can **"work at it with all your heart, as working for the Lord"** (Colossians 3:23). Be a light in your corner of the world—on the factory floor, behind the customer service counter, or in your laundry room—even if it's unnoticed and underappreciated.

God notices. He will bless you for it.

Boast in the burn
Pastor Mike Novotny

About twice a week, my wife and I have the same conversation. She says, "My workout at the gym was so hard today." And, after hearing the details, I say, "That does sound hard." And then she says, "I can feel the ache already." And I say, "It will hurt even more tomorrow." And she says, "I know. It will be terrible." And I say, "How much are we paying these people?!"

Because we are! Every month the Discover card statement reminds me we are paying someone to put my wife through pain. In fact, some gyms these days even boast about their sinister plans to hurt our loved ones, naming themselves Burn Boot Camp or Fire Fitness.

But you probably know the reason why. As the old saying goes, "No pain, no gain." You know that if you want to be able to play sports in your 40s or wrestle with your grandkids in your 60s or hike the hills of Jerusalem in your 70s, you need to have a strong body. And strength, as science tells us, comes after we put our bodies through pain.

According to the Bible, your faith works the same way: **"We also glory in our sufferings, because we know that suffering produces perseverance; perseverance, character; and character, hope"** (Romans 5:3,4). Think about your current sufferings, inconveniences, and frustrations. What might God be producing through them? Scribble a few blessings God might be giving on the other side of your pain.

Then, like Paul, you can boast in the burn.

Just enough
Pastor Jon Enter

There's a comforting promise given by your Good Shepherd, Jesus, in Psalm 23 that's often overlooked. In verse 3 David wrote, **"He guides me along the right paths for his name's sake."** The right path. The needed path. Daily. Continually.

Verse 1 of this beautiful psalm connects the word pictures within to a shepherd and his sheep. Verse 3 is no different. Sheep can go months without drinking large amounts of water. Most people don't know this; shepherds do. Shepherds rise early to lead sheep along right paths at the right time (early hours) to graze on dew-covered grass. That little water sustains the sheep. It's just enough to sustain life until they are able to drink deeply from an abundant water source. But this small amount of water is needed daily.

You need to graze on the gospel-covered words of the Bible. Daily. Continually. Nourishment in the Water of Life sustains. Jesus guides you to it. There's a thirst inside you for refreshment. Jesus satisfies your quench. He is always there for you, with you, leading you in his Word on the right path.

Here's a refreshing sip of grace: **"Repent, then, and turn to God, so that your sins may be wiped out, that times of refreshing may come from the Lord"** (Acts 3:19). Live refreshed, forgiven, and knowing you are filled and fueled by the daily, continual mercy of Christ.

Tucked away safely
Pastor Clark Schultz

The rain poured down in buckets with no sign of letting up. The boy and his father waited in the store entrance. Through the pelting water droplets, they could see the minivan that looked like it was miles away. A quick check on the smartphone weather app revealed that this front was only beginning and was likely to get much worse.

Option 1: Wheel the cart of groceries back into the store and be late for a party. Option 2: Brave the elements. The father didn't mind the rain, but the four-year-old was afraid of storms. The father, who had a moment of brilliance, tucked his son's head under his shirt, hoisted the bags of groceries into his hands, and went into the rain. The little boy giggled because he could hear the rain but couldn't feel it touching his head. What looked silly to many watching proved to get the boy to safety.

We are caught in the storm of our sins; however, when Christ died, we died with him. His death is our death, and our debt is paid in full. **"For you died, and your life is now hidden with Christ in God"** (Colossians 3:3).

No matter how silly that first Good Friday looked or looks to many, our heavenly Father safely tucks us in his arms. As God's children, we are now hidden under the robe of Christ's perfection. So it's okay to giggle like a child because you are safe with Christ.

God is on your side
Pastor David Scharf

Frederick Douglass said, "One and God make a majority." The idea is that in the face of insurmountable odds, even if you only have God on your side, you will prevail. Sometimes it's easier said than believed.

At his ascension, Jesus told his followers they would be his witnesses in Jerusalem, Judea, Samaria, and to the ends of the earth. What an army Jesus must have been addressing when he gave the church her marching orders! Well, actually . . . **"In those days Peter stood up among the believers (a group numbering about a hundred and twenty"** (Acts 1:15).

So 120 people would be his witnesses to the whole world? It sounds like an impossible task, doesn't it? And yet, remember who our God is? He is the God who parted the Red Sea. He turned water into wine. He fed thousands with just a few loaves of bread and some fish . . . twice! That is who our God is!

How often you and I forget that or doubt it or fail to appreciate it. We worry. We get anxious. Have you forgotten that the almighty Creator of the world doesn't just have muscles but also a heart . . . a heart for you? It led him to a cross for you. And now this all-powerful God, the God who can accomplish the "impossible," is on your side.

What did those 120 accomplish? By the end of their lives, the Word had reached as far as Asia Minor, North Africa, and Europe. Impossible? Not with God on their side!

Lessons from Satanism
Linda Buxa

In July 2015, the Detroit chapter of the Satan Temple unveiled a bronze Baphomet statue. The nine-foot tall, one-ton monument pays homage to Satan. As opposed as I am to anything that glorifies the enemy, this lifeless statue reminds me that there is real and active evil power in this world—and I need to take it seriously.

A man who lived two thousand years ago took Satan seriously and wanted to remind us, **"Your enemy the devil prowls around like a roaring lion looking for someone to devour"** (1 Peter 5:8).

Satan is after you and would love to tear your world apart, to tear your eternity apart too. As scary as that might seem, Jesus has a reminder for you. After Jesus paid for your sins and then rose from the dead, he went and proclaimed victory to those in hell. Because Jesus secured your position in God's family, nothing can separate you from the love of God—neither heights nor depths nor powers.

One last thought: It's good to be appalled by an idol dedicated to the father of lies. However, this is also an opportunity to see if we have any idols in our hearts that exalt things in this world—even good things— and make them the Most Important Thing. Tear those down because they won't save you or love you. Only Jesus does that.

Stress and rest
Pastor Mike Novotny

Set down your devices and devotional booklets for a second and flex with me. Feel that bicep as you curl your fist close to your ear. Do you know, mechanically, how that muscle gets bigger? Two things have to happen—stress and rest.

First, you need to put your body under intense stress. Curling your phone up to your face won't do it. The exercise has to be the kind of new pain that shocks your system and causes microscopic tears in your muscles. Second, you need rest. A day or two away from the gym and lots of protein and sleep allow your body to fix that tear in a way that makes you stronger than ever before.

Your soul works the same way. In order to grow spiritually, God has to put you through stressful situations you're not used to. He has to stretch you and force you into uncomfortable positions. But then—and this is a massive truth—God has to give you rest, the kind of relief that comes through knowing Jesus is with you, for you, and working through you.

Paul describes the two parts of growth like this: **"We also glory in our sufferings, because we know that suffering produces perseverance; perseverance, character; and character, hope. And hope does not put us to shame, because God's love has been poured out into our hearts through the Holy Spirit, who has been given to us"** (in Romans 5:3-5).

Stress and rest. That's how you grow with God. Remember that and you'll be able to thank God on good days and bad.

What's gone is gone
Sarah Habben

Once while snorkeling, I adjusted my mask and knocked out an earring. It spiraled down to the ocean floor, where it was quickly covered by shifting sand. When it comes to the sea, what's gone is gone.

When a gracious God handles our shame, the same is true. **"You will again have compassion on us; you will tread our sins underfoot and hurl all our iniquities into the depths of the sea"** (Micah 7:19).

If we don't hunger for forgiveness, those words don't mean much. Micah lived during a time of prosperity. God's people were living the kind of comfortable lives that people of all-time figure God owes them. Easy lives led God's people to put him on a shelf and instead worship idols, money, and social position. They paid pastors to preach what they wanted to hear. They trampled society's underlings underfoot.

Micah warned the people of God's disastrous anger, but he also reminded them of God's compassion.

Micah's world sounds awfully familiar. We comfortable Christians often give God less adoration than we give our social media accounts. But when guilt and shame invade our hearts, our Instagram followers can't help us. We need a God of compassion.

And we have one. God sent his Son, who took the heat of hell in our place. He takes our sins and hurls them into the sea. We are forgiven, and how this lightens our hearts! Don't fish for the sin and guilt Jesus has removed.

What's gone is gone.

He's up!
Jan Gompper

Commercial insurance broker Sam Castronova posted the following on his weblog back in 2010: "*To all my Brothers out there trying to win the battles! Be the kind of man that when your feet hit the floor each morning the devil says, 'Oh crap; he's up!'*"

When I first read that quote, I couldn't help but wonder what Satan says about me when my feet hit the floor each day. Sadly, I feel he might often say, "Oh well, she's up again. No big deal. She poses no real threat to me."

And that's exactly how Satan wants me (and you) to feel. He wants us to think that we can never be the type of Christians we should be. He wants to sow the deadly seed of guilt in our hearts so that we may just want to stay in bed altogether.

But what makes Satan nervous is when we step out of bed, reminding him (and ourselves) that Christ has already given us the victory over him. And he trembles even more when we take our first steps with confidence, knowing that that the Holy Spirit walks with us and that **"it is God who works in** [us] **to will and to act in order to fulfill his good purpose"** (Philippians 2:13).

Christ's resurrection has already made the devil say, "*Oh crap; he's up!*" And every day we step out of bed, we have the privilege of rubbing that amazing salt into Satan's wounds.

Stop babbling in prayer
Pastor Mike Novotny

Have you ever noticed how hard it is for kids these days to get their dads' attention? In our smartphone, bring-work-home, screen-staring world, the average son has to wear his father down with many words. "Dad. Dad. Daddy. Dad! Hey, Dad. Look, Dad. Dad!" Maybe after babbling for a bit, his father will look up from his pixels and pay attention to his kid.

Our Father is not like that. Just before giving us the Lord's Prayer, Jesus taught, **"And when you pray, do not keep on babbling like pagans, for they think they will be heard because of their many words. Do not be like them, for your Father knows what you need before you ask him"** (Matthew 6:7,8). The pagan people of Greek culture believed that the gods were busy and didn't like to be bothered.

But the one true God is infinitely better than that. He wants to be interrupted. He wants you to knock on his door. He wants you to call upon him in your day of trouble and cast all your anxiety on him and keep asking him for the Holy Spirit. He is not an earthly father with a limited attention span but a Father in heaven who can't wait for you to open your lips and ask him for every good and perfect gift.

So pray. You don't need to repeat "Father" to get his full attention. What a promise! What a gift!

Pain is a tough test to pass
Pastor Mike Novotny

I so desperately want to remember God works spiritual gains through physical pains. Just like a tough workout leaves me sore today but stronger tomorrow, the sufferings of life are God's unique way of giving me a faith stronger than ever before.

But that's hard to appreciate in the moment, because Jesus doesn't let us control our pain. At the gym, we can slow down on the treadmill, lower our reps, or go home if we don't want to feel the burn anymore. But life isn't like that. You aren't in control of how much it hurts to lose a job, go through chemo, or struggle to pay the bills. Therefore, the pain can feel so overwhelming that we lose sight of what Jesus might be doing through it.

Perhaps that's why the apostle Paul couldn't talk too much about the purpose of pain before bringing up the promise of love. Romans chapter 5, an incredible section on what our Father does through our suffering, ends up here: **"God's love has been poured out into our hearts through the Holy Spirit, who has been given to us"** (Romans 5:5).

When pain gets the best of you, know the Holy Spirit is still with you. When your grumbling has out-worded your gratitude (again), know God's love is still being poured out. When you fail the test of pain, know Jesus endured his pain so you would always end up with a Father in heaven who loves to call you his dear child.

October

"Very truly I tell you," Jesus answered,
"before Abraham was born, I am!"

John 8:58

The archaeological gospel
Pastor Mike Novotny

In the spring of 2020, in a quiet museum in Jerusalem, I saw the price Jesus paid for our peace. Back in 1968, some building contractors stumbled upon a tomb just east of the city, and in the tomb they found a nail stuck through bone, the first surviving evidence of a crucifixion. That chunk of human heel and first-century metal now sits in a glass case, inviting museum goers to draw near and consider the horror of death on a cross.

As I inched my nose closer to that glass, I thought about the price Jesus paid so we could have peace with a perfect God. Isaiah's words felt fitting: **"The punishment that brought us peace was on him, and by his wounds we are healed"** (Isaiah 53:5).

I can't fathom the pain of having a nail driven through flesh and nerve and bone, but that is what Jesus chose. The God who owed us nothing, who himself needed nothing, gave up everything to put us first. The Prince with the crown laid it all down, laid himself down, and was himself lifted up so you could be first. The first to know you are forgiven. The first to know God isn't mad anymore. The first to know even if there's drama everywhere out there, there is none here, not with God.

This is why we marvel at the gospel and call Jesus our Prince of peace!

Pray the fine print
Pastor Daron Lindemann

Joab was a successful military commander in King David's army. His faith was bold. He was a fighter. Sometimes he struggled to keep his own ambitions in check. And sometimes he yielded his own preferences in faith to where God might lead.

This is one of those times. Joab was leading military campaigns to bring peace to the land for the building of the temple. He was speaking to Abishai, another commander, before each led a contingent of Israel's army to defeat enemies.

"If the Arameans are too strong for me, then you are to rescue me; but if the Ammonites are too strong for you, then I will rescue you. Be strong, and let us fight bravely for our people and the cities of our God. The Lord will do what is good in his sight" (1 Chronicles 19:12,13).

Sometimes we pray God into a corner. We become too attached to our own ideas and plans, and we don't reach out in faith to what God can do.

It's okay to pray for your ideas and plans. Just add some fine print, like Joab trusted in the Lord to do "what is good in his sight."

Joab was prepared to yield to the Lord's answer.

Dear God, thank you for hearing my prayers. You always hear and always answer in your perfect wisdom and love. Help me yield to your possibilities and purposes beyond my ideas and to trust you in them. Amen.

A new master
Sarah Habben

Imagine a certain sin. You're not just tolerating it like a stray dog that occasionally squeezes under your fence. But you feed it. Adopt it. *Adore* it. Maybe it's scorn for others who aren't as cool. Maybe it's an addiction to drink or drama or porn. Maybe it's lust or lies.

Soon enough, that sin isn't your pet but your master. You know it's wrong, but it brings you satisfaction . . . acceptance . . . *happiness.*

Or does it?

No.

Sin can only do what all sin does—separate you from your God forever. That sin you adore will be the death of you.

Maybe you've begged God to remove your temptation, to take the taste for it out of your mouth. Sadly, that's not how it works. Sin will dial your number as long as you live in this world. But that sin has no clout because of Jesus. **"Those who belong to Christ Jesus have crucified the flesh with its passions and desires"** (Galatians 5:4).

You belong to Jesus. He nailed your sinful passion to his cross; it dangles there, a pathetic master. Oh, it still has breath—it coaxes and threatens and beckons. But you don't need to listen. In your heart sits another Master—your risen Savior. He hasn't just set you free from the penalty of sin. He's set you free from its *power.*

When temptation crooks a finger your way, nail it to the cross. Your heart belongs to someone better: your faithful, forgiving, forever-loving God.

Rising above
Pastor Jon Enter

Have you experienced the Ark Encounter in Kentucky? It's near impossible to walk through this built-to-size replica of Noah's ark without being in awe. 450 feet long. 75 feet wide. 45 feet tall. The volume God planned for this floating zoo is massive: 1.5 million cubic feet of storage. That's the capacity of 569 railroad stock cars creating a train 5.5 miles long!

God had a plan, a big plan, to save humanity. But it was going to take work, big work, from Noah's family. They had to hand cut all those trees. Move them by animal. And somehow shape them and lift them into place with no modern machinery. Then they had to collect pitch/tar to coat the boat inside and out and grow, gather, and store all the food for all the animals for all the days on the ark.

Do you remember why this happened? **"Every inclination of the thoughts of the human heart was only evil all the time"** (Genesis 6:5). How many times was Noah's lumber stolen or harvested crops eaten? Frustrating! But for those animals, all they needed was to be in the ark. The work was done for them.

It took a lot of work, big work, to save you. Jesus cut down your sin. He moved you into faith with the Holy Spirit. And he feeds you daily in Word and sacrament. Jesus did all the work of saving you. As long as you are within the holy ark of the church in faith, you will rise above and be safe!

Almost sunk
Pastor Jon Enter

In yesterday's devotion, we discussed the massive work Noah's family dedicated for decades building the ark. The ark was so huge it could fit seven college-sized basketball courts on each of its three levels! I can't imagine what it took to complete.

What accomplishment are you particularly proud of? Your culinary skills? A sports championship? First chair in band? An academic award? Your career? Your kids?

We tend to find our worth in what we do. When we're asked to tell others about ourselves, we often start with our work. We look to see how we measure up to others and then base our value on that comparison. The devil knows this and feeds into our insecurity or pride, depending upon whom it is we're comparing ourselves to.

That's why I love what God did with Noah. Noah built a floating zoo and saved humanity. But to stop Noah from sinking into pride, watch the brilliance of God's wisdom. All the animals marched two by two into the ark. The rains were coming. **"Then the Lord shut him in"** (Genesis 7:16). The door to the ark was wide enough for an elephant and tall enough for a giraffe. Without the Lord sealing them in, Noah's work was worthless.

The same is true for you. Use well the abilities the Lord has given you, but don't find your worth in your work. Your worth is in the Lord, in his love for you as he seals you in faith and gives worth to your work.

A sincere relationship
Andrea Delwiche

Have you received a beautiful gift from someone and thought, "Instead of this, I would rather have had a chance to sit and talk to you for a couple hours" or, "I would rather you showed by your words and actions that you respect and love me"?

God says something similar in Psalm 50: **"I have no need of a bull from your stall or of goats from your pens. 'Sacrifice thank offerings to God, fulfill your vows to the Most High, and call on me in the day of trouble; I will deliver you, and you will honor me'"** (verses 9,14,15). Rather than a showy sacrifice, God would love a real relationship with you where you talk with each other and do things for each other in an exchange of gratitude, love, and trust.

God deeply desires a sincere relationship with you and me. Everything else is meaningless if it isn't from a heart that loves God above all else.

What if we don't know if we love God in this way? What if we suspect that we *don't* love God in this way but we would like to change?

We learn to love someone in a steadfast way by spending time with them, listening and responding with interest to what they tell us about themselves. Similarly, the more time we spend with our Lord, the better we will know him and come to love him with a deep and grateful heart and worship him in an honest way that will delight him.

Helping each other up
Linda Buxa

I was running on a treadmill across the gym from a weight-lifting club. (I used voice-to-text to get my devotional thoughts down on my phone!) During warm-ups, the members of the club chatted, stretched, and laughed. As the workout began, everyone was at her own bar, lifting lighter weights. But as each lifter went for a higher and higher number, the group dropped their own weights, surrounded the lifter, and shouted like crazy. Nobody could step in and lift the weights for her, because it was her workout. But the heavier the weights, the louder they cheered.

It's the same when you are part of a group of people who believe in Jesus. God puts people together so you are surrounded by people who will laugh with you during the easier parts of life. The minute things get heavy, they will drop everything to surround you. They can't do the hard work for you, but they are cheering you on.

Cheering when life is hard looks a little different though. It most often means sitting next to you, crying with you, taking you to rehab, sending you a text, cleaning your house, holding you accountable, or praying with you. And you do the same for them. **"Two are better than one, because they have a good return for their labor: If either of them falls down, one can help the other up"** (Ecclesiastes 4:9,10).

Hope will not be canceled
Pastor Mike Novotny

2020 was the year of the cancellation. Vacations were canceled. Sports seasons were canceled. Conferences were canceled. The coronavirus meant that nearly everything was "wait and see" at best and already canceled at worst.

But that is why I love Joe's T-shirt. Joe is part of the *Time of Grace* camera crew who uses his gifts to get the message from my church to your screen. He is also the guy who has an impressive collection of really cool Christian T-shirts. One of my favorites from Joe's wardrobe is a simple black shirt that declares, "Hope will not be canceled."

Hope is a for-sure future, a guarantee that is only possible because our God knows and controls the future. The author of Hebrews reminds us, **"Let us hold unswervingly to the hope we profess, for he who promised is faithful"** (10:23). You can hold tight to the promises of God because the Promiser is faithful. What God says, God does.

So take heart. All the things in your life will work out for good (even the divorce you didn't choose). Your labor to love that prickly neighbor next door is not in vain (even if he refuses to warm up to you). Your habitual prayers are powerful (even if you feel like you're talking to the air and nothing more).

The hope of future blessings will not be canceled, because the God who promised is faithful.

Jesus is the middleman
Pastor Clark Schultz

Being caught in the middle isn't the most enjoyable position to be in. A traffic cop directing cars at a busy intersection where an accident has occurred can have it tough. A mom working out the differences between two siblings doesn't have an easy task. In a contract dispute, an arbitrator has to tread lightly so as not to show favoritism. Being a middleman or a go-between isn't always the spot people want to be in. The Old Testament leader Moses knew what that was like, but the Lord knew why Moses was there. **"For this is what you asked of the Lᴏʀᴅ your God at Horeb on the day of the assembly when you said, 'Let us not hear the voice of the Lᴏʀᴅ our God nor see this great fire anymore, or we will die.' The Lᴏʀᴅ said to me: 'What they say is good. I will raise up for them a prophet like you from among their fellow Israelites, and I will put my words in his mouth. He will tell them everything I command him'"** (Deuteronomy 18:16-18). Moses was the middleman delivering the Lord's message to his people.

Now take a trip past Sinai to Calvary, where we see God's ultimate mediation. Jesus, God's own perfect Son, took the full wrath of God for the sins of the world. And that one-time sacrifice has ongoing effects. Today our Savior continues as he sits at the right hand of his Father, pleading and putting in a word for you every day until he welcomes you into his arms.

So much love
Pastor Mike Novotny

Three weeks ago, I visited a woman from our church who was dying of cancer. We crowded into her bedroom—me, her daughter, her son, her son-in-law, and her two grandkids—and I wish you could have been there because there was so much love in that room. You could see how much she loved her family and how much they loved her right back. Even better, there was no doubt this family loved God, quoting promises from his Word and confessing with their lips that they worshiped Jesus Christ as the sin-erasing Lord and death-conquering Savior.

But the best part was hearing how much God loved them. The dying woman smiled and asked, "Pastor, why does God love us? I'm kind of a pain in the backside." Yet, despite her amazement at grace, she knew all about Jesus' unconditional love. Maybe that's why her granddaughter suddenly burst out singing, "Yes, Jesus loves me! Yes, Jesus loves me! Yes, Jesus loves me! The Bible tells me so."

Yes, the Bible does. And, yes, Jesus loves you. **"This is love: not that we loved God, but that God loved us and sent his Son as an atoning sacrifice for our sins"** (1 John 4:10). Praise God for being our unfailing source of unfailing love. And may that love compel us to fill more rooms and more families with so much love.

As good as it gets
Pastor Matt Ewart

Sometimes I empty the dishwasher even though I could have pretended I didn't know it was clean. Sometimes I clean out the garbage from the family car even though 99% of it isn't mine. Sometimes I hold the door open for a few more people than common courtesy calls for.

Why do I do those things? Sometimes it's because I want to reflect the love God showed me. But if I'm honest, sometimes I do them out of selfish pride.

Pride loves to be in charge of our motives. And even though you and I know better, pride wants everyone to think that when it comes to people in this world, *we are as good as it gets*.

King Solomon, who was way more "as good as it gets" than you and me, learned something important when it comes to the pride that loves to take hold of our motives:

"When pride comes, then comes disgrace, but with humility comes wisdom" (Proverbs 11:2).

Some forms of pride are outwardly obvious. But most forms of pride can only be detected through personal introspection. Today, think about why it is you do the good things you do. Remember that when it comes to what is at the center of your life and when it comes to everything your achievements stand for, Jesus is as good as it gets.

Assigned reading
Pastor Daron Lindemann

It feels like a grueling reading assignment. Ever had one of those?

You have to finish the book. Not by your choice. No, your supervisor at work or your therapist demands it.

It's like a year that has brought us some problems, a bit of pain, and the aftershock of various troubles. We didn't choose it. But it is our assignment.

As with most difficulties and disappointments in this life, we just want them to go away. Because we assume that without them, life will be better.

Please pay attention here. God doesn't see it that way.

God isn't interested in removing everything unpleasant from your life. Because he sees a better version of you than you can see. He knows you can grow, become stronger, and be filled with much more grace, kindness, and forgiveness than you think you can.

The apostle Paul was imprisoned for being a Christian. He didn't ask for it. But there he was. How did he see his unpleasant and painful assignment?

"I have learned the secret of being content in any and every situation, whether well fed or hungry, whether living in plenty or in want. I can do all this through him who gives me strength" (Philippians 4:12,13).

Instead of seeing the past year as a bad book, see it with the faith that can say, "I learned something. It taught me about myself and my God. I discovered what is truly important. I found strength in Jesus Christ more than my circumstances."

The cross—A compilation
Pastor Mike Novotny

One of my favorite parts of being a pastor is having the time to pull on the threads of the Bible. Every few days, I open a website that allows me to type in a Bible word—like *grace* or *faith* or *kingdom*—and see precisely how many times it shows up, which books of the Bible use it the most, and how often Jesus himself quoted that word. Recently, I did the same with the word *cross*.

Ready for a lot of good news? According to some of the 33 appearances of cross, **"'he himself bore our sins' in his body on the cross"** (1 Peter 2:24). **"[He] canceled the charge of our legal indebtedness, which stood against us and condemned us; he has taken it away, nailing it to the cross"** (Colossians 2:14). "[God made] **peace through his blood, shed on the cross**" (Colossians 1:20). **"To us who are being saved** [the message of the cross] **is the power of God"** (1 Corinthians 1:18). Through the cross, we have peace, healing, forgiveness, sins taken away, no condemnation, more peace, salvation, and power. That's what's loaded in the cross!

Take a moment to meditate on the passages above. Perhaps pick just one and let its truth soak down into your soul. Because there are many powerful words in the Scriptures, but few are as inspiring to our souls as the cross.

Fear of missing out
Pastor Matt Ewart

"So the Lᴏʀᴅ God banished him from the Garden of Eden to work the ground from which he had been taken" (Genesis 3:23).

You have it in every stage of life. As a child, you don't want to go to bed while the adults are still awake. A little older, and you get a sick feeling when your friends are at a party but you were not invited. When older, you don't want to miss out on time with the young people you love.

Fear of missing out looks different for everyone, but it is always there in one form or another. What does that currently look like for you?

The reason I am so convinced that everyone wrestles with this is because it goes back to the very beginning. We were created to dwell with God in his paradise. But sin changed that.

Adam and Eve were the first to experience the loss of God's presence in the Garden of Eden. Ever since then, we have within us a spark of fear over all the other things we stand to lose.

Maybe your fear of losing something stems from the fact that you have already lost something or someone precious. I understand how fear can be part of you.

But because of Jesus, fear does not have to rule over you. He promises to restore everything that was lost in Eden. Live by faith in the One who conquers every fear.

See the unseen
Pastor Jon Enter

The stars are magnificent. When it's a crisp, clear night with twinkle-twinkly stars glowing bright, you get a glimpse of the expanse of God's greatness. In one day, just one 24-hour period, God spoke, and it was. The universe was and is and continues to be.

Look up and see God's handiwork for you. Look up and know God pinpointed each star into its place, each planet into its existence. You see the unseen. Oh, the stars are beautifully visible, but you didn't see God plop them into place. Yet your faith trusts he did. You see the unseen. Oh, the sun is unmistakably present, but you didn't witness God setting it ablaze. Yet your faith trusts he did. You see the unseen. You see with eyes of faith the brushstrokes of God's loving hand in each sunset. You see the unseen power of the all-powerful as your eyes marvel at creation.

There are many times when you can't see how life will work out. The devil whispers that God is not powerful enough or present enough to help. **"The heavens declare the glory of God; the skies proclaim the work of his hands"** (Psalm 19:1). Creation commands that God is powerful. After thousands of years, creation is still balanced and beautifully proclaims God is present. You are not alone. If he took so much care creating the cosmos and even crawfish, how much more care does he have for you, whom he sent his Son to save!

Peace has a price
Pastor Mike Novotny

I have a theory as to why there are so many wars between countries, so much drama within families, and so little love in our local communities. My theory is that peace has a price. If you and I truly want to live in peace with each other, we both need to pay a hard-to-swallow price—our own desires.

Think of all the wars that erupt when two parties both prioritize "me first." Two preschoolers both want the same plastic dump truck. Two sisters both want to take the first shower. Two brothers both want their idea for how to care for their mother. Two significant others want the other to apologize first. Two nations both want the same land. Pick any topic—a church budget, where the dishes go after dinner, how often spouses are intimate—and "me first" will make a mess.

This actually isn't my original theory. Jesus' half brother James said it first: **"What causes fights and quarrels among you? Don't they come from your desires that battle within you?"** (James 4:1).

Today I want you to think about any less than peaceful relationships in your life. Is part of the problem your own desires to get what you want? Take some time to talk it over with God, asking him for forgiveness for your sins as well as the power to pay the price for peace. The price isn't cheap, but seeking peace is always worth it.

Seeing the future
Linda Buxa

Most of our stress is because of the unknown. How will the kids turn out? What will retirement look like? Will I be able to make rent this month? Will our relationship survive?

So much is unknown that our prayers get a little panicky. "Dear God, what am I going to do? How is this going to work out? Please just fix it."

Really, we are asking God to let us see the future. That's not how it works. You know what though? We can see the past.

In his Word, God reminds us of the great things Jesus has already accomplished: living a perfect life (and giving us credit for that), dying a painful death (so we don't have to), and rising from the dead (so we can be with him forever). Which, really, gives us a glimpse of our eternal future.

"In his great mercy he has given us new birth into a living hope through the resurrection of Jesus Christ from the dead, and into an inheritance that can never perish, spoil or fade. . . . In all this you greatly rejoice, though now for a little while you may have had to suffer grief in all kinds of trials. These have come so that the proven genuineness of your faith—of greater worth than gold, which perishes even though refined by fire—may result in praise, glory and honor when Jesus Christ is revealed" (1 Peter 1:3-7).

God and the 5 love languages
Pastor Mike Novotny

Have you ever heard of or read the book the *5 Love Languages*? This classic on relationships has sold more than 13,000,000 copies because of its simple but powerful concept. The concept is that we each tend to show love and feel loved in one of five ways—gifts, time, touch, works, and words. When your mom or your best friend or your boyfriend speaks "your language," you will feel incredibly loved. (Anyone who likes touch and has recently gotten a back rub is saying, "Amen!")

It hit me that the God of love speaks all the languages. God sent his one and only Son into the world as the best *gift* ever in order to spend quality *time* with people as he walked the earth. In his conception and birth, Jesus took on flesh and blood, which meant you could *touch* his hands and side after he was risen from the dead. On the cross, our Savior did the ultimate *work*, proving that he did not come to be served but rather to serve us. Through faith in his sacrifice, believers get to hear the stunning *words* of the gospel—you are loved, forgiven, and safe from sin and death and hell.

I don't know your love language, but I do know that the God of love speaks it. So, beloved, be loved today, knowing that God is speaking your language. **"This is how God showed his love among us: He sent his one and only Son into the world that we might live through him"** (1 John 4:9).

He loves me!
Karen Spiegelberg

"He loves me; he loves me not. He loves me; he loves me not." This is a common phrase spoken by adolescents as they pluck one petal at a time from a daisy to determine if their crush indeed cares for them. It's not really a surefire determination of one's love for another, but it's a fun game nonetheless. Okay, okay, I'll admit that I even indulged in that silly game in my younger years.

Thankfully, I don't have to destroy a flower to determine if God loves me! In Psalm 23:6 David assures me, **"Surely your goodness and love will follow me *all* the days of my life, and I will dwell in the house of the Lord forever."** This is a promise I can cling to. God's love is always present and never changing. He has loved me from eternity and throughout my entire life. He loves me every day as much as he did on Good Friday, the day he died for my sins. More than that, God's love for me isn't based on how good I am but solely on his promise to be merciful to me. And he will still love me on the day that I die. Then, I will dwell in his presence forever!

Adolescent games of love predictions can be put aside. God loves me; he loves me; he loves me! And he loves you just the same.

God holds the cards
Pastor Daron Lindemann

What do these four kings have in common: David, Charlemagne, Caesar, and Alexander? These are the kings of hearts, spades, diamonds, and clubs in a deck of cards. But where is the King of kings? Where in a deck of cards is the supreme Commander of the universe?

Any ruler in our world may have authority over a certain domain, but ultimately Jesus Christ has authority over all domains and rulers—even corrupt rulers who abuse their authority and power.

Pharaoh chased down Moses and the Israelites, but the Lord used Pharaoh for his own purposes, saying, **"I will gain glory through Pharaoh and all his army, through his chariots and his horsemen"** (Exodus 14:17).

Martin Luther once remarked, "God looks upon kings as children look upon playing cards."

The slavery in and exodus from Egypt served God's plan of salvation for sinners. The destruction of Jerusalem and foreign captivity served God's plan of salvation for sinners. The pharaohs and Nebuchadnezzars of today continue to serve God's plan of salvation for sinners.

God has every government and government leader in his hand to help him accomplish his saving plan.

Read Psalm 118:9 and meditate on it in prayer. Be honest and confess where you have trusted in this world's governments to give you what only God can give you. Turn to him in repentance, and trust God more than government.

With God's help, you can change
Andrea Delwiche

Psalm 51 is famously a song and prayer of repentance. I encourage you to read all 19 verses. God had allowed King David's life to unravel because of David's violations of God's own good guidelines. With his life at rock bottom, David turned to God for help.

David may have looked the perfect king as he walked the halls of his palace, but God was not interested in a pretty exterior. Under the surface, David was dwelling in deep sin and self-deception. He had cut himself off from God's transformative peace. Similarly, when power plays, deceit, and disgust toward others runs rampant in our hearts, our soothing words and plastered smiles don't fool God.

God doesn't just plaster over our cracks to make us look like good Christians. He wants to work at our foundation to build us into individuals who dwell in the deep truths of his kingdom. This is good news! Building something beautiful is slow work, but each day, with effort and the Holy Spirit providing the power, we do change.

Daily we can pray this prayer of David's: **"Enter me, [Lord]; conceive a new, true life"** (Psalm 51:6 MSG).

Grace = "no way!" love
Pastor Mike Novotny

There are many helpful ways to define the word *grace*. I grew up reciting, "Grace is undeserved love." Others have suggested that grace is an acronym—GRACE—which stands for "God's Riches At Christ's Expense." If I could add to those helpful definitions, I would propose that grace is love that makes you say, "No way!"

Jesus chose Matthew, a Jewish sellout who worked for Rome just to fill his pockets? No way! Jesus chose Mary Magdalene, once possessed by seven demons (imagine her past profile pictures!) to be the first witness of his resurrection? No way! Jesus chose Peter, a Galilean verbal processor who spoke before he thought or prayed? No way! Jesus chose Paul, a violent, obsessed, ignorant murderer of the church to be on the leadership team of Christianity? No way! But, as you may know, that's exactly what Jesus did, because he is a Savior who is full of grace.

For you too. Christianity is not an Ivy League religion but one for killers and critical people, tax collectors and troublemakers, prostitutes and people who've slept around, for sex offenders and bulldozer moms. This faith doesn't give people a second chance to get things right but instead declares at the cross that we are God's own, once and for all. Jesus chooses people like us to be holy, blameless, and pure in the sight of God, and he died and rose to get the job done.

Logic would object—No way! But Jesus smiles and says, "Yes way. That's grace."

Replacing thieves
Pastor Matt Ewart

We usually reserve the term *addiction* for the really bad stuff. Being labeled as an *addict* carries with it many stigmas.

But in a way, everybody suffers from addictions in one way or another. It's just that most of our addictions are so hidden that they are hard for anyone to notice—sometimes even ourselves.

An addiction is anything that takes time, energy, or focus away from the most important things in your life. I like to think of an addiction as a thief. It takes more than it gives, even if it always promises the opposite.

We often think of things like drugs or alcohol. Addictions to substances can rob a person of resources, energy, time, and focus.

But there are also addictions to good things and good tools, such as recreations, exercise, electronics, and hobbies. Good things can rob your attention from the best things. Things the Bible doesn't label as "sinful" can be thieves that promise you happiness and fulfillment but only leave you empty.

If you are thinking of something in your life right now that might be a thief, don't just get rid of it or delete it. Replace it with grace. Meditate on the fullness of life that Jesus has already given to you through his forgiveness. Redirect your whole being to find its peace and purpose in one place:

"Love the Lord your God with all your heart and with all your soul and with all your strength" (Deuteronomy 6:5).

Free!
Pastor Clark Schultz

The Judiciary Act of 1789 was passed by Congress and signed by President Washington, establishing the Supreme Court of the United States as a tribunal made up of six justices who were to serve on the court until death or retirement. This court grew into the most important judicial body in the world in terms of its central place in the American political order. In times of constitutional crisis, the nation's highest court has always played a definitive role in resolving, for better or worse, the great issues of the time.

Naturally, if the Son of God was to be put on trial, he would be worthy of the highest court. Instead, he got Caiaphas, a corrupt high priest who succeeded his more corrupt father-in-law, Annas.

After a slew of false witnesses couldn't collaborate their stories, Caiaphas pulled his last card: **"The high priest said to him, 'I charge you under oath by the living God: Tell us if you are the Messiah, the Son of God.' 'You have said so,' Jesus replied"** (Matthew 26:63,64). Irony of ironies, Jesus was and is the Son of God, and his very confession is what convicted him.

Okay, our turn. Our trial is coming on the Last Day, when all our sins will be exposed. What will our plea be? Not Guilty. Huh? Friends, that is the beauty of the cross. What laws did Jesus break? None. By faith the Father credits Jesus' perfection to us. Because Christ paid the price, we leave the judgment day courtroom of the Judge not guilty and free!

Jesus sticks close
Pastor Mike Novotny

I was preparing to teach a message about choosing friends wisely when I had a scary thought—Would Jesus want to be friends with me? If he was listening to me quote the proverb about choosing friends carefully, would Jesus invite me out for coffee or would he stay far, far away from me? After all, the Bible warns about getting close to fools, and I have certainly done my share of foolish things in life. Solomon, in his wisdom, encouraged us to walk with wise people, but I don't often look back at my week and consider it brimming with wise choices. So what would Jesus do with me? Or with you?

Thankfully, this passage gave me hope: **"There is a friend who sticks closer than a brother"** (Proverbs 18:24). There is someone who will stick by you even when flesh and blood keep their distance. His name is Jesus. Even though our Savior knew that a companion of fools suffers harm (Proverbs 13:20), Jesus became the companion who would suffer for our sake. Despite knowing everything about us, he still chose to be with us. As we work on our "walk," he graciously insists on walking with us, forgiving us when we stray off the path and strengthening our spiritual muscles with his Word and Spirit. When all other friends fade and fall away, our Savior stays.

What a friend we have in Jesus!

Don't be you
Pastor Mike Novotny

One of the most offensive things Jesus ever said was, **"Whoever wants to be my disciple must deny themselves and take up their cross and follow me"** (Mark 8:34). Ponder the words *whoever, must, deny,* and *themselves,* and you'll realize why *offensive* is the right description of Jesus' teaching.

In saying this, Jesus is rejecting the number-one theme of modern culture—Be you. Be true to yourself. Embrace yourself. Live your truth. The theme of nearly every movie we market at children is, apparently, the exact opposite of what Jesus said. Do you know why Jesus said it? Two reasons come to mind:

First, because we are creatures of comfort. If a sin makes us feel good, we will choose it, regardless of what Jesus has to say on the matter. Therefore, to follow Jesus down his road, we must deny the desire to take our own road and trust he is leading us to the greatest long-term comfort.

Second, because grace is not logical. Our brains can't make sense of a love that is given to people who absolutely don't deserve it. So if we are to find any comfort in being loved for ever and ever, then we must deny our natural inclinations of earning/deserving/being worthy and instead follow Jesus to his cross and empty tomb. It might be irrational for God to forgive us freely for everything, but this is the foolishness of the gospel.

Don't be yourself. Be what God has called you to be—a repentant sinner who becomes a saint through Jesus.

Heaven ahead
Sarah Habben

Antigua boasts 365 beaches, one for each day of the year. I dispute the math, but I do have a favorite beach. It's called Seaforth. Picture an almost-deserted mile of curving white sand cupped by lumpy green mountains and water in deepening shades of turquoise. It's a slice of heaven.

But there's a problem. This beach is tucked away in the backlands at the end of a hazardously rocky road. Our van bounced along that road like an unbroken horse, bottoming out on rocks. Just when our nerves couldn't handle another second—there was the ocean.

Heaven awaits those who put their trust in Jesus. He's the only Way there. But there's a problem. The road to heaven is narrow and rough. Christians don't have it easy just because we trust the King of kings. In fact, Jesus tells his followers to expect the road to be plenty rough.

"Blessed are you when people insult you, persecute you and falsely say all kinds of evil against you because of me. Rejoice and be glad, because great is your reward in heaven" (Matthew 5:11,12).

Ask Christians around the world whose lives and vocations bottom out because they confess Christ. Ask university students who are demeaned for their faith and labeled as haters and bigots. Ask those who are ridiculed by family members for needing a "crutch" like religion.

But then ask Jesus. He looks at your emotional scratches and dents and calls you blessed. When life gets rough, he says, "Rejoice."

At the end of the road is a great reward.

Jesus is more than a carpenter
Pastor Daron Lindemann

Last year my wife and I had a new home built for the first time in our lives together. Our builder has handled some warranty repair issues gladly and completely. But sometimes the warranty department supervisor has to take it to the next level with some contractors to get things done. I'm glad for his authority and responsiveness (and for a home warranty, although it expires soon).

But get this; there is a supervisor of the supervisor. His authority and responsiveness are even better and will not expire at all. His name is Jesus. He is more than a carpenter. He's more than a supervisor who can take things to the next level. He is the builder's Son, his right-hand man, and he personally has authority and responsiveness for everything in my life.

Better yet, Jesus isn't building me a place to live where I can cook a scrumptious meal or sleep soundly in a comfortable bedroom. Jesus is building me. I am "his house."

Jesus is given responsibility by the Father to take care of me, to bless me with his grace even though I sin and fail, to fix me and heal me, and to make sure I meet God's standards.

"For every house is built by someone, but God is the builder of everything. But Christ is faithful as the Son over God's house. And we are his house, if indeed we hold firmly to our confidence and the hope in which we glory" (Hebrews 3:4,6).

Final words
Pastor Jon Enter

Only two people haven't experienced death and are physically enjoying heaven. Just two. Enoch, who walked with God right into heaven (Genesis 5:24), and Elijah, who was carried past death into glory in a whirlwind (2 Kings 2:11). Unless the skies peel open and you see Jesus descending with all the heavenly hosts with him, there's a pretty good shot that you'll experience death.

That can be a scary thought. Death. So final. So inescapable. Many Christians fear death itself and then feel guilty. They wonder, "Do I have weak faith that I'm honestly afraid of death?"

Have peace; you can fear death and still have strong faith. There's nothing wrong with fearing the possible pain and process of death. That's natural. That's human. We are built with a natural fear of death to stop us from doing dumb, reckless things that kill us. But if you don't fear what happens eternally after death, you have confident faith. In the end your soul will speak with the same boldness as your dear Savior, **"Father, into your hands I commit my spirit"** (Luke 23:46).

Faith speaks as we spend our last minutes on earth. Author Heinrich Heine proclaimed, "God will forgive me. It is his profession." Pastor John Newton, author of the famous hymn "Amazing Grace," declared in faith: "I am in the land of the dying, and I am soon going to the land of the living." Faith speaks.

What do you want your final words of faith to be?

What are you ashamed of?
Karen Spiegelberg

Is there anything that you are ashamed of? Apparently, my oldest daughter could answer that question emphatically. I was parked with our family minivan outside of a dance studio waiting for my youngest daughter. The other two kids were waiting with me. Suddenly, the 12-year-old unbuckled her seat belt and started scurrying around picking up empty snack wrappers, fast-food bags, and random garbage. I asked, "What are you doing?" She very sternly replied, "Mom, I am not ashamed of the gospel, but I am ashamed of this van!"

I'm not sure that the apostle Paul, as he addressed the Gentile believers in Rome, could have imagined his words being used in such a sentence. He couldn't even have imagined a motorized vehicle like a van! He probably did pray that his unabashed love for the good news of Jesus Christ would live on in believers around the world. When Paul stated in Romans 1:16, **"For I am not ashamed of the gospel, because it is the power of God that brings salvation to everyone who believes,"** he explained why proclaiming Jesus' message was his life's work. And our life's work.

It was an unexpected gift to have my daughter clean up our messy van that day, but the bigger gift was hearing her proclamation of confidence in the gospel message. Let us all proclaim with childlike boldness the truth of God's Word. No fear and no shame!

Faith in what?

Pastor Mike Novotny

Our culture is infatuated with faith. An 80s pop song told us, "You just gotta have faith," and Disney constantly preaches, "Just believe." College sports teams hang "Believe" banners over their locker room doors. But what does that mean exactly? Believe in what? in whom? and why? After all, faith in the wrong person can leave you deeply disappointed. Good faith needs the right something to hold on to, the right someone to trust in.

That's why the Christian faith is about trusting Christ. When it comes to being right with God, we don't trust in ourselves, our hearts, our moral resumes, our ethical stats, or our best efforts to be good. No, we trust in Jesus. We have faith in Jesus. We rely upon the perfect life of Jesus, the sacrificial death of Jesus, and the glorious resurrection of Jesus. We believe the only way we can escape the danger of our sins and the only way we can see God's glorious face is through faith specifically in Jesus Christ, the Son of God.

This is why Paul got specific when speaking about faith. He wrote to the Romans, **"This righteousness is given through faith in Jesus Christ to all who believe"** (3:22). Catch that? Faith *in Jesus.*

Everyone has faith in something. Everyone relies on someone to give them hope. The next time someone says they "have faith" or are a person "of faith," ask them a simple question—Faith in what? Then tell them about whom your faith is in.

November

Enter his gates with thanksgiving and his courts with praise; give thanks to him and praise his name.

Psalm 100:4

What scale are you using?
Linda Buxa

I stepped on the corner of our scale in the dark, and the plastic foot broke. Great. No woman really wants to confess that she broke the bathroom scale, but I did. So off I went to the store to get a new one.

We took the new one out of the box and used it the next morning. Immediately my husband and I gained three to five pounds. What in the world?!

Did we really gain weight? Nope. We were just using a different standard. Even though I knew I hadn't actually gained weight, I still felt a little discouraged. (I know. That's weird.)

Depending on what standard you use for your identity, it's easy to get discouraged too. You might get the feeling that your value is based on your weight or your income or your marital status or your ability to reproduce or your age or how good of a pray-er you are.

It's wiser and leaves you feeling more at peace if you use God's standard for your identity. **"But now, this is what the LORD says—he who created you, Jacob, he who formed you, Israel: 'Do not fear, for I have redeemed you; I have summoned you by name; you are mine'"** (Isaiah 43:1).

You are his. No matter your income, popularity, weight, or health status. He felt you were valuable enough to form you, redeem you, and call you his child. This is the only scale that ultimately matters.

Shame is an essential worker
Pastor Mike Novotny

This might seem odd to say, but shame is an essential worker in the kingdom of God. If the sinful actions that came from the sinful desires of your sinful heart never grieve or humiliate you, you might be in a dangerous spiritual place. This is why the prophet Jeremiah lamented, **"Are they ashamed of their detestable conduct? No, they have no shame at all; they do not even know how to blush"** (6:15). Blushing isn't always bad. There are times, according to God, when we should be ashamed.

During my first years of ministry, I met the strip club fiancé. A young woman from our church got engaged to a guy who, right there in the pastor's office, locked eyes, grinned, and told me (and his bride-to-be) that he liked strip clubs. He was not ashamed. Later, I saw them in the parking lot. While I couldn't hear their words, I could see her slumped shoulders and hanging head. Their relationship couldn't survive when he felt no shame for his shameful acts.

A relationship with God is the same way. While Jesus knows that you will struggle with many sins in many ways, he wants you to be ashamed of them. So if you have chosen your way instead of God's way, if you have talked back to the mother who sacrificed so much for you, if you get more excited about a game than God, blush about it. Sin is shameful, so be ashamed.

You will find that our gracious Savior will lift up your head and take your shame away.

Read. Write. Worship.
Sarah Habben

Sometimes I feel too busy to read my Bible. But I came across this passage about God's expectations for the kings of Israel, men who had their hands full:

"When he takes the throne of his kingdom, he is to write for himself on a scroll a copy of [God's] law, taken from that of the Levitical priests. It is to be with him, and he is to read it all the days of his life so that he may learn to revere the LORD his God and follow carefully all the words of this law and these decrees and not consider himself better than his fellow Israelites" (Deuteronomy 17:18-20).

Imagine if that was the first thing on our national leaders' agendas . . . copying a significant portion of the Bible with their own pens. Who knows how their strategies might change?

Imagine if that was your boss' first priority each day—to "read and obey" God's Word. How might your workplace change?

Now imagine if *you* were to write a passage a day and reflect on it. How might that change the way you speak to your spouse, encourage your children, do your duties, or pray for your leaders?

Imagine knowing God better: the God whom angels worship, whom Satan couldn't defeat nor death hold.

Imagine the Spirit working through your daily study so you have power—not to please yourself but to do what is pleasing to God.

Now stop imagining and start reading . . . writing . . . worshiping.

Tune your ears to hope
Pastor Mike Novotny

Back in 1982, the Wisconsin Badgers played Michigan State in a Big Ten football game on the same day the Milwaukee Brewers played the St. Louis Cardinals in game 4 of the World Series. Since local fans couldn't be both places at the same time, many attended the football game but listened in on small radios to get the play-by-play of the baseball game, which made for one of the more interesting events of the year. On certain plays where the Badgers were a mess, the fans roared with joy because the radios brought the news of a Brewers' hit. There was another source of good news that those fans couldn't see but they could hear.

Sound familiar? If you open your Bible (or Bible app) during the week, you are like those Badger fans in the stands. **"But those who hope in the LORD will renew their strength. They will soar on wings like eagles; they will run and not grow weary, they will walk and not be faint"** (Isaiah 40:31).

What you see in front of you might make you weary—an endless list of to-dos, tests, projects, and parenting tasks. But when your ears are tuned in to the promises of God, you have an alternative source of good news. God's love for you in Christ renews your strength and enables you to walk, run, and eventually soar by the Spirit's power.

If life is complicated right now, please prioritize time with the "radio" of God's Word. Your heart will thank you later.

Firmly rooted
Andrea Delwiche

There are different ways to approach life. One approach is to amass power, wealth, influence, and knowledge to have an edge over others. It's a life that positions us against anyone who might possibly have any sort of advantage over us or our loved ones.

We may have grown up in homes where this was a hidden family value. Perhaps you or I have passed this mentality on to our own children, and they too live in constant competition, an elaborate manipulation of power and reputation.

And then there's the other way. The way of Christ and his followers. **"I am like an olive tree flourishing in the house of God; I trust in God's unfailing love for ever and ever. For what you have done I will always praise you in the presence of your faithful people. And I will hope in your name, for your name is good"** (Psalm 52:8,9).

An olive tree is firmly rooted in its native soil. An olive tree depends on its roots and leaves to drink in water and sun. It grows and thrives with the vital nutrients that God gives.

How can we, like the psalmist, be olive trees in God's kingdom? Take time to explore with the Holy Spirit this image of grace-filled sufficiency. What would it look like to think of yourself as an olive tree planted and rooted in God's provision?

Good or good?

Pastor Mike Novotny

Years ago my daughter went to the store with her grandma and wanted to buy a new toy. Thankfully, my baby had money in her pocket, so she pulled out the two pennies and one dime to show off. Twelve cents, which was pretty good for a kid her age. But grandma had to explain that what was good for a little girl wasn't good enough for a big store. She was about one percent of the way there for the $12 toy. When Maya heard the news, she broke down crying.

That story reminds me of the difference between being a "good" person and being "Good" enough to get into heaven. This is why Jesus once told a relatively good guy, **"One thing you lack"** (Mark 10:21). This is the same reason why Jesus would say the same thing to you. You could be as compassionate as Mother Teresa and as courageous as Martin Luther King Jr., but you would still lack something if you want to be with God. You might feel like a fairly good person, but God lives in an ocean of Goodness. If you want eternal life, life that Good, you can't just be good. You must be Good like God.

Here's the bad news, according to Jesus: **"With man this is impossible"** (Mark 10:27). Here's the good news, according to Jesus: **"But not with God; all things are possible with God"** (Mark 10:27). So cling to Jesus today. He's the only one who can make both bad and good people "Good."

Family history
Pastor Matt Ewart

Being a Jew in the first century included with it a certain amount of pride in your ancestors. Jewish families would tell stories about the patriarchs of old times: Abraham and his daring faith, Isaac and his miracle birth, Jacob and his wrestling with God. And you can't forget the heroism and leadership of King David.

It was expected, then, that when Matthew wrote an account of Jesus' life, he would begin with a list of Jesus' ancestors. And he did. But what was unexpected were the ancestors that Matthew highlighted. Here are just a few names from Matthew chapter 1: **"Judah the father of Perez and Zerah, whose mother was Tamar. . . . Salmon the father of Boaz, whose mother was Rahab. . . . David was the father of Solomon, whose mother had been Uriah's wife"** (verses 3,5,6).

What's the point? Matthew didn't shy away from the darker side of Jewish history. By referencing Tamar, Rahab, and Uriah's wife (feel free to research their stories later today), Matthew made one thing abundantly clear: The kind of people Jesus came from were far from perfect. In fact, Jesus' family history contained some embarrassing stories and questionable characters.

So why would God want Matthew to highlight these people from Jesus' family tree? If you keep reading about Jesus' life, the point makes itself clear: The kind of people Jesus came from are the kind of people Jesus came for.

It doesn't matter how embarrassing or questionable your past is. Jesus came for people like you. And people like me.

Jesus: The sequel
Pastor Clark Schultz

Recently, our family watched a blockbuster sequel movie online. The movie was . . . not good. Sequels often don't live up to the original. The expectations are high, and that leads to a major letdown.

Wait; did that just describe your day? You and I expect one day to be better than the last. Then, roll camera; we are hit with a diagnosis, an annoyance, a remembrance of our past, a disagreement with our spouse. Letdown City, here we come! But allow the prophet Isaiah to give you some comfort as he speaks to a generation about to be taken into captivity. This is written to the original audience! The sequel audience would be those returning from captivity years later. We are part of that sequel audience.

"Comfort, comfort my people, says your God. Speak tenderly to Jerusalem, and proclaim to her that her hard service has been completed, that her sin has been paid for, that she has received from the Lord**'s hand double for all her sins"** (Isaiah 40:1,2).

Israel's captivity would be over. They would be free to go home. No matter the day you are having, you are NOT a slave to anyone. Why? Calvary's cross shouts, "It is finished!"

Israel was to be free. God so loved you that his Son freed you from Satan's grasp.

Israel would get "double." The sequel = We are doubly blessed—redeemed and restored daily until Christ's second coming, a sequel that will exceed all expectations.

Jesus' favorite topic

Pastor Mike Novotny

You can't really understand Jesus until you understand the thing that Jesus talked about the most. Do you know what that is? If your guess is love, that's a good guess but not at the top of the list. If you guess money, you are biblically educated, since Jesus constantly talked about gold, silver, taxes, and treasures, but you still aren't quite there. Ready for the real answer? The thing that Jesus talked about the most was the kingdom of God/heaven.

Let me prove it—One of Jesus' first-ever messages was, **"The kingdom of God has come near"** (Mark 1:15). One of the earliest summaries of Jesus' ministry said, **"Jesus went throughout Galilee . . . proclaiming the good news of the kingdom"** (Matthew 4:23). Nearly all of Jesus' parables started with, **"The kingdom of heaven is like . . ."** (Matthew 13:24). At the start of Acts, after Jesus rose from the dead, we read, "[Jesus] **appeared to them over a period of forty days and spoke about the kingdom of God"** (1:3). So if you want to get to know Jesus, get to know the kingdom of God.

What exactly is the kingdom? My favorite summary is this: The kingdom of God is a place of authority and safety. The heart that believes in Jesus as both its Lord and its Savior, the One who gets the final word and the One who promises to keep us safe from sin, death, and hell—that's the kingdom of God.

Is the kingdom within you?

Not afraid
Pastor Jon Enter

I can't imagine the decision Moses' parents had to make. They were blessed with the joy of pregnancy while in slavery in Egypt. Babies are always a blessing, a gift, no matter the circumstances that surround how a baby enters the world. But the pharaoh felt differently. He commanded all the Hebrew boys be murdered at birth. **"By faith Moses' parents hid him for three months after he was born, because they saw he was no ordinary child, and they were not afraid of the king's edict"** (Hebrews 11:23).

Not afraid? They didn't fear the most powerful man on the planet? Countless babies were lost to his cruelty. Families that defied him were likely tortured to strike fear and obedience. But not Moses' parents. By faith they followed God's commands rather than fear the pharaoh's wrath.

It's extremely difficult to stand up for what's right when that means standing against those who can hurt you. College tests are failed for expressing your faith. Job promotions are lost when you refuse to be unethical. Romantic relationships end abruptly when you refuse to cross the Lord's boundary on sex. Lives have been lost for simply loving Jesus.

Don't be afraid. Jesus can overcome every evil the devil deploys against you. Even if you lose your life, you instantly enter heaven! And the devil still loses! Nothing will separate you from the love of Christ. Nothing. When you face adversity—pray, trust, and step forward in faith for you never walk alone.

Fanny & Jesus
Pastor Mike Novotny

Have you ever heard of Fanny Crosby? She was a Christian songwriter who produced more worship music than Martin Luther, Chris Tomlin, and Hillsong combined. By the time she died in 1915, Fanny had written over 8,000 hymns and gospel songs. If you've ever sung "Blessed Assurance" or "Take the World but Give Me Jesus" or "To God Be the Glory," you've sung a Fanny Crosby hit. But the craziest part is that Fanny was blind for almost all 94 years of her life.

You might expect her to be bitter, but she wasn't. At age 8, Fanny wrote these faith-filled words: "It seemed intended by the blessed providence of God that I should be blind all my life, and I thank him for the dispensation. If perfect earthly sight were offered me tomorrow, I would not accept it. I might not have sung hymns to the praise of God if I had been distracted by the beautiful and interesting things about me." That's some faith for a third grader!

The apostle Paul wants you to have the same kind of trust in God's purposes for your pain. After rejoicing in our peace, our access to God, and the love we have in Jesus, Paul boasts, **"We also glory in our sufferings, because we know that suffering produces perseverance; perseverance, character; and character, hope"** (Romans 5:3,4).

Like Fanny Crosby, Paul knew that God is always working for the good of his people. What kind of good work might God be up to on your bad days?

God, what should I do?
Pastor Daron Lindemann

At some point, even the smartest of us faces a dilemma. A decision that could go either way. Should I grab a cup of coffee or keep working at my computer? Should I reply to that email with strong words or gentle words? Should I really be spending this money? Should I reach out to the person who hurt my feelings?

These are just the beginning. Think of all the major life decisions. Get married? To whom? Take the job offer? Sign the papers? Move to California? Move from California?

God loves it when you don't know what to do. Here's why. He is God, and you're not. You don't know everything, and he does. You don't know everything there is to know about any of the decisions you make today. Sometimes that frustrates you. Sometimes that overwhelms you. Sometimes that influences you toward a bad decision.

God doesn't shake his head, roll his eyes, and think, "Not again. Can't you just make a good decision for once?" Instead, God helps. He usually doesn't take the decision away from you but allows you to work through it even when it's difficult. But he does equip you with what you need to decide well.

"If any of you lacks wisdom, you should ask God, who gives generously to all without finding fault, and it will be given to you" (James 1:5).

Since you lack wisdom, admit it and ask God for help.

Stop the leak
Pastor Matt Ewart

Thankfulness is a powerful thing. There are books written about the impact it makes when you are intentionally thankful. I highly recommend trying it out. Be filled with thanks.

If you are struggling to be as filled with thanks as you want to be, it might be because something is causing a leak. You can't be full of thanks if you've sprung a leak.

The most common culprit that causes us to be less than full of thanks is something called discontentment. If not addressed, discontentment can make your heart like a bucket full of holes. Any thanks you pour into it will quickly leak out.

Discontentment is the belief that your circumstances need to change before you can be thankful. It's the belief that you need more money, more respect, more house, etc. Until you get more, discontentment will ruin you.

The bad news is you often can't control your circumstances. The good news is you don't have to: **"I have learned the secret of being content in any and every situation, whether well fed or hungry, whether living in plenty or in want. I can do all this through him who gives me strength"** (Philippians 4:12,13).

Trusting in Jesus' promises can fill the holes caused by discontentment. He promises never to leave you or forsake you. He promises that he works all things out for your good, even unfavorable circumstances. When it comes to being filled with thanks, stop the leak with Jesus' promises.

Celebrate the managers
Linda Buxa

At the conclusion of the Wisconsin boys high school state Division 3 basketball championship game, all the players had been awarded their medals. It was time for Nick Bennett, the head coach from Racine St. Catherine's to walk out on to the court, pick up that state championship trophy, take it back to his team, and celebrate.

Instead, he sent the manager. When the young man with Down Syndrome walked out to pick up the trophy, the crowd and team cheered like crazy—and the celebration became even sweeter.

Too often, managers get none of the attention or respect they deserve. They take care of all the details, check in on the coaches before they leave school for the night, and do all the things nobody pays attention to. They're the most faithful fans—with none of the glory.

The Christian pastor or TV preacher or blogger or teacher might get all the attention, but there are faithful "managers" working every day to build God's family—and they shouldn't be overlooked. They quietly pray for their friends and family and text encouragement. They open the doors and count the offerings at church. They serve at food pantries and homeless shelters. Look for these managers, and let them know how valuable they are.

Remind them God loves their humble service and can't wait to give them the ultimate trophy of eternal life when they get to heaven. **"For the Lord takes delight in his people; he crowns the *humble* with victory"** (Psalm 149:4).

Acknowledge your God
Andrea Delwiche

"The fool says in his heart, 'There is no God.' They are corrupt, and their ways are vile; there is no one who does good. God looks down from heaven on all mankind to see if there are any who understand, any who seek God. Everyone has turned away, all have become corrupt; there is no one who does good, not even one" (Psalm 53:1-3).

This indictment against the human race and each of us individually is pretty hard for our human natures to swallow. All human hearts are curved away from God rather than toward him. We give ourselves and our interests the place of God in our lives.

But through God's goodness and love, we are changed creatures, capable of showing love for God through loving action toward God and each other. But now that we've been brought to faith, we might ask, "How does this psalm speak to me?"

Perhaps we claim faith in God but tend to live as what has been described as "functional atheists." We speak the words of faith, but our daily lives demonstrate we actually believe in and depend on ourselves. With this attitude, we *are* fools, saying to God, "I don't believe you exist in any way that's meaningful for how I choose to operate."

This thought pattern does not *surprise* God. Our heavenly Father knows our weaknesses and yet loves us with an everlasting love. He continually calls to us to acknowledge him and live in his wisdom. May our hearts and ears be open to hear him and respond!

Care less about failure
Pastor Daron Lindemann

My superstar college roommate would say, after breaking scoring records on the basketball team, "You miss 100% of the shots you don't take."

We need to care less about failure and live more carefree because God cares. Nehemiah, a social reformer and spiritual leader, did this. He cared less about failure because, he said, **"The gracious hand of my God was on me"** for **"what God had put in my heart to do for Jerusalem"** (Nehemiah 2:8,12).

When your God is gracious, your failures aren't failures but learning experiences for growth.

Nehemiah faced fears of failure with passion for God. He admitted, **"I was very much afraid"** (Nehemiah 2:2). Whatever causes you pain and fear is a passion. As a passion for what's important to God, it translates into courage.

And courage says, "God, because this is important to you, it's important to me."

Nehemiah faced fears of failure with purpose from God. He told the king (his boss), **"Send me to the city in Judah where my ancestors are buried so that I can rebuild it"** (Nehemiah 2:5). Nehemiah's ancestors were buried in Jerusalem because God gave that city a special purpose. Eventually, Jesus would die and be buried there.

When your purpose is from God, you say, "God, let's do this!"

Trying and failing is better than failing because you never tried at all. Take intelligent, intentional risks for God because he cares.

Just let me cry

Karen Spiegelberg

Some years ago when a Christian family member passed away suddenly, I was moved to tears in my grief. Another family member told me very sternly that Christians should keep those emotions in check and be joyful for those who have gone on to eternal life. I silently screamed inside, "Just let me cry!"

Is it okay for Christians to cry or grieve at the death of another Christian? The simple answer is yes. God has blessed us with a natural affection for our families and friends. Of course we'll feel pain when we lose them. We shouldn't feel we are doing wrong by experiencing those emotions. The psalms are full of expressions of grief. We also know from the book of John that Jesus wept with Mary and Martha at the death of their brother, Lazarus.

But the Bible tells us we should not grieve without hope. In 1 Thessalonians 4:13,14, we are told, **"Brothers and sisters, we do not want you to be uninformed about those who sleep in death, so that you do not grieve like the rest of mankind, who have no hope. For we believe that Jesus died and rose again, and so we believe that God will bring with Jesus those who have fallen asleep in him."** As Christians, we can feel sadness when someone dies, but we also have the knowledge of the hope of eternal life for those brothers and sisters in Christ!

So cry away if you feel like it . . . and while you're at it, hand me a tissue too.

The rope of hope
Pastor Mike Novotny

I recently bought a 150-foot rope on Amazon and wrapped a tiny piece of black tape around the first inch of it. That might seem like a misuse of both rope and tape, but I would disagree. Because that rope reminds me of biblical hope.

That tiny inch of black tape reminds me that few things are for sure while we are here on earth: Your family may or may not be healthy. Your friends may or may not stick with you after high school. Your bank account may or may not be better than the average. One of the hardest parts of life is the uncertainty of whether tomorrow will be any better than today.

But that's why I love the rope of hope. After this life is over, there is a for-sure future that is drastically better than your current experience. God has promised us lifetime after lifetime after lifetime (how does one describe eternity?) where there is pure joy, perfect community, indescribable rest, and a front-row seat to see the face of God. Zero of these blessings are up in the air; 100% of them are for sure. This is why I wanted to decorate my last Christmas tree with the rope of hope!

"Let us hold unswervingly to the hope we profess, for he who promised is faithful" (Hebrews 10:23). Have hope, Christian. Your God is faithful, so your future is for sure.

What are you giving?
Pastor Jon Enter

Isn't it amazing how children born to the same parents and raised in the same home can turn out so differently? It happened in the first family. **"Abel kept flocks, and Cain worked the soil"** (Genesis 4:2). This shows different careers, not different character. Yet God accepted Abel's offering and rejected Cain's. Why? **"Without faith it is impossible to please God"** (Hebrews 11:6). The difference in the brothers' characters, their trust in God, was revealed in their offerings. Abel gave God the choicest meat of his flock. Meanwhile, Cain . . . eventually . . . when he finally felt like it, gave God the leftovers.

"In the course of time Cain brought some of the fruits of the soil as an offering to the LORD. . . . But on Cain and his offering [God] did not look with favor" (Genesis 4:3,5). Cain's offering was not joyful or thankful. It was given by guilt and reluctant obligation. Abel was commended; Cain was criticized.

What you give, how you give, and how joyfully you give your offerings paints a clear picture. **"For where your treasure is, there your heart will be also"** (Matthew 6:21). Very few times does the Lord give a command and then couple it with a promised blessing. Proverbs 3:9,10 and Malachi 3:10 proclaim when we step into faithfulness with joyful, generous, and regular offerings to the Lord, amazing blessings follow. How? You can't out-give God. His goodness is overpoweringly good. His abundance is immeasurably abundant. His love unrelenting. What are you giving God?

Everything good is from God
Pastor Mike Novotny

When I was a kid, my mother insisted I write a thank-you card for every birthday, Christmas, and graduation gift I got. As a rather ungrateful youth, I hated her policy, but now I understand why she wanted to instill a spirit of gratitude in my heart. Giving thanks not only is the right thing to do, but it also strengthens your relationship with the One who gave the gifts.

Imagine if you wrote a thank-you card to God for one of his gifts! James writes, **"Every good and perfect gift is from above, coming down from the Father of the heavenly lights"** (James 1:17). Everything good and beautiful and funny and interesting and comforting and relaxing is from God. Everything that makes you smile and laugh and breathe a sigh of relief is from God. Every birthday wish from someone who cared enough to write. Every day you're able to work and earn your daily bread. Every time the car starts, there's food in the fridge, or you sleep through the night. Every friend who has time to talk. Every hug from your granddaughter. Every video of puppies. Every sin forgiven. Every transgression erased. Every mistake whisked out of his holy sight. Everything good is from God!

What could happen to our relationship with God if we paused to thank him for everything good around us? I have a hunch it would not only show him great honor but also make us love him more than ever before.

Give thanks today. You have been greatly gifted!

Forgive because
Pastor Matt Ewart

I'm sure you've heard something similar to at least one of these things:

- You will be controlled by the grudges you hold.
- Refusing to forgive will only make you miserable.
- Grudges commit you to a direction that will never heal your hurt.
- Failing to forgive others puts a burden on you.

Sometimes those things are true because with some grudges, the only person you are hurting is yourself.

But I have yet to find a Bible passage that commands us to forgive others because of the benefits it will bring to us. I have found a lot of passages that say the opposite.

The greatest example of this is God's forgiveness for you. His act of forgiving you didn't lift a burden off his shoulders. In order to forgive, God had to deal a blow to himself. Jesus had to carry a cross. You can look at all the things listed above, and none of them applied to the act of God forgiving you.

Forgiving someone might cost you something. It might cost you an opportunity to make things even. It might cost you some money or time. Forgiveness might mean you carry a burden that rightfully belongs to someone else.

Sometimes your decision to forgive someone will benefit you. But don't let that be what compels you. Forgive because you've received the benefit of forgiveness from God. Or as the apostle Paul put it, **"Forgive as the Lord forgave you"** (Colossians 3:13).

Thanks for ~~nothing~~ everything!
Pastor Mike Novotny

The pastors at our church gathered together to talk about grumbling, gratitude, and God. I asked them, "Who is the most grateful person you have ever met?"

One of my colleagues paused thoughtfully and replied, "My mother." Despite dealing with chronic and increasing back pain in her older years, this dear saint refuses to give in to a grumbling spirit. In fact, as my friend recounted, she will catch herself getting close to the edge of grumbling but then pull herself back on to the holy ground of gratitude. "This is not how I envisioned retirement . . . but God is good!"

I love stories like that, perhaps because I'd love to mature into that kind of Christian. You too? If so, maybe we can start in the same place this sister in Christ does, that is, with Christ himself. Through Jesus Christ, God has an overwhelming number of good things to say about us. He promises we are chosen, holy, blameless, predestined, adopted, redeemed, graced, forgiven, saved, included, marked, and filled with the Holy Spirit. If that isn't enough, he also declares we are justified, sanctified, purified, and will soon be glorified, the blood-bought gifts labeled "To: You" and "From: Jesus."

Zip through those last two sentences, and the pain will probably pull you into grumbling today. But slow down and savor the goodness in them, and you might end up like my friend's mother, giving thanks to God.

"Give thanks to the Lord, for he is good; his love endures forever" (Psalm 107:1).

Loved by the Shepherd
Pastor Clark Schultz

As if our life wasn't hectic enough with three toddler boys, we got a puppy. We threw into the mix an energetic, black, scruffy goldendoodle named Winston who sees a whole world needing to be chewed. A puppy, much like a child, needs to be fed and instructed. Soon the puppy learns to listen to the voice of its master. Commands such as sit, stay, do not eat Momma's slippers are learned and understood. Outside we have an underground fence, not just to keep the puppy inside, but it also helps keep others safe.

A word from the master and a hand that provides a fence to keep safe is not just reserved for man's best friend. It's used for God's best creation—you! **"My sheep listen to my voice; I know them, and they follow me"** (John 10:27).

Our Good Shepherd has given us his Word, and his Word is not just a list of dos and don'ts but a list of love for us. Following God's commands is meant to keep us safe and not to harm us. Time hearing the Master Shepherd's voice in Bible study and prayer reassures and feeds our hungry and tired souls. Fencing ourselves in the loving arms of our Savior reminds us we are protected. The world will look to lead us away. Staying close to the Shepherd does not mean life will always be easy, but it does mean you are loved unconditionally.

God's ~~not~~ good!
Pastor Mike Novotny

In my office you'll find an ancient scroll snatched from the fires of hell (or, perhaps, created by a local artist with some paper and a lighter). That scroll contains the greatest deception of the devil, the lie that lures countless souls away from God: "God's not good."

Behind every temptation is the belief that God's not good, that our Father doesn't want what's best, that there's a better way to live than following his rules. That same lie is peddled every time you're in pain. "If God was good, he would use his power to cure your cancer and heal your grandson and give you a promotion. Yet here you are suffering again. Maybe God isn't as good as you thought." If you've ever suffered, and especially if chronic pain is part of your story, I bet you've felt the magnetic pull of that thought in your heart.

But James won't let you be lied to. Jesus' brother writes, **"Don't be deceived, my dear brothers and sisters. Every good and perfect gift is from above, coming down from the Father of the heavenly lights, who does not change like shifting shadows"** (James 1:16,17). The unchanging God who is the giver of every good thing in your life must be good. No one that generous could possibly be labeled evil.

And if the perfect gift of a Savior came down from the Father, the devil must be lying to you. God must be good. All the time. Even now. Believe it.

Grow in faithfulness
Sarah Habben

A dad takes his daughters to the zoo, as promised. He is faithful to his word.

A couple celebrates their 50th anniversary. They have been faithful to their vows.

A congregation works hard to reach out to their community. They are faithful with the gospel.

More often than not, faithfulness comes at a price. The dad at the zoo gave up much-needed overtime. The husband chose to honor his marital vows despite his wife's past infidelity. The congregation sees no visible results despite all their faithful work.

Sometimes the price of faithfulness can seem too steep. Sometimes we may go through the motions of faithfulness with a deep frown. Sometimes we blame circumstances for making faithfulness impossible.

Now consider God. He makes some hefty promises. "I will supply all your needs. I will work evil for your good. I will forgive your sins. I will raise you from your grave." The price he paid to keep those promises? His Son's life. The attitude behind his faithfulness? Steadfast love. The circumstances that can prevent his faithfulness? Nothing in heaven or on earth or hidden in the human heart. Even **"if we are faithless, he remains faithful, for he cannot disown himself"** (2 Timothy 2:13).

God has declared his faithfulness. History proves it. It should be enough, but God does even more. To deepen our trust, he calls us his own, forgiven people in Baptism and in Lord's Supper. We are convinced of his faithfulness. And out of such faith, *our* faithfulness grows.

A prayer of thanks
Pastor Daron Lindemann

Loving and generous Lord, at this time of thanksgiving we remember with grateful hearts all the blessings you have showered on our nation.

Help us receive all your blessings with humble hearts. Destroy our sinful pride, and protect us from temptations of greed, materialism, and selfishness. May our choices and lives of faith be our offerings of thanks and praise.

As we count our blessings and acknowledge your goodness, our hearts go out to those who do not have what we enjoy and are in need. Care for them in your divine ways and through us as your agents.

We thank you, Lord, for opportunities and choices, for meaning and challenges. We pray you would lead us into your designs and purposes for us, our community, our church, and our country.

We thank you for family and friends who love us and care for us and pray you would be a Friend to those who are alone.

Loving God, in this season and all year long, give us the gift of thankful hearts so that we appreciate all your blessings, especially the gift of salvation through Jesus Christ. May we live in a spirit of gratitude to you and generosity to others. Amen.

Always
Sarah Habben

I have a video of him clowning around in grade 6. Floppy hair, enormous grin. His arms are thrown over his friends' shoulders. They are beautifully carefree.

Five years later, he committed suicide.

His parents and brothers were blindsided. They knew he had his ups and downs. But they had no idea he was struggling enough to end his own life. Now, as his father describes it, "Carnage has been set free on more hearts than I can count." They face a lifetime of asking *why?*

Why didn't he tell us just how badly he felt? Why did a loving God allow this? Why?

Are you asking *why?* Have you lost something or someone of utter importance to you? Do you wake up each day only to feel your heart implode again?

When we howl our grief in God's direction, it sometimes feels like the only response is a mournful echo. Some questions aren't answered this side of heaven. The Bible doesn't spell out why God allows emotional carnage. Nor does God offer platitudes for our pain. He gives us something much better in response to our gutted lives and unanswered *whys* . . . he gives us himself.

Look—he's there in the manger, sharing your mortality. He's there on the cross, bearing your sins. He's standing beside the empty tomb with his foot on death's neck. He's with you in your delight and in your desolation. Look—he's there. He's there because he promised.

"Surely I am with you *always*, to the very end of the age" (Matthew 28:20).

Pick up your Legos
Pastor Daron Lindemann

Grandpa and Grandma are coming over. However, kids' toys, games, and a bunch of Legos (dangerously painful to step on) are strewn all over the living room.

Do you tell your kids, "Go ahead and leave those Legos on the floor. When Grandpa and Grandma come, they can walk around them"? No! You say, "Please pick up your Legos because Grandpa and Grandma are coming."

Why? Because Grandpa and Grandma are special. When they come into the house, you want them to have a clear and open path. It prepares the way for a big welcome of love and hugs. "Grandpa and Grandma are here!"

Do you need to pick up your Legos? **"Prepare the way for the Lord, make straight paths for him"** (Luke 3:4).

Remove sinful obstacles of pride or despair that get in the way. Clear a path with repentance and humility. Don't ask Jesus to work his way around your priorities, but work your priorities around Jesus. He's special.

Prepare the way and clear a path for his big welcome of love, forgiveness, and salvation. "He's coming!"

During the four-week prelude to Christmas called Advent, Christians prepare to celebrate the birth of Jesus.

Are you familiar with any kind of Advent celebrations? Google a few of them like an Advent wreath, Advent candles, or an Advent calendar (a countdown to Christmas that works great with the kids). Give one a try this Advent season.

Nothing to lose
Pastor Matt Ewart

My family has a dog. When she was a puppy, she would snarl and snap at us when we got too close to her favorite bone. (We were quick to train her out of that behavior.)

As I thought about this all-too-common behavior in dogs, I began to wonder why it is they do that. I think it is simple: They are afraid of losing something they love.

You and I do not literally snarl and snap at people. (If you do, I hope someone trains you out of that soon.) But we do have defensive mechanisms in place when people get too close to something we are afraid of losing.

Some people lash out. Some people shut down. Some people assume an intimidating stance. Some people keep their distance. We all have our own way of snarling when we are vulnerable with something we don't want to lose. So I have just one question for you: What if you had nothing to lose?

In one of his letters, the apostle Paul acknowledged he had a weakness that made him vulnerable. But instead of snarling at people when they got too close, this is what he did: **"Therefore I will boast all the more gladly about my weaknesses, so that Christ's power may rest on me"** (2 Corinthians 12:9).

Whatever you are afraid of losing, commend it to Jesus. He can make it so that your vulnerabilities are an opportunity for his power to work.

Everything good is a gift
Pastor Mike Novotny

I recently texted my mom about the day of my birth. November 18, 1980. Sheboygan, Wisconsin. Clifton Avenue (I was born at home). My mom reminisced, "Everyone said you were a big baby. . . . It sure felt like it!" Judy pushed 7 pounds, 12 ounces out of her body and now, 40 years later, to thank her for her suffering, I get a bunch of stuff. Isn't that insane?! "Mother, you endured the worst pain of your life, so I think I should get a cake."

The same thing happens at Christmas. Jesus Christ, the Son of God, leaves the pure happiness of heaven to be born in a manure-scented cave at a time in history when there was no air conditioning, cars, or Netflix. And to remember all that Jesus suffered for us, every Christmas we . . . get stuff! Isn't that doubly insane?!

But maybe that's the point. That's why we call it a "gift." It's just given. It's not earned or deserved or worked for. It's not a paycheck. It's grace. And James says that everything good in your life is a gift. **"Every good and perfect gift is from above, coming down from the Father of the heavenly lights"** (James 1:17).

You and I have sinned against God. Despite the endless list of our errors, however, God has gifted us with every good thing. What kind of God would respond to sin in such a way? Only our God.

What grace! What a Savior!

December

In him was life, and that life was the light of all mankind. The light shines in the darkness, and the darkness has not overcome it.

John 1:4,5

Jesus > Hallmark
Pastor Mike Novotny

Why do you suppose Hallmark Christmas movies have become so popular? These low-budget, incredibly predictable, big-city-girl-falls-for-small-town-guy-with-great-hair films have taken over the holiday broadcast schedule for months at a time. How?

According to some media analysts, Hallmark offers us a few things that resonate deep within our souls—safety, warmth, and love. In our dangerous, cold, and unloving world, Hallmark allows us to sit back, relax, and rest without fear of a dark ending or a serious twist in the happy plot. Yes, it may be 90 minutes of predictable fiction, but it sure makes us feel good.

The nonfictional Jesus, however, offers us something better. **"Jesus Christ is the same yesterday and today and forever"** (Hebrews 13:8). The unchanging nature of Jesus is the safest, warmest, most secure source of love in all the universe. Yesterday, he loved you. Today, he loves you. Tomorrow, he will love you. You never have to doubt, question, or wonder about his commitment to his relationship with you because he is the God who does not change, whose grace is always the same.

One of the harder parts about life is that anything can change in an instant—your health, your job security, your friendships. But one of the best parts about trusting in Jesus is that none of life's changes can change his promise to be with you, now and forever.

More than milkshakes
Sarah Habben

In a lifetime of reading and writing, American author John Irving has noticed there are a greater number of "meaty" novels on best-seller lists in Europe and Canada than in the U.S. "Most Americans," he says, "read junk." According to Irving, Americans' reading tastes are lazy, infantile, and "lemminglike."

The writer to the Hebrews had a similar, unfiltered observation about his readers—they had a bad habit of not even *trying* to understand parts of the Bible. **"Though by this time you ought to be teachers, you need someone to teach you the elementary truths of God's word all over again. You need milk, not solid food!"** (5:12).

Craving the pure gospel milk of "Jesus loves me this I know" is not junk. It's the foundation of our faith. But the Jewish Christians lacked spiritual drive. They were content to call their foundation a building. They failed to add the frame and brickwork of *all* God's words.

Maybe we don't even *try* to understand what God says regarding sexuality, the roles of men and women, Baptism, or church fellowship. Maybe we are content to stick to spiritual basics because our full days leave us too tired to chew on God's Word.

But building spiritual muscles requires more than milkshakes. Weathering life's hurricanes requires a foundation with walls. Resisting the lemming urges of the world requires a heart that knows a cliff from solid ground.

This week, dig into God's Word. Commit to a Bible class. Build on the sure foundation of Jesus' love.

A clean whiteboard
Linda Buxa

I left dinner instructions on a whiteboard for my family and then headed out to run errands. At the end of the night, I went to wipe off the whiteboard—and the words remained. Oh no. I had used a permanent marker instead of a whiteboard marker.

That's when I remembered a tip shared on Facebook. I traced over those permanent letters with a whiteboard marker and—amazingly!—the permanent marker came off.

The same happens in our lives. The sins (the permanent marker in this story)—angry words, drunk nights, arrogant pride, hypocrisy, affairs, addictions, lies—leave stains on our lives.

Thankfully there's good news for that too. Jesus (the whiteboard marker in this story) covers them. Now when God looks at us, the stains—amazingly!—are gone because **"the blood of Jesus, his Son, purifies us from all sin"** (1 John 1:7).

Let's be realistic though. We might feel some nagging guilt every day. We still have to live with consequences from our choices. We do the same stupid things again (and again and again), even though we know better.

Does Jesus really cover those things? Yes.

Is he going to run out of patience? No.

Why? **"Because of the Lord's great love we are not consumed, for his compassions never fail. They are new every morning; great is your faithfulness"** (Lamentations 3:22,23).

Every day, thanks to Jesus, you have a clean whiteboard.

Unlike any other name
Andrea Delwiche

Psalm 54:1,2 says, **"Save me, O God, by your name; vindicate me by your might. Hear my prayer, O God; listen to the words of my mouth."**

What does it mean when the psalmist prays, "Save me, O God, *by your name*"? God's name is a recognition and demonstration of God's characteristics.

So who is God? God described himself to Moses in this way: **"The Lord, the Lord, the compassionate and gracious God, slow to anger, abounding in love and faithfulness, maintaining love to thousands, and forgiving wickedness, rebellion and sin. Yet he does not leave the guilty unpunished"** (Exodus 34:6,7).

When the psalmist asks God to save him "by his name," he is recalling all these qualities of God that make God trustworthy.

How does this affect you and me? We are continually in situations where we ask for God's assistance. When we ask, do we consider what we know about God that gives us confidence that he is taking care of us?

The list of attributes the Lord gave to Moses also indicates what we know about Jesus, God's Son, and about the Holy Spirit. Christ's life, death, and resurrection show us he is like his Father, our champion, Savior, and friend. The Spirit's continual presence in our hearts is a manifestation of God's tenderness and deep desire for us to grow and bloom under his care.

Our God's name is unlike any other name. God's name contains everything we need for daily protection and flourishing. How can this change your day today?

Jesus and prayers for justice
Pastor Mike Novotny

I long for a world that's filled with justice, don't you? Justice is that deep desire we have that all the innocent people are protected and all the guilty people are punished, the ache we all feel for things in this life that are simply unfair.

We don't want to live in a world where innocent people are assumed to be dangerous or where parents have to warn their sons about where to keep their hands when caught speeding. No, we want justice. And we don't want to live in a world where wearing blue is bad, where people who risk their lives to serve are assumed to be evil. No, we want justice. Justice is what we want in our communities, homes, schools, and churches.

Thankfully, Jesus wants justice too. **"And will not God bring about justice for his chosen ones, who cry out to him day and night? Will he keep putting them off? I tell you, he will see that they get justice, and quickly"** (Luke 18:7,8). While "quickly" might mean something different to the eternal God than it does to temporary humans like us, Jesus' promise still gives us hope.

God's people will see justice. God will not put off our cries forever. The God who chose us despite our sin will one day make sure that sin disappears forever.

So, chosen one, keep praying. God hears your cries. Your Father will see that we get justice, and quickly.

God sees, knows, and cares
Andrea Delwiche

Have you fallen victim to the lie that trusting in God is for those who can't make it on their own? Do you ever think God might get tired of hearing you pour out your grief to him or that he doesn't pay attention or care?

Take this exquisite image from Psalm 56 and hold it in your mind and heart: **"When I am afraid, I put my trust in you. In God, whose word I praise, in God I trust; I shall not be afraid. What can flesh do to me? You have kept count of my tossings; put my tears in your bottle. Are they not in your book?"** (verses 3,4,8 ESV).

Your Lord sees, knows, and cares about every circumstance of your life. Your God sees, cares, and *knows* you, down to the freckles on your face and the joys and griefs that permeate your bones. Your heart is an open book to him. His face shines with love for *you*. When you cry, or even *wish* to be able to cry tears of grief or anguish or frustration, he is not only aware of your tears, but he keeps count of your anguished tossings and tears. He puts them in a safe place and records them as important and noteworthy. He sees; he hears; he helps.

The psalmist closes this picture of our loving God with this testimony: **"You have delivered my soul from death, yes, my feet from falling, that I may walk before God in the light of life"** (verse 13 ESV).

May God's peace dwell within you.

December 7

Merry dictionary Christmas!
Pastor Mike Novotny

As a pastor, I get concerned every time December rolls around. It's not the presents and the busyness and the Santa dilemma that worry me the most; it's the words.

I'm worried that we've lost the meaning of four of the Bible's best words—*hope, peace, joy,* and *love.* Have you ever noticed how some combination of that quartet shows up in every Christmas card, Christmas ad, and Christmas letter, and yet we rarely slow down and define them? The result is, like a phone that has been unplugged from the outlet for days, those words lose their power, no longer able to bless us in the ways God wants.

Could you give a simple definition to those words if I put you on the spot? If not, can I encourage you to add a dictionary to your holiday reading list? Imitate the attitude and the action of the Ethiopian who admitted, **"'How can I** [understand what I'm reading]**,' he said, 'unless someone explains it to me?'"** (Acts 8:31).

This year, take time to plug four of God's favorite words back into their biblical meanings. If you do, you might just find your life filled with more hope (a for-sure future), more peace (a warless, unity-filled relationship with God), more joy (happiness that isn't based on happenings), and more love (doing what's best for another, like God did for us).

Have a merry dictionary Christmas!

The truth about lying to yourself
Pastor Daron Lindemann

Most of us grew up with parents who warned us about telling lies to others.

One time I disobeyed my parents and, without their permission, went to the house of a friend of a friend. We misbehaved, I tried to cover it up, my parents found out, and I got into big trouble.

Not many of us, however, grew up learning that one of the biggest mistakes we can make is lying to ourselves. We do this every day, many times a day, and these lies get us into big trouble.

We rationalize sinful behavior. We analyze God's promises and conclude they are wrong. We minimize the danger of our bad habits. We neglect broken relationships.

When Jesus said, **"I am the way and the truth and the life. No one comes to the Father except through me"** (John 14:6), he gave us a promise and also a prohibition. He doesn't allow any kind of lying to get us closer to God, including lying to ourselves. It only distances us from God.

Jesus promises a better way. When we trust him, we will strive for truth. We will repent of our lying tendencies. We will live in the grace of his forgiveness.

There is only one letter that makes *lie* different than *life*. So replace lying to yourself with faith in Jesus that loves him and his ways. Instead of trouble, you will find the blessing of a better, richer, and more abundant life.

Like a tube of toothpaste
Pastor Clark Schultz

Here is what I learned about the Bible from a tube of toothpaste. My wife and I have conflicting views of how to squeeze the tube. She grabs the tube at the end and slowly works her way through the tube. My boys and I grab the middle and squeeze away. She and the boys will take the toothpaste when nearing the end and chuck it into the garbage, whereas I will take it, squeeze it, and twist it into an origami shape to get the last bit of cavity-fighting goodness out of it.

Do you and I do the same with our time in God's Word? Do we take shortcuts? Do we chuck it to the side when we have more important daily tasks to get to? Or do we read it, soak it in, and squeeze every last bit out of those pages of life? If you haven't read the Bible in some time, take heart! There's no wrong way to read it. It's not too late to give it a go.

You can start in the middle, perhaps in the psalms. Psalm 139 reminds us God doesn't make junk. Or you can start at the beginning and slowly work your way through. The American Dental Association recommends brushing your teeth twice a day with fluoride toothpaste for two minutes each time. What would happen if we matched that brushing time, brushing up on God's amazing grace in the Scriptures? **"Now the Berean Jews . . . received the message with great eagerness and examined the Scriptures every day"** (Acts 17:11).

God makes you new
Pastor Jon Enter

There are only 17 people mentioned specifically by name in Hebrews chapter 11 as great heroes of faith. From the beginning of time until Jesus' birth, less than two dozen made the cut. What if God wrote a second list and only 17 people were recognized? From Jesus' ascension until now, who do most Christians think would make the new Heroes of Faith List? Paul? John? Constantine I? Martin Luther? Billy Graham? How about you? Would you make the list?

I'm guessing you're laughing to yourself right now. "Me? Yeah, right! Do you know what I've done? I'm no hero of faith. Too often, I'm more of a zero." I feel the same. I am the same.

But do you know who made God's original list of 17 big-faith believers? Rahab. She was a prostitute! **"By faith the prostitute Rahab, because she welcomed the spies, was not killed with those who were disobedient"** (Hebrews 11:31). She made the list because Jesus' forgiveness is bigger than Rahab's past.

Jesus' forgiveness is bigger than yours too. What makes you feel downright dirty before God? What makes your soul ache at the mere thought of your past unrighteousness? God doesn't judge you by your past. He judges if you have faith. Your past is gone. It doesn't define you or confine you to disgrace. You have grace, and that lands you on a bigger list, a better list. Your name is written in Jesus' book of life in heaven, and it's the list that matters eternally!

We want to be happy

Pastor Mike Novotny

St. Augustine, a famous Christian who lived around A.D. 400, wrote, "Every man, whatsoever his condition, desires to be happy." Isn't that true? Whoever we are, whatever our age, and whatever we do, don't we all want to be happy?

Think of your annual birthday list, handpicked in your personal pursuit of happiness. A 75" 8K UHD QLED TV or a kitchen makeover or a dinner where everyone lingers and no one is in a rush to leave. I don't know your list, but I do know you made your list because you want to be happy.

This might surprise you, but God wants you to be happy too. Not in the shallow, purchase-based way of our world, where happiness is tied to what is happening in your life. But in the depth of his love, in the purchase that Jesus made on the cross to make you part of God's forever family.

Most mornings, in my daily pursuit of happiness, I pray these words: **"Satisfy us in the morning with your unfailing love, that we may sing for joy and be glad all our days"** (Psalm 90:14). Moses, the author of this psalm, didn't fill his prayer list with a new staff or a kitchen upgrade but with a long look at unfailing love.

Let's do the same thing today: *Father, satisfy our souls with the profound thought that we are loved by you. Make us happy by fixing our eyes on the only thing in life that will never fail—your love for us through Jesus. Amen!*

The purpose of rules
Pastor Matt Ewart

Every family has its own set of rules. Rules dictate proper behavior, govern screen time, and establish daily schedules. Each family is a little bit different, but every family has rules.

Here's a silly question: *How long did you have to keep the rules before you were brought into your family?*

You know the purpose of rules is not to bring people *into* a family. Rules indicate you are already *in* the family, and they provide a baseline for showing respect to everyone in the house.

Here is the same question but on a spiritual level: *How long did you have to keep God's rules before you were brought into his family?*

Well, that's not what his rules are for either. His rules were not designed to bring people in. Before God gave a single commandment to the Israelites, he established the basis for his relationship with them:

"I am the Lord your God, who brought you out of Egypt, out of the land of slavery. 'You shall have no other gods before me'" (Exodus 20:2,3).

God put his act of redemption before mentioning a single rule, because keeping rules does not bring you into God's family. Only Jesus does.

The Holy Spirit gave you the gift of faith, which essentially means you are now God's child. Jesus obeyed the rules perfectly for you, which means God is pleased with you. God's rules can now serve as your guide to reflect the love that brought you into this family.

Baby Yoda and baby Jesus
Pastor Mike Novotny

Have you ever heard of Baby Yoda? He is the adorable character from Disney's show the *Mandalorian*, the little guy who turned into an American cultural sensation (google "Baby Yoda," and you'll see what I mean).

Technically, as the show begins, the name of this creature is not Baby Yoda but simply The Child. While the first episodes don't reveal much about him, we do know something—this child could change everything. There is some abnormal force within the child, something in its blood that has power to change things.

Hmm. That sounds familiar, doesn't it? A child whose blood has the power to change things? The prophet Isaiah speaks of a similar child when he says, **"For to us a child is born, to us a son is given, and the government will be on his shoulders. And he will be called Wonderful Counselor, Mighty God, Everlasting Father, Prince of Peace"** (Isaiah 9:6).

B.C. believers sat on the edge of their seats, waiting for "the child" whose birth and blood would bring them peace with God.

If you're looking for more peace this time of year, you don't have to escape to cute fictional figures to find it. Open your Bible and read about the birth of Jesus, the Son born to us, to you. He is wonderful. He is mighty. He is God. He is the Prince of peace.

God's true north
Pastor Daron Lindemann

How certain are you—right now—of direction? Try this: Can you point straight north? Go ahead and point. Now check your compass app on your phone to see how close you are.

Knowing your direction makes all the difference.

What happens if a ship sets its bearings from Galveston, Texas, to Miami, Florida, and in the middle of the Gulf of Mexico, it storms during the night? Winds and waves push the ship's direction slightly south by only a few degrees.

The ship will end up in Cuba.

If the captain is checking his compass regularly, however, he will be resisting the storm's direction constantly and steering the ship in the right direction.

By design, compasses already navigate true north. You don't have to design or discover true north. Just face that direction, trust it, check your compass regularly, make adjustments when circumstances try to alter your course even a few degrees, and keep going.

God's truth, God's character, and God's promises are timelessly consistent. Like true north, he never changes.

"For the word of the LORD is right and true; he is faithful in all he does" (Psalm 33:4).

Is your life heading where it should? Do you even know where that is?

God is your compass. Without your design or doing, he has established himself as your true north. Know him, and you know the way. Follow his faithfulness, and you will go in the right direction.

It's so worth it
Pastor Clark Schultz

Ask a cancer patient if it's worth it to put up with chemotherapy when the treatment often makes him or her feel worse than the disease. Ask an Olympic athlete if it's worth it to endure grueling years of athletic training that is often as monotonous and repetitious as it is painful. Ask a soldier if it's worth it to risk life and limb amidst the dangers of the battlefield. The life of a Christian is no different. **"Whoever wants to be my disciple must deny themselves and take up their cross and follow me"** (Mark 8:34).

This teaches us that the path of glory comes through the cross. Simply put, this means the life of a Christian will not always be easy. As Jesus followers, we will suffer depression, deal with death, and see brokenness in our own families. However, there is a difference in suffering because you are a Christian and suffering because of a sin.

Follow me for a minute. Where in your life do you allow the creation to become greater than the Creator? What has the power to make you sad or happy? Is it that your cat post didn't get the number of likes you wanted? Did the performance of your favorite sports team send you into a tailspin? What defines your happiness? Creation or Creator? Suffering will happen; loss is inevitable. No pain, no gain. Christ endured all the pain so we have everything to gain! Is it worth it? You bet!

What does God want for Christmas?
Pastor Daron Lindemann

When I was a kid, my parents helped me and my sisters set out cookies and milk for Santa. Before we went to church on Christmas Eve, we'd put them on the hearth of the fireplace. My childish heart was glad I could do something for that jolly giver.

What can you give the one, true Giver of Christmas?

About the same time the virgin Mary became pregnant by a miracle of God, another woman named Elizabeth also became miraculously pregnant. An angel announced the news to her husband, Zechariah: **"Your wife Elizabeth will bear you a son."** Zechariah asked, **"How can I be sure of this? I am an old man"** (Luke 1:13,18).

Similarly, when the angel told Mary, **"You will conceive and give birth to a son,"** Mary asked, **"How will this be . . . since I am a virgin?"** (Luke 1:31,34).

The Bible reveals what was in the hearts of Zechariah and Mary; they both questioned the angel but with different motives. Zechariah **"did not believe"** (Luke 1:20) the angel's announcement. Mary, on the other hand, continued, **"May your word to me be fulfilled"** (Luke 1:38).

So what does God want for Christmas?

Faith. Instead of questioning if God *can* do what he says, like Zechariah, you can process God's promises, like Mary, while believing God *will* do what he says.

Faith agrees that what God says is always true, that his Word is always fulfilled, even when it seems impossible.

You are significant
Pastor Matt Ewart

There are plenty of things in life that leave you feeling insignificant. It could be something complicated like losing out on a promotion, or it could be as simple as someone not replying to your text message right away.

Think of the last time you were feeling insignificant. What caused it, and what did that feeling lead you to do?

The Bible tells the story of a man who dared to believe he was significant to God, even though he was insignificant to the world around him.

The man's name was Bartimaeus. He was blind, and because of that, he was a beggar. He had nothing to offer the world around him. In fact, he depended on others' generosity to survive.

But one day a crowd was passing by, and I'll let Mark tell the story from there: **"When [Bartimaeus] heard that it was Jesus of Nazareth, he began to shout, 'Jesus, Son of David, have mercy on me!' Many rebuked him and told him to be quiet, but he shouted all the more, 'Son of David, have mercy on me!'"** (Mark 10:47,48).

Bartimaeus may have been blind, but he could see he was significant to God. He believed that vying for Jesus' attention was better than winning the approval of the crowd.

What if you could do the same? Plenty of things in life can leave you feeling forgotten and insignificant. Dare to live as if you are significant to God. Because in Jesus, you are.

Leaving a legacy
Pastor Jon Enter

Life is temporary. Life is short. What are you living for? Mark Twain once said, "The two most important days in your life are the day you are born and the day you find out why." What legacy will you leave?

Jacob's son Joseph knew the legacy he'd have. God revealed it in a dream when he was just 17. His dad, mom, and brothers would bow down to his power. If you know Joseph's story, it took a long, long time through lots and lots of pain before that happened. Joseph became the world's second-most-powerful person and saved countless lives from a region-wide drought.

But that's not what God commended in the life of Joseph. It wasn't his determination despite adversity or his integrity or humility. It wasn't even his incredible forgiveness of his brothers who sold him into slavery. **"By faith Joseph, when his end was near . . . gave instructions concerning the burial of his bones"** (Hebrews 11:22). Joseph left a legacy of his faith in his funeral plans.

Families who plan their loved one's funeral can't. They're emotional messes. Leave a legacy of faith. Grab your Bible. Inside the front cover, write "MY FUNERAL PLANS" and list what passages give you comfort and your favorite hymns. There is deep peace when you know the hymn or the Scripture was picked by your loved one who is now enjoying heaven with Jesus. Leave that legacy. Plan your funeral, and point your loved ones to Christ!

Love your neighbor
Karen Spiegelberg

It's such a lovely Bible passage, one that even non-Christians try to embrace: **"Love your neighbor as yourself"** (Matthew 22:39). But what does it really mean? Some theologians say it might be the most important question we ask about Christ's gospel.

Jesus was being tested by the Pharisees, the chief religious rulers of the day: **"'Teacher, which is the greatest commandment in the Law?' Jesus replied, '"Love the Lord your God with all your heart and with all your soul and with all your mind." This is the first and greatest commandment. And the second is like it: "Love your neighbor as yourself"'"** (Matthew 22:36-39).

When I was a kid, that entire passage confused me greatly. Many times I didn't really love myself, and I certainly didn't feel lovable before God. So was I supposed to love others as poorly as I loved myself? It didn't make sense. But when I realized that if I focus on his greatest commandment to love him, his perfect love then flows through me—to not only love myself greatly but in turn to love other people just as strongly.

What a joy it is to be able to understand what it means to love God with all my heart and mind, although imperfectly. Through that understanding, I have grown to recognize that each person around me is a soul for whom Christ died and one to be loved as I am now loving myself!

God doesn't mind
Pastor Mike Novotny

Of the many things I love about Jesus' mother, near the top of the list are the lyrics to her famous song: **"My spirit rejoices in God my Savior, for he has been mindful of the humble state of his servant"** (Luke 1:47,48).

I picture pregnant Mary smiling as she ponders God's promise. "Look at this place—Nazareth. Nowheresville. The armpit of Galilee. Look at me— Another Mary. Another nobody planning a wedding on a next-to-nothing budget. But God has been mindful of me. I'm not much, but God doesn't mind."

God doesn't mind choosing, using, and saving the nobodies of this world. Maybe you're just another teenager who will never become a social influencer. Or another employee who could be replaced by next Monday. Or another resident in another nursing home who needs another pill. Maybe people have to ask, "What's your name again?" because they forget you far too quickly.

But—listen—God doesn't mind. God is mindful of you, conscious of your existence, and concerned about your experience. You being nobody won't stop God from being the somebody who sought you, brought you into contact with the gospel, and created faith in your heart to believe it. God doesn't mind. In fact, it brings a smile to his face to call you his own beloved child.

Smile today, even if you are a nobody in the eyes of the world. God doesn't mind.

More than simple

Pastor Daron Lindemann

The Bible says, **"The complacency of fools will destroy them"** (Proverbs 1:32).

Complacency means being entirely satisfied with where I am, even if it isn't where I should be. It is the path of least resistance.

Complacency is the smoker who has had a heart attack saying, "I know I should quit," but not doing anything about it. Complacency is the A student being satisfied with Bs. Complacency is a Christian accepting their level of biblical understanding with no concern for spiritual growth.

God's wisdom calls out, **"How long will you who are simple love your simple ways? . . . Repent at my rebuke! Then I will pour out my thoughts to you, I will make known to you my teachings. But . . . since you disregard all my advice . . . I in turn will laugh when disaster strikes you; I will mock when calamity overtakes you"** (Proverbs 1:22-26).

Christians cannot safely say, "I was baptized and confirmed and know enough about the Bible to be saved." Christians cannot repeatedly ignore Bible study and worship and personal time in God's Word and prayer without a disastrous result.

God forgive us for such foolish complacency in our Christian homes and churches. Respond to God's rebuke and see his heart pour out to save you from complacency.

God promises to make his own, divine thoughts known to you! You are more than simple. You are wise with God's own thoughts.

School of grace
Pastor Matt Ewart

Eventually we all must navigate how to discipline those who are under our authority when they need a change in behavior. What I know is that I naturally gravitate toward the easy way of doing that.

If you want to change someone's behavior very quickly, instill fear in them. Threaten to give them something or take something away that will create discomfort. Make them afraid enough to change what they are doing, and they will change right away.

It is natural to see God that way. Many people see him as an angry God who threatens us with punishment unless we change our behavior. While it is true that God lays out the consequences of sin, his goal is not to change our behavior.

God's goal is to give us a new heart that is aligned with him. His goal from the very beginning of this creation was that mankind would reflect his love to him and to one another. And through Jesus, he has restored that kind of heart for us.

"For the grace of God has appeared that offers salvation to all people. It teaches us to say 'No' to ungodliness and worldly passions" (Titus 2:11,12).

It was God's grace that changed who we are. And it is his grace that compels us to choose a path through life that reflects love back to him. God does not conform our behavior through fear. He transforms us through grace.

Wear God down
Pastor Mike Novotny

Have you ever heard of Andy Bernard? Andy is one of the more persistent and annoying characters from the show the *Office*, a man whose personality could be summarized by one of his best quotes: "Every success I've ever had at my job or with the lady folks has come from my ability to slowly and painfully wear someone down."

Ha! I love that line. And I love it even more when Jesus connects it to prayer. After telling the humorous parable about a persistent widow who wore down a local judge with her constant cries for justice, Jesus said, **"And will not God bring about justice for his chosen ones, who cry out to him day and night? Will he keep putting them off? I tell you, he will see that they get justice, and quickly"** (Luke 18:7,8).

Jesus' point was not that our Lord is like an unjust judge, a grouchy God whom you have to wear down with a thousand prayers. No, this is an argument from the lesser to the greater. If a bad guy is moved by persistence, how much more a good God? Won't God answer the people he chose to be his children? Won't God make sure they get justice? When you cry out to him, won't he do something about it? Of course he will. He will see to it that you get justice. So "wear God down" and keep praying. Jesus promises that God will, when the timing is perfect to carry out his plans, answer your prayer.

Know. See. Yearn.
Sarah Habben

It's Christmas Eve. The tableau is set: a baby's soft cheek against a bed of hay, a wondering mother, wide-eyed shepherds who have seen heaven turned inside out.

But let's leave that stable for a moment and visit a scene two thousand years earlier. Sitting on the ground is a husk of a man. Job is a believer who is being sifted by Satan. He's lost almost everything—his children, his wealth, his health. Job is struggling. Who wouldn't? Sometimes he clings to God as his advocate, his friend. Other times he feels God has abandoned him.

And then, from a chasm of loss, comes a confession: **"I know that my redeemer lives, and that in the end he will stand on the earth. I myself will see him with my own eyes. . . . How my heart yearns within me!"** (Job 19:25,27).

It's Christmas Eve. Tonight, that Redeemer lies in a manger. An unseen enemy stirs in the shadows. Satan wants to sift the Savior, to test and tempt and kill him and doom you to hell.

And indeed, the Redeemer will be abandoned by God. He'll suffer. He'll die. But he will not allow Satan to win. Jesus' victory over sin, death, and Satan will be etched in the emptiness of his stone tomb.

It's Christmas Eve. Whether your heart is bubbling over or heavy with loss, look at that baby and know *your* Redeemer. Look at his tomb and see *your* pardon. Look to the skies—he's coming back for you.

How our hearts yearn within us!

The insulting and amazing birth of Jesus

Pastor Mike Novotny

Has anyone ever offered you a breath mint? Even though they are giving you a gift, free of charge, there is something rather humbling about the offer. It implies that something is wrong with you, offensive and off-putting, something that needs to be fixed through a gift.

Christmas is like that. The angel said, **"Today in the town of David a Savior has been born to you; he is the Messiah, the Lord,"** and we smile in response to the good news (Luke 2:11). But implied within that good news is the sobering statement that we needed to be saved. We were in such danger that only God in human flesh—a Lord who could be touched, crucified, and killed—could save us. If our spiritual lives needed only a slight adjustment, an angel could have given us a self-improvement tutorial. But that's not what the angel declared. God came down from heaven, the only doable solution to our dangerous situation.

I pray you are humble enough to admit that you, by nature, are so bad that you need to be saved. I also pray you realize that God, by his nature, is so good that he came down from heaven so you could be with him forever. Be humble and be happy—a Savior has been born to you! He is the Messiah, the Lord!

What's that smell?!
Karen Spiegelberg

Taste, touch, hearing, sight, and smell. Those are the five senses. Each is important in some way. The sense of smell has been called the underrated sense, until you stop and think about it. Smell is the sense most strongly associated with our memory. The smell of baking cookies can remind us of our grandmother's home. But the smell of rotting food can remind us that we forgot to take the garbage to the curb. "What's that smell?" we ask as we open the garage door.

The people of Corinth might have figuratively asked that same question of the apostle Paul when they received his first letter. There were many issues that needed to be dealt with—divisions in the church, open immorality, abuse of the Lord's Supper. Paul had to confront them head-on, but his message was repulsive to their nostrils. It stunk. They didn't want to be called out for their iniquities. In his second letter, smell what Paul says we are as God's messengers: **"For we are to God the pleasing aroma of Christ among those who are being saved and those who are perishing. To the one we are an aroma that brings death; to the other, an aroma that brings life"** (2 Corinthians 2:15,16).

So what's that smell? It's the sweet smell of the gospel message, and it wafts among us. Its odor attracts some and repels others. But let us never give up on breathing it in and sharing it with others. It's even better than the smell of Grandma's cookies!

Listen when he speaks
Pastor Clark Schultz

There was an old TV commercial about a financial firm named E.F. Hutton. It showed Mr. Hutton in a busy restaurant or on a crowded street, and as soon as he opened his mouth, there was silence. The ad slogan was this: "When E.F. Hutton talks, people listen."

There was no greater Old Testament prophet than Moses. All the others who followed directed the people to follow what he had written in the first five books of the Bible. He deserved the attention.

But he didn't deserve the ultimate attention. That was reserved for someone else: **"The Lord your God will raise up for you a prophet like me from among you, from your fellow Israelites. You must listen to him. The Lord said to me: '. . . I myself will call to account anyone who does not listen to my words that the prophet speaks in my name'"** (Deuteronomy 18:15,17,19).

That someone else, "a prophet like me," is Jesus. But does he get your attention? Today many other things vie for our attention. I've made plenty of excuses for why I don't have time to study God's Word. I've made excuses for why I haven't given God my best. I am the master of convincing myself that I just don't feel like being a servant anymore. However, Jesus' perfect life is credited to you and me by grace. God's attention is all on us as dearly loved children. So when he speaks—listen.

Why does God wait?

Pastor Mike Novotny

Why doesn't God just end injustice? If our Father knows about all the unfair things that happen in our communities and in our lives, why doesn't he just push the "end the world" button today? The answer to that simple question is simple—because God loves people who don't love him just yet.

The other day I had coffee with a young woman who didn't understand what had happened to her. "I haven't been using drugs, Pastor," she beamed. "I don't even want to. And I haven't been hooking up, Pastor. Wait; can I tell you that? And this Bible app. I've been reading it every day." I smiled in celebration with the angels in heaven. This lost soul had been found, saved, and changed.

Here's my point—That just happened. If Jesus would have come back six weeks ago, I don't know if she would have been ready for his return. Every day God is doing that same thing, opening people's eyes to their need for Jesus and the gift of eternal life through faith. But God's desire to save more people means that we, in sacrificial love, have to wait in this broken place, trusting that God will bring justice and truth and love soon.

Would you wait for their souls' sake? **"The Lord is not slow in keeping his promise, as some understand slowness. Instead he is patient with you, not wanting anyone to perish, but everyone to come to repentance"** (2 Peter 3:9).

Healing for broken relationships
Andrea Delwiche

In the upheaval of the past year or two, most of us have been touched by divided opinions and stress buildup leading to angry words or altercations.

In Psalm 55, David speaks to such a situation—his life was marred by anger and violence with a close friend:

"My companion stretched out his hand against his friends; he violated his covenant. His speech was smooth as butter, yet war was in his heart; his words were softer than oil, yet they were drawn swords. Cast your burden on the Lord, and he will sustain you; he will never permit the righteous to be moved" (verses 20-22 ESV).

How does he handle it? **"I call to God, and the Lord will save me. Evening and morning and at noon I utter my complaint and moan, and he hears my voice"** (verses 16,17 ESV). He then encourages all who will hear his song to **"cast your burden on the Lord, and he will sustain you"** (verse 22). These vulnerable words of a warrior-king reassure us that none of us are too big for God or able to carry our own burdens.

Are you haunted by broken relationships that need to be healed? We know God desires that we love each other, but it's more than we can do on our own.

Where do you need to pour out grief to God over a broken relationship? Where do you need God's courage to heal hurt and division in your life? The Lord longs to step into that grief with you and work it for good.

Jesus is God's greatest gift

Pastor Mike Novotny

Sometimes you need about 40 years to really understand a Bible passage. That's what happened with me and James 1:17. Ever since I was a kid, I knew the wonderful words from Jesus' half brother James: **"Every good and perfect gift is from above, coming down from the Father"** (James 1:17). First as a teenager, then as a Christian adult, and finally as a pastor, that passage was my go-to verse for Thanksgiving Day and devotions on gratitude.

But it wasn't until I turned 40 that something fairly obvious hit me. "*Hmm* . . . out of all God's good gifts, which gift is the best? What gift could be so good that James would call it 'perfect'? Which perfect gift came down from the Father so we would be guaranteed to believe that God is good? Oh! Jesus!"

For four decades, I had used James 1:17 to make lists of all my physical and financial and relational blessings, but now I can't read those words without thinking of the greatest gift of all, the perfect gift who came down from heaven to become my Savior and Redeemer—Jesus!

I'm not sure how this year has been going for you. You might be flying high or in chronic pain, but Christians always have the greatest reason to fall on their knees and give thanks to the Father. You have Jesus. You always will.

His hands
Linda Buxa

Hands show the work you do. Farmers have dirt under their nails perpetually. Artists will always have paint on their hands. My neighbor is missing some fingers because of the work he used to do. A mom's hands are often dry and cracked from all the handwashing. A boxer's hands will show the effects of many broken fingers. A devotion writer's hands, well, there's nothing that really sets mine apart.

Jesus' hands show the work he did too. When he visited the temple, Jesus' hands unrolled the scrolls to read from the Scriptures. His hands embraced little children and infants. Jesus' healing hands touched lepers and blind people and sick people. His hands handed out food to the disciples so thousands who had come out to listen to him share God's words could eat. His hands broke bread and gave us the Lord's Supper—telling us that it is his body and blood given for our forgiveness. He has scars where soldiers drove nails into his hands to hang him on a cross, finishing the work of buying you back from evil. Finally, **"when he had led them out to the vicinity of Bethany, he lifted up his hands and blessed them"** (Luke 24:50).

Now we get to be Jesus' hands to the people around us. We get to pray for them, baptize them, open Scripture with them, and point them to the saving hands of Jesus. The hands that bless them too.

Devotions
for
Special Days

Bring your doubt

Easter Sunday

Pastor Matt Ewart

I don't remember much about my Sunday school experiences as a kid, but I do remember one lesson in particular. The lesson was about Jesus' resurrection, and the point I remember is that one of the disciples doubted that Jesus could be alive. We call him Doubting Thomas.

Now as I look at that story as an adult, I wonder if we could have given him a better nickname: *Honest* Thomas. He didn't hide the doubt that was in his heart. He verbalized doubt more honestly than I do. While it's not beneficial for us to question what God declares to be true, it's also not healthy for us to ignore doubt when it settles into our hearts.

At least Thomas was honest. He wanted to see and touch Jesus before he could believe in a resurrection. His honesty gave Jesus an opportunity.

"Then [Jesus] **said to Thomas, 'Put your finger here; see my hands. Reach out your hand and put it into my side. Stop doubting and believe'"** (John 20:27).

Jesus does not deny doubters. Jesus is not intimidated by your doubt. When you are honest like Thomas and bring your doubt before Jesus, it will not last long. Jesus is alive. Doubt cannot survive where death has been defeated.

One day you will see Jesus with your own eyes and touch him with your own hands. Until then, don't be afraid to expose your doubt to the power of Jesus' resurrection.

Convicted yet forgiven
Mother's Day
Ann Jahns

When my boys were younger, I took them to swimming lessons. One day I talked about my church to another mom. She responded, "I could tell you're a Christian by the way you talk to your kids."

Now this statement didn't have the effect on me you might expect. I went home and cried tears of conviction and shame. What about the harsh way I spoke to my kids in the privacy of my home? Despite my patient and loving words in public, I was also *that mom* behind closed doors.

That mom could yell in anger. *That mom* sometimes showed favoritism and held grudges. *That mom* was me.

I was like the Pharisees who earned Jesus' harshest rebukes: **"On the outside you appear to people as righteous but on the inside you are full of hypocrisy and wickedness"** (Matthew 23:28).

Have you ever been *that mom* ? There are days when the magnitude and exhaustion of caring for young lives presses down on us and we snap.

But I bet you've also been the mom who whispers, "I love you" and shares stories of Jesus and prays fiercely over a sleeping teen. This mom was also me, and I know you are this mom too.

Show yourself some grace, for that's what Jesus died to give you. On the tough days, remember this: **"As far as the east is from the west, so far has he removed our transgressions from us"** (Psalm 103:12).

Happy Mother's Day, dear momma. You're right where Jesus wants you to be, doing what he designed you to do.

A father who makes the Lord his trust
Father's Day
Andrea Delwiche

"Blessed is the man who makes the LORD his trust" (Psalm 40:4 ESV). In addition, blessed is the *family* of the man who makes the Lord his trust. Everyone connected with the man who truly makes the Lord his trust will be blessed by that man's faithfulness to God.

The characteristics of someone who makes the Lord his trust are named throughout Psalm 40. The man who trusts the Lord waits patiently for the Lord; he acknowledges and praises God; he looks to God for his self-worth and patterns of wisdom; he follows the will of God in his dealings with other people; he asks God to walk with him throughout his life.

Some of us strive to be fathers in this model. Some of us *have* fathers who, by God's grace, modeled this sort of integrity as they parented us. Some of us have not known an earthly father who in any way, shape, or form modeled this Christ-like example. May God's blessing and healing rest with you.

For all of us, the prime example of fatherhood is found in God the Father. He loves us, provides for us, enjoys spending time with us, and listens to us. He delights in calling us by name.

Do a search of the word *father* in the New Testament to explore our heavenly Father's characteristics. Remember that Jesus said of himself that **"whoever has seen *me* has seen the Father"** (John 14:9 ESV). The steadfast and loving characteristics of Jesus are also true of our Father God.

A Thanksgiving Prayer
Thanksgiving Day
Sarah Habben

"Oh, give thanks to the Lord, for *He is* good! For His mercy *endures* forever" (1 Chronicles 16:34 NKJV).

Heavenly Father, before I get distracted by my plans for this day, I want to give you thanks.

Thank you for my blessings of food, family, and freedom; for my health and work; for my warm bed. When those blessings seem in short supply, thank you for the gifts you've provided in their place: help, encouragement, courage, or perseverance that keeps me going.

Help me listen for your footsteps of mercy each day. A sinner lives here, and yet mercy comes. It perches on the edge of my bed. It keeps no record of last night's foolish worries, of yesterday's grumbling, of last week's indiscretions. The evidence of my idols does not keep mercy's feet from standing at my side. The smell of my sin does not dissuade it.

Lord, if I ever feel that I have earned this mercy, remind me that your grace isn't gullible. You know I'm a miserable being. I don't deserve my daily bread, let alone the feast of forgiveness I have in Christ or the joy that awaits me in heaven. I deserve to be consumed, to be crushed. Instead you give me your great love. You assure me of your faithfulness in your Word, in the waters of my baptism, in the meal of your Holy Supper.

Even if your mercy is all that I have, I know it is forever, and it is more than enough.

Thank you, Lord. Amen.

About the Writers

Pastor Mike Novotny has served God's people in full-time ministry since 2007 in Madison and, most recently, at The CORE in Appleton, Wisconsin. He also serves as the lead speaker for Time of Grace, where he shares the good news about Jesus through television, print, and online platforms. Mike loves seeing people grasp the depth of God's amazing grace and unstoppable mercy. His wife continues to love him (despite plenty of reasons not to), and his two daughters open his eyes to the love of God for every Christian. When not talking about Jesus or dating his wife/girls, Mike loves playing soccer, running, and reading.

Linda Buxa is a freelance writer and Bible study leader. She is a regular speaker at women's retreats and conferences across the country, as well as a regular blogger and contributing writer for Time of Grace Ministry. Linda is the author of *Dig In! Family Devotions to Feed Your Faith, Parenting by Prayer,* and *Made for Friendship.* She and her husband, Greg, have lived in Alaska, Washington D.C., and California. They now live in Wisconsin, where they are raising their three children.

Andrea Delwiche lives in Wisconsin with her husband, three kids, two dogs, cat, and a goldfish pond full of fish. She enjoys reading, knitting, and road-tripping with her family. Although a lifelong believer, she began to come into a deeper understanding of what it means to follow Christ far into adulthood (always a beginner on that journey!). Andrea has facilitated a Christian discussion group for women at her church for many years.

Pastor Jon Enter served in West Palm Beach, Florida, for ten years. He is now a campus pastor and instructor at St. Croix Lutheran Academy in St. Paul, Minnesota. Jon also serves as a regular speaker on Grace Talks video devotions and a contributing writer to the ministry. He once led a tour at his college, and the Lord had him meet his future wife, Debbi. They are now drowning in pink and glitter with their four daughters: Violet, Lydia, Eden, and Maggie.

Pastor Matt Ewart and his wife, Amy, have been blessed with three children who keep life interesting. Matt is currently a pastor in Lakeville, Minnesota, and has previously served as a pastor in Colorado and Arizona.

Jan Gompper spent most of her career teaching theatre at Wisconsin Lutheran College in Milwaukee. She also served six years as a cohost for *Time of Grace* during its start-up years. She has collaborated on two faith-based musicals, numerous Christian songs, and has written and codirected scripts for a Christian video series. She and her husband now reside in the Tampa area, where she continues to practice her acting craft and coach aspiring acting students as opportunities arise. She also assists with Sunday school and other church-related activities.

Sarah Habben is a pastor's wife and mom of four daughters. She and her family have been blessed to call several beautiful places "home": Alberta, Canada; the Caribbean island of Antigua; and most recently Flagstaff, Arizona. Sarah is the author of *The Mom God Chose: Mothering Like Mary* (2015, Northwestern Publishing House) and the coauthor of *The Bloodstained Path to God* (2012, Northwestern Publishing House).

Ann Jahns and her husband live in Wisconsin as recent empty nesters, having had the joy of raising three boys to young adulthood. She is a marketing coordinator for a Christian church body and a freelance proofreader and copy editor. Ann has been privileged to teach Sunday school and lead Bible studies for women of all ages. One of her passions is supporting women in the "sandwich generation" as they experience the unique joys and challenges of raising children while supporting aging parents.

Pastor Daron Lindemann serves in Pflugerville, Texas. Previously, he served in downtown Milwaukee and in Irmo, South Carolina. Daron has authored articles or series for *Forward in Christ* magazine, *Preach the Word*, and his own weekly Grace MEMO devotions. He lives in Texas with his wife, Cara, and has two adult sons.

Jason Nelson had a career as a teacher, counselor, and leader. He has a bachelor's degree in education, did graduate work in theology, and has a master's degree in counseling psychology. After his career ended in disabling back pain, he wrote the book *Miserable Joy: Chronic Pain in My Christian Life*. He has written and spoken extensively on a variety of topics related to the Christian life. Jason has been a contributing writer for Time of Grace since 2010. He has authored many Grace Moments devotions and several books. Jason lives with his wife, Nancy, in Wisconsin.

Pastor David Scharf served as a pastor in Greenville,

Wisconsin, and now serves as a professor of theology at Martin Luther College in Minnesota. He has presented at numerous leadership, outreach, and missionary conferences across the country. He is a contributing writer for Time of Grace and a speaker for Grace Talks video devotions. Dave and his wife have six children.

Pastor Clark Schultz loves Jesus; his wife, Kristin, and their three boys; the Green Bay Packers; Milwaukee Brewers; Wisconsin Badgers; and—of course— Batman. His ministry stops are all in Wisconsin and include a vicar year in Green Bay, tutoring and recruiting for Christian ministry at a high school in Watertown, teacher/coach at a Christian high school in Lake Mills, and a pastor in Cedar Grove. He currently serves as a pastor in West Bend. Pastor Clark's favorite quote is, "Find something you love to do and you will never work a day in your life."

Karen Spiegelberg lives in Wisconsin with her husband, Jim. She has three married daughters, four grandchildren, and has been a foster mom to many. Years ago she was encouraged to start a women's ministry but was unsure of the timing. When her brother died suddenly, it hit her hard—that we can't wait until the time seems right for our ministry; the time is now. And so in 2009, with God's direction, A Word for Women was born. Karen finds great comfort in Psalm 31:14,15: "But I trust in you, O LORD. . . . My times are in your hands." www.awordforwomen.com

Christine Wentzel, a native of Milwaukee, lives in Norfolk, Virginia, with her husband, James, and their fur-child, Piper. After two lost decades as a prodigal, Christine gratefully worships and serves at Resurrection in Chesapeake, Virginia. There she discovered latent talents to put to use for the Lord. In 2009 she began to write and create graphic design for an online Christian women's ministry, A Word for Women (www.awordforwomen.com), and now also joyfully serves as a coadministrator for this ministry.